As I Walked Out Through Spain
in Search of Laurie Lee

P. D. MURPHY

AS I WALKED OUT THROUGH SPAIN IN SEARCH OF LAURIE LEE

SilverWood

Published in 2014 by the author
using SilverWood Books Empowered Publishing®

SilverWood Books Ltd
30 Queen Charlotte Street, Bristol, BS1 4HJ
www.silverwoodbooks.co.uk

Copyright © Paul Murphy 2014
Map © Katie Stewart, Magic Owl Design 2014

The right of Paul Murphy to be identified as the author of this work
has been asserted by him in accordance with the
Copyright, Designs and Patents Act 1988.

ISBN 978-1-78132-207-9 (paperback)
ISBN 978-1-78132-208-6 (ebook)

British Library Cataloguing in Publication Data
A CIP catalogue record for this book is available from
the British Library

Set in Sabon by SilverWood Books
Printed on responsibly sourced paper

Contents

If ever I saw blessing in the air
I see it now in this still early day
Where lemon-green the vaporous morning drips
Wet sunlight on the powder of my eye.

Blown bubble-film of blue, the sky wraps round
Weeds of warm light, whose every root and rod
Splutters with soapy green, and all the world
Sweats with the bead of summer in its bud...

From "April Rise" by Laurie Lee, on Lee's headstone

Foreword

24 April 2014

I am writing this story for the people that I love.

I am writing this for my wife: the girl I fell in love with; the woman who shared my life; and the stranger who divorced me three years ago.

I am not sure whether, in fact, some or all of them ever really knew me, or perhaps knew me only too well. The emotions that remain are mixed and complex, but there is love still there amongst them. I don't think you ever really stop loving someone who stole your heart. Laurie Lee could never quite forget Lorna, never mind Rosie.

I am writing this for my father, who, like Lee, had a secret from which he could never quite escape. I would have liked my father to read this story; we never really knew each other, and now never will.

I am writing this for my mother. I promised her a book. I doubt it will help her to know me better; she is a mother, after all.

I am writing this for my five brothers who I hope will forgive me for telling my story as I saw it. They no doubt will have their own stories of our unfolding lives.

I am writing this for my daughter, who loves and trusts me enough to allow me to write this book.

I am writing this for Laurie Lee, for Yasmin, Jessy and Kathy.

And I am writing this for all those who fell in love with Laurie Lee's writing. He still speaks to so many from his grave in Slad, although not many talk back to him. I hope this changes as we celebrate his centenary on 26 June 2014.

This is a story of two journeys on two levels: Laurie Lee's through Spain in 1935 and how it profoundly shaped the way his life unfolded; my journey following in his footsteps across Spain in 2012 and how it has given me a second chance in life.

One of the things I learnt along the way is that heroes often have feet of clay and writers often manipulate the truth to serve the story.

Laurie Lee, in his account of the journey in *As I Walked Out One Midsummer Morning*, told a story that had its narrative roots in the actual experience of his time on the road. However, he played around with time and space and characters to tell a universal truth about what he saw and heard. He did the journey as a young man of twenty-one and wrote about it as a middle-aged man of fifty-five; no doubt his recollections of the time he spent in Spain in his youth would have been filtered through the experience that comes with age.

I have chosen to tell a story written in a creative non-fiction style. I immersed myself in a country for a summer and an autumn and whilst looking for the spirit of a troubled writer encountered many characters from the present and the past. I have relied on imagination and fictional craft techniques to delve beneath the surface to portray the hidden depths of a poet's soul, to uncover a country's spirit and to show how some endings are also beginnings.

My story is also a personal one, so some names have been changed and not everything takes place in the time and locations indicated. Some events never actually happened, but nevertheless they are an important part of the story I have chosen to tell and help to depict what I have learned during my journey.

It is true that I was lost and my life at a standstill. It is true that I had to walk out and make something happen. It is true that my life has changed as a result.

My thoughts on Lee and views on how and why his life took the course it did are not truths, for only he knew the truth. I have interpreted the events in his life in a way that I felt made sense.

I have been faithful to the story that I wanted to tell. Stories have their own way of evolving to tell a universal truth.

Introduction

So how did I, a middle-aged man from the English home counties, end up in Vigo in the north-west of Spain, at the start of the biggest adventure of his life, in the early summer of 2012? Well, the story started a long time ago...

A book read at a certain time of a young man's development can be pivotal in terms of his direction of travel through life. It can switch on a light at a dark period and illuminate a path. So it was with me and Laurie Lee. It all started in 1974 when I was nineteen and chanced upon a copy of Lee's classic rite of passage book *As I Walked Out One Midsummer Morning*.

Laurie Lee was born in 1914. He wrote about his childhood in his first memoir, *Cider With Rosie* (1959), of an upbringing that was simple and at times hard. Abandoned by a father he never really knew, he grew up in a household of sisters and a loving mother. As a young man he left his home and walked to London. He lived there for a year before setting off to Spain to walk across a country on the verge of a civil war. He fought briefly for the Republican government against General Franco's fascist rebels, but returned home to England before the war ended. Franco's side went on to win and a dictatorship was imposed on Spain for 36 years.

Laurie Lee wrote about his life-changing walk across Spain in his memoir *As I Walked Out One Midsummer Morning* (1969), but waited until he was fifty-five to do it – almost my age now. He was seventy-seven when he wrote the story of the role he played in the Spanish Civil War in *A Moment of War* (1991). This trilogy of memoirs was his life's crowning achievement. His experiences before, during and after the Spanish Civil War had defined his life. The three books covered his life from the age of three to twenty-four.

Did I see in Lee a father figure? Or the young man I wanted to be? Was it simply his words that took my breath away? Possibly all of these. All I know is that he once took me with him to a new world for a summer, a time and place that I have never forgotten.

I left behind my English schooldays of cricket in the outfield, strains of Jerusalem floating on the breeze outside the school chapel, and the daily devotions to Catholic saints. And with Laurie Lee in my rucksack, I discovered a new country – Spain – and a new freedom. With Lee as my companion, I experienced the country through his curious "bright and strange" eyes.

That first visit to Spain for me was like Lee's "first bite of the apple" with Rosie: "Never to be forgotten, that first long secret drink of golden fire." Lee has been a reference point for me at key periods of my life ever since. Now, at a crossroads in my life, I have again turned to Laurie Lee.

Map of Route

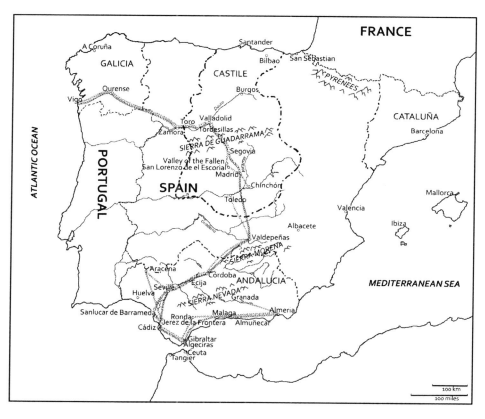

xxxxxxxxx   Laurie Lee's Route 1935 June to September
>>>>>>>>>   Paul Murphy's Route 2012 June to November

Into Spain

First Light

4 June 2012, Vigo, Galicia, North-West Spain

I sit high above the bay of Vigo on a June day in 2012. It is just after dawn. It is quiet and cool and there is little activity on the water below me. This is the beginning of a journey that will take me 600 miles and across three mountain ranges, from the misty hills of Galicia to the sun-drenched Mediterranean.

My pale fingers stray across the hard contours of a shell, tracing the fluted pattern of ridges; I can detect still the elusive trace of the Atlantic Ocean on its porcelain skin. The scallop shell: the symbol of Saint James carried by pilgrims en route to Santiago de Compostela. When it was alive it would have had over a hundred reflective eyes, assembled around its circumference like a string of rosary beads.

I imagine Laurie Lee sitting in this same spot nearly 80 years ago, high above the crashing waves, looking down on the town of Vigo enveloped by a fine Galician mist. His fingers, hardened and calloused from the London building site and the strings of his fiddle, caressing the feminine pink-fleshed shell, dreaming of loves left behind in England and looking ahead to walking down a long, dusty road all the way to the Mediterranean sea.

For Laurie Lee it was a momentous coming-of-age adventure: "As I left home that morning and walked away from the sleeping village, it never occurred to me that others had done this before."

I have realised, as I have grown older, that every new stage of life feels new and uncharted and as I set out on my quest I, too, am sure that nobody has done this before. I want to feel what Lee felt and, if I am honest, I want some of his magic to rub off on me as I walk out in search of that dusty road shaded by groves of orange trees that Lee dreamed of seeing.

Like a solitary monk praying, my fingers trace their way along the inlets of the shell; a shell that perhaps clung, wide-eyed, onto an offshore rock back in 1935 and brought all one hundred of its eyes to bear on the panorama of that moment of arrival.

In 1935 the Royal Mail Line steamer picked its way through the islands in its approach to Vigo. Its black hull snaked through the blue Atlantic waters, its trademark bright yellow twin funnels standing out against the white clouds. The ship was en route to Buenos Aires and had started its journey in Tilbury, London, where Laurie Lee boarded – a £4 one-way ticket in his hand – his savings from a year's labouring.

As the ship docked at Vigo, Lee recorded in his diary: "Out of the unconscious rocking of sea and sleep I was simultaneously woken and hooked to the coast of Spain by the rattling anchor going over the side."

I see, in my mind's eye, a fair-haired, tall, pale-skinned, slim young man step off the boat carrying a knapsack, a blanket and a fiddle. He looks around at the sight of the first foreign town he has set foot in. It is a gentle introduction to a harsh and alien landscape. The soft green hills above the port, so reminiscent to him of the Malverns, shade him from the fierce Spanish sun. The early morning mist rising from the Galician *Rías* – an intricate network of deep fjords – envelops him in a misleadingly cool cocoon of comfort. He stretches his coltish young limbs, cramped from two days on board. His first faltering steps on his journey across Spain are those of sea legs on dry land.

In the wake of the liner whirlpools of white frothy emotions are strewn all the way back to London and beyond: Betty and Molly (Marquita) Smart, sisters from the Slad Valley, both smitten by Laurie and wracked with pain and longing; Rita Louise, who turned down Laurie's plea to accompany him to Spain; 16-year-old Cleo, daughter of a communist agitator; Mollie, whose gymslip-clad sea-wet body kept him warm on Bognor Regis sands. Laurie Lee was on the run: "I was learning how much easier it was to leave than to stay behind and love."

His thoughts turn to Sophia Rogers – "Sufi" – an exotic Argentinian who had moved to Slad from Bueños Aires. Sufi had taught him the few words of Spanish he knew, including what he prized as the most important, given his imagined journey down through the sun-scorched desert plains of Spain: "*¿Un vaso de agua, por favor?*" (A glass of water, please?).

It was his dream to walk down through Spain to Moorish Andalusia and the tip of Africa. Now, as he stands beneath the green Galician hills, he is more likely to be serenaded by the plaintive whirling tones of the *Gaita* (the traditional Galician bagpipes) than the *duende* (the magical spirit) of the flamenco gypsy guitar of southern Andalusia.

He looks up at me, high above him on the hill, and for a moment, as our gaze meets, I see a hint of panic. He is alone, wondering perhaps whether he should have listened to those siren calls of fair English girls, begging him to stay at home or take them with him. He is looking at me, but thinking of his mother and the last time he saw her as he left Slad a year earlier: "The stooping figure of my mother, waist-deep in the grass and caught there like a piece of sheep's wool."

Lee had left home in 1934 at the age of 19. Like Lee, I too had left my home. A year ago. I was 56. Lee chose to go, I did not.

I walked down the stairs for the last time. Pausing, I slowly scanned the montage of photographs that lined the stairway and told the story of my life to date. As I descended they followed me, framed images of my life hanging on the wall, hanging in the air, chronicling the passage of time and the story of a family: my family. Silent timeless observers of modern lives, lives that had been lived at pace, in the moment, for the moment, hurrying up and down the stairs, like high-speed trains rushing past glimpses of green countryside and deserted platforms.

My life was all there in those photographs: a young boy learning about failure; a man finally making that commitment; my two girls collecting memories; my grandfather breaking bread with the leader of a fragmented nation.

A freckled face squinting at the sun, smart blazer hanging down over frayed cuffs, scuffed shoes, cap perched unsteadily and tie askew, stretching out, in vain, for the ripe apple from the tree.

Bride and groom under the oak tree, 5 August 1994. Daniella's bridesmaid dress rustling in the cool summer breeze as she kicked her legs high on the swing underneath the branches.

A long summer day in west Wales, drawing to a close, Elizabeth and Daniella on the beach, collecting shells.

Granddad George, who grew up in Cardiff in the 1900s – Welsh Chicago they called it then, a hard place to start out. He has a kind comfortable face. He is drawing on a Player's Navy Cut Number 6, untipped, and inhaling deeply and satisfyingly. He is sitting in a bar, fob watch dangling from his waistcoat, next to Pandit Nehru. Where and when and why is lost in the mists of time. Pandit Nehru had been the Prime Minister of India at the time of Partition, the bloody fragmentation of one nation into two.

Partition happens to families too. After the door had clicked closed behind me for the last time, Dani sat on the stairs with her knees drawn up tight to her chin. She loved the picture of her on the swing with her mum and her new dad at the nice hotel. She thought of the first time I had come to see her mother at the house.

"Give Paul a tour of the house, Daniella," her mum said casually, as if it had not been practiced many times over. She summoned up all of her six years, three months and 21 days and still I towered over her. She knew I was special, Mum hadn't said as much, but she knew.

"Come on then," she said and pulled me up the steep stairs past the freshly-painted blank white wall.

"This is my room." She threw open the door to reveal a pinkish room that she shared with an assortment of animals and dolls who all knew their place.

"This is Mummy's room," she continued, indicating a firmly shut door. "It's a mess and I mustn't show it to you."

Back then something had told her that with me around her mum would not be quite so sad. And now I was gone, Dani thought that her mum, once again, would not be quite so sad.

As I left my home for the last time, I left behind the ordered chronological timelines of my family life and instead took with me, in an old box under my arm, a random collection of old sepia tinted photos, curling at the edges, fragments of my life as jumbled and faded in the box as they were in my head.

I removed my gold wedding ring for the last time. Over the past 18 years I had played with it, dropped it and lost it so many times. Now I consigned it to a drawer.

Unthinkingly I rub the grooved surface worn into the fabric of my left ring finger, a pale circle of nothing.

I fell over today, climbing up here to my pitch high above Vigo. A nasty fall. My left leg went numb as I was clambering up the stone steps and I was suddenly flat on my back. Nobody was there to see, but you don't need an audience to feel foolish. Lee, of all people, knew that. I thought of him at that moment, the falls that he must have had on his walk. He kept quiet about those and for a fleeting instant I was a little bit closer to understanding why.

My stumble only served to heighten my sense of mortality, the realisation that my body is slowing down. I am not ill, just ageing. I feel like I have to make this journey and am aware that it will be difficult, but as the sun breaks through the clouds, a rare green shoot of optimism pushes through my brittle outer shell, causing a crack to form. I slither and clatter down the scree slope from the hills of Vigo, breathing in the fresh mountain air.

It's as if Spain and I are meeting each other for the first time. There is still snow on the top of the distant hills. Under the white blanket a pink streak of rural life runs through the green fields. Farmers' wives squeeze thick slices of blood, sawdust and entrails into black stockings, hands covered in the sticky red gore. Yesterday was *Matanza*, the killing of the pigs, and not one sinew of the body is spared in making the sweet, black blood-pudding, *morcilla*, the delicacy of the region.

I cross a bridge over the mountain stream, trout playing life and death with men waist-deep in the fast flowing waters. The market stalls in the small town are piled high with pungent blue-veined round cheeses. The *queso* is wrapped in moist green leaves, slugs peering out from underneath. When the slugs appear, the cheese is ripe and the prices, like the smell, go sky-high.

Entering a small *pueblo*, I pass down the narrow streets, grateful for the brief respite from the sun. Sizzling olive oil sings from a kitchen, smoke curls out into the street; you can taste the sharp bite of garlic. I pause by some shaded gardens for a rest. There is a fountain carved out of a grey block of granite set into a stone wall, a jigsaw puzzle of stones of all shapes and sizes, cemented together. It is rough and uneven and beautiful.

Through an archway, framed by a black grille, I spy the hand of a young girl. Her face is obscured by gypsy black hair and her fingers are trailing deliciously through the fresh clear water as it runs down a slight incline before being collected and diverted into a pool.

I am finally on my way.

Two months earlier...
23 April 2012, Dorchester-on-Thames, Oxfordshire
What does a poor boy do in troubled times? He goes back to his mother. I did just that at the age of 57, returning to a small Oxfordshire village, a village that I had gone back to many times over the years as my life unfolded. This time, however, I had no idea when I would leave again.

I passed a troubled few months in the quiet tranquil surroundings of a perfectly still village, trying to wrap myself into the thatch of the sloping roofs that hemmed in the narrow winding streets and its denizens. Winter had turned into spring. I worried that I was becoming invisible, slipping away into an old sepia tinted photograph I needed to resist this urge to settle in and hunker down. I needed to slip out of its clutches before its grey blanket descended upon me and choked off all escape.

I am walking down the high street, heading out of the village. I have been walking this path for much of my life, from the village up to the heights of Wittenham Clumps, 394 feet above sea level. The Clumps have a mystical, timeless presence rooted in Old England. I would sometimes walk up to them before dawn, just as the birds were awakening, their arias floating in the air, an ethereal moon still visible, bathing the scene in a yellow wash.

The Abbey bells are calling me on my way. Miss Marple stories are filmed here, brown-coated and hatted men periodically wander around, pipes in their mouths, tipping their hats to pencil-skirted, rouge-lipped young ladies called Dorothy, as the cameras roll.

I pass the George Inn with its bright red and white sign depicting Saint George astride his gleaming charger. It is his day today; the flag flying above the Abbey confirms this. For centuries people have made pilgrimages to the Abbey in search of relics, sanctified fossils, old bones. I am not looking for bones or saints; I am searching for a lost soul of an ordinary man with extraordinary powers. I am looking for the spirit of a man who once showed me the way forward. He is dead now and I recently visited his grave in another small English village.

All of a sudden, I am aware of the sweet aroma of wood burning. It is a revelation – the rediscovery of a vital sense. Since my wife divorced me a year ago my senses generally have dulled into indifference by a life that has stalled. The divorce came just two years after redundancy and early retirement had been foisted upon me unexpectedly; the shock was huge. Overnight I lost my sense of smell. For over a year I had withdrawn more and more and this loss just quickened the retreat.

As the wood smoke settles into the distant recesses of my being and the bells continue to toll, I am taken back to that first visit to Spain, a young man walking along a bed of autumn leaves, shed from golden branches. The leaves crackle underfoot in the crisp Spanish air. Wild boar, *jabalís,* are roaming in the forest, pigs are snuffling for acorns.

I pass by Rotton Row and enter Bridge End with St Birunus Catholic Church on my left. I had carried the coffin of my father into this church. Elizabeth, my wife, had sung *Ave Maria,* her perfect phrasing sending my father's lost spirit soaring heavenwards.

I approach the river now down Wittenham Lane, pink cherry blossom carpeting the road, lilac and mulberry trees lining the way. Seeded blackberry jam is on offer, honesty box to hand. Crossing the first bridge over the stagnant creeky-brown water, for a brief moment I think I glimpse Miss Flynn, fresh from the pages of *Cider With Rosie,* hidden below the surface, "a green foot under," with the long tapered hands of the willow softly caressing her pale torso.

It was my mother who told me once that weeping willows were almost certainly feminine, that *Cider With Rosie* was written by Laurie Lee and that poor Miss Flynn had drowned herself in a pond in Slad. My mother, who had borne five sons to my feckless father, and then briefly raised another, my father's love child. It had not occurred to me until now how similar my mother was to Annie, Lee's mother. Circumstances were different: I had a comfortable middle class upbringing, while Lee's was a humble hand-to-mouth existence. Annie had been let down by Lee's father who left her and went to London, leaving her to bring up his children from two marriages.

My father was a constant presence during my childhood. Lee was abandoned early by his father who he never really knew. Like me, he never had his father's blessing nor received absolution, the sign from a father to a son that he is wanted and loved, his sins forgiven. This must have hurt him and yet I wonder if he had the better deal. My father was a distant figure, a doctor who suffered from depression and phobias. He came into contact daily with disease and bacteria and was convinced that his skin was contaminated; he would shun any contact with his children for fear that his touch would taint.

I walk over the curved bridge, the sluicing of the lock gates a distant murmur. Peering over the edge of the bridge, I can feel again the damp hand of my young daughter clutching on to mine as she anxiously watches her stick float away on the water.

The earth of the path below me is baked and dusty, its thin capillary-veined cracks branching off in all directions. Do people cleverer than I interrogate the land I wonder, like a clairvoyant would read the lifelines of hands? Can the earth retain the secrets of the past, foretell the future? I gaze up at The Clumps as Nash would have done in the last century. In the period leading up to the Great War, Nash, the Slade School-educated English landscape artist painted The Clumps in all seasons. He was part of a set of artists of the time, known as the Crisis of Brilliance School. Lee and Nash would have known each other in the 1940s. Nash was an English artist of great sensitivity and drawn to surrealism. I wonder if, like me, and possibly Lee, he felt uncomfortable in a body bound by English tradition and reserve. Lee could see beyond the English and Spanish superficial façade and as an artist Nash delved into the inner recesses of the English landscape.

A solitary walker is halfway up The Clumps incline, stoically walking up those 394 stone-dry yards away from the liquidity of sea level. He will have walked up them many a time before, like me, like all the solitary English walkers. Did Nash ever capture the image of such a man in a painting? I do not want to be that man, the solitary man halfway up the hill never destined to reach the top.

The steep slope comes tumbling down towards me. As a young girl, Daniella would roll down the hill with her friends, gathering speed, hair caught in the rays of the setting sun, like the "flaming cartwheels" of Nash's vivid oil painting.

Over the years the steep final leg of the climb has got harder. At the top I sit and rest, drawing down great gulps of air as the wind whistles about me.

"*Sancta Maria, Maria ora pro nobis, nobis peccatoribus,*" the strains of "Ave Maria" drift up from the past, from the empty church below. Elizabeth saw something vital in me once that over the years has ebbed away and lies twitching, all washed up on the riverbank down below me.

I look down upon England. The lukewarm, thin, red liquid ambles through my veins, barely warming my English skin to room temperature. It creates the reserve, the polite veneer, the doubt, the superiority, the caution. I long to surprise myself, and her – Elizabeth. But I fear it is too late for her.

Nash would climb to the top of The Clumps and experience a sense of flying through the air over his cobalt-green fields below. He would prepare his painting oils with an explosive mix of linseed, poppy oil and petrol. With my newly restored sense of smell I can almost taste the heady concoction.

Over to the north lie dreaming spires, away to the west, the dried up source of the Thames, further west still lies Laurie Lee, in a sunken green valley called Slad. The sleepy Cotswolds village is set between two other villages, Paradise and Purgatory.

It is hard even to confess this to myself but I probably fell in love with him that long ago summer and the feeling has never quite worn off. If, that is, you can fall in love with the words of a pale ghost. Words that ignited a spark of recognition. The sort of words never spoken in my house – a place of silence and one bereft of touch. A place where the edge was never quite taken off the chill.

The breeze at the top of The Clumps dances through the lushness of the copse, nudging aside the bluey-yellow butterflies intent on their wingtip-to-wingtip chase. A hundred metres and more above the world below, I sit and gaze towards Slad. A decidedly unpoetic name for the home of a poet. I went there recently for the first time. "He lies in the valley he loved", it says on his gravestone. I drank in his pub, knelt in his church, gazed through the April-yellow stained glass; a window not created for a medieval English saint but for Laurie Lee, who would have been one hundred years old in 2014.

Lee, in his own valley of dreams. Laurie Lee who witnessed the dying of the light of the English village, the last years of a place and time where people were born, lived and died in the same long shadows cast by the local church and squire.

I want, need, to walk away from the present and seek out the world that Lee had found in Spain that changed his life forever. I need to retrace his steps and see if I can bring him – and myself – back to life.

I sit for some time at the top of the hill as the day comes to an end. My ageing eyes are still just sharp enough to home in on a narrow slit between the grey cloud cover under the ash-blue sky and the black Thames below.

The sky to the west darkens above the setting sun hovering above the horizon, or "as far as the eye can see" as my mother used to describe it when I was a child. The sun is losing its golden core and turning crimson as it sinks towards the lip of the end of the world. A pink strip of dissolving cloud stretches either side of the sun, dividing the earth from the sky. Just above the melting sun, in the still of the sky, is a display of silent lightening flashes. I look away from this scene towards the dreaming spires of Oxford, the last rays of the sun still glinting off my glasses. I track a young couple as they walk along the top of the hill, into the sun. They seem to walk right into its molten centre and disappear for an instant before emerging the other side.

The sun is about to slip away from the day and right through my fingers. I pour myself in, drink from its cup and emerge into the dawn of a Spanish summer June day in Vigo.

South from Vigo

And Did Those Feet in Ancient Time

6 June 2012, Allariz, Galicia

It is hot, very hot, the temperature nudging 40 degrees, very unseasonal for Galicia in June. Walking into the headwind of centuries of faith seems like an extra force of nature to contend with, alongside the heat, lack of shade and the relentless trajectory of the snaking incline ahead. Today, though, I am a solitary figure, no other soul brave enough or foolish enough to walk out in the murderous heat of the day. I embrace the experience: this is what I have come for.

The views to the valley below compensate, as does the shade of the occasional inn and the taste of ice-cold sparkling water on parched lips. As I walk out I find solace in the sound of the Spanish word for cold, *frío*. I repeat the cooling syllables to myself.

I lunch at a small inn in a village. The elders have gathered for their afternoon game of cards. Voices are raised, tables thumped, fierce curses ring through the air, *ostia, coño, joder,* while their grandchildren play happily at their feet.

Outside the afternoon sun is still splitting the pavement. Life comes down to two essentials: water and shade. I stagger eventually across a Roman bridge into the *pueblo* of Allariz and up through winding cobbled streets into the tiny main square and the welcoming sign of the Bar Central. It is 5pm and as I revive myself with a cold beer, my overheated brain and body start to cool down and I can appreciate my surroundings. Allariz is a slice of Spain's past perfectly preserved. I feel it is older now than at any time in the last century.

I see a notice on the wall of the bar – it is a fiesta weekend, the annual festival of bulls, *La Festa da Boi*. It is written in *Gallego*, the local dialect. Lee loved the traditions that grounded the culture of Spain to its pagan past. Even this far north in Spain, the bull is still king. Blood and sand, fear and honour, passion and pride are all part of the spectacle and death is always close at hand. Lee's favourite Spanish poet, Federico García Lorca, wrote a classic poem about the spectacle, *La Cogida y La Muerte* (Goring and Death), a tale of the Sevillian bullfighter Sanchez Mejias who was gored to death in August 1934 by a bull called Granadino. Its haunting refrain *"A las cinco de la tarde"* ("It was five o'clock in the afternoon"), underscores a beautiful but sad tale of pointless death:

> *A lo lejos ya viene la gangrene a las cinco de la tarde*
> *Trompa de lirio por las verdes ingles a las cinco de la tarde*
> *Las heridas quemaban como soles a las cinco de la tarde*
> *el gentío rompía las ventanas a las cinco de la tarde*
> *A las cinco de la tarde*
> *Ay que terribles cinco de la tarde*
> *Eran las cinco en todos los relojes Eran las cinco en*
>   *sombra de la tarde.*

> *Gangrene hovers on the horizon at five o'clock in the*
>   *afternoon*
> *A lily seeps from the green-turning groin at five o'clock in*
>   *the afternoon*
> *The wounds were burning up like suns at five o'clock in*
>   *the afternoon*
> *The crowd shattered the windows at five o'clock in the*
>   *afternoon*
> *At five o'clock in the afternoon*
> *Ay that terrible five o'clock in the afternoon*
> *It was five o'clock by all the clocks*
> *It was five o'clock in the shade that afternoon.*

Gallego is the first Spanish language that Lee would have heard following his arrival in North-West Spain. Spain is home to a rich melting pot of languages – *Catalán, Basque, Andaluz* – and many people have died over the years to protect their right to speak them.

Many were executed in the civil war for their allegiance to their region rather than to the centre. Ironically, Franco himself was born in Galicia.

When in Orense yesterday, the day of 40 degrees plus, I came upon a plaque and a trail commemorating a local activist, singer and writer, Alexandre Bóveda. He was executed by Franco's troops on 17 August 1936, simply for being a local patriot. The date is now designated a *Dia da Galiza Martir* (Day of Galician Martyrs). It is a salutary reminder that one did not have to be a cultural icon like Lorca to be hunted down in the early days of the civil war. In those desperate times, as Lee would come to know, being a simple man with values who believed in something was enough to seal your fate.

Federico García Lorca was, himself, executed just two days later by the nationalists, on 19 August 1936 in Granada. His body, along with those of the schoolteacher and two *banderilleros* killed alongside him, has never been found.

Recently a referendum was carried out in a small province in southern Spain by a local council. Given the austerity programme of cuts all across the country, councils are having to make hard choices. This particular council polled its community about preferences for using one section of the budget. The choices were to repair school buildings, to extend capacity for day centres for the elderly or to put on a programme of fiestas including bullfights. The community voted clearly for the fiestas. I am not sure how to interpret this. Does it show that the Spanish still love a party or that the public do not trust their politicians to deliver on spending promises so settle for having a good time? I suspect the latter but at the moment am prepared to believe the former.

I gather that the Allariz bull running is not to be compared with San Fermín in Pamplona. There, the bulls run freely through the streets in the annual festival, chasing young men and older tourists, most fuelled by a high octane mix of alcohol and machismo. This will not be like that, but I choose to stay for the first day nevertheless.

I had heard Lee recently, speaking on an old crackly BBC radio tape, recorded in the 1970s, talking in his Gloucestershire burr, of a similar visit to a small village bull festival in the Basque region by the Pyrenees.

He told of his experience in taking part as an honoured guest, an Englishman from far away: "We arrived, myself and my two attractive young companions. It was late in the season and the sun had lost its bite, it was a morning of green rain. There was to be a *corrida* that afternoon, with a special open event to precede it at noon. A young bull would be released into the main plaza. An old crone by my side smiled and said, 'There will be some broken heads later, God willing'. By that time I had decided to give it a go and before I could change my mind the word had got round that El Inglés was going to fight. My two companions looked at me with a new respect and with what looked like bloodlust in their eyes."

The tale he told, a hint of a smile playing on his lips, was one of the English guest taking on the experienced and wily bull that the locals would not touch with a *banderilla* (the sharp barbed stick employed by the *banderillero* to weaken the bull before the entry of the matador into the ring), and emerging as a much feted hero.

Lee's account of his one and only encounter with a bull was the second I had come across. As a young man I read a book describing the experiences of a young American journalist who in 1922 went to Pamplona, to the San Fermín festival. He ran with the bulls and wrote about it in his novel *The Sun Also Rises*. His name was Ernest Hemingway.

Lee continued: "I was warm with cognac and felt no fear, I was aware only of the high pitched screams of the women in the crowd as the young bull eyed me. The promises and bravado of the dandy young locals had come to nothing. I was alone in the Plaza with my nemesis. He came at me and caught me a glancing blow. I gathered myself, stamped my foot and shouted, though not very loud and the bull turned, looked at me and did nothing. The sun shone blue on his steaming flanks and he came at me again. It was all over very quickly as I bit the dust again and leapt to safety, his hot breath on my heels. My sense of shame did not last. I found myself feted as a hero. The two girls draped themselves over me, flushed with the spectacle. I was pronounced a man of valour, though like all Englishmen, one who lacked grace. A choir gathered around and sang songs of death and martyrdom and maidens wronged far from home. We departed for home, my two companions and I, with a gift of a roll of film that never saw the light of day!"

On balance, I think I prefer Lee's tamer, tongue-in-cheek account to Hemingway's bravado version full of blood and sand.

As the excitement builds in Allariz and the town waits for the first bull to be released into the small winding streets, I shelter in a tiny packed bar in the main square. I am hiding there, not just from the bulls, but from the incessant downpour that has followed the heat wave.

Everyone is wearing their bright red fiesta *pañuelos* (neckerchiefs) tied around their necks in what could be called "cravat style".

The stylish young women are back home in their *pueblo* for the Corpus Christi holiday, escaping from their professional careers in Madrid, some of the few in their age group to have jobs. Astonishingly, 50 per cent of 16-25 year olds are unemployed in Spain at the moment. They mix with their brothers, sisters and nieces and nephews. The chatter is a mix of *Castellano* – purely spoken Spanish – and *Gallego*.

"*Qué tal en Madrid... no me digas que tengas empleo. Aquí, no hay nada.*"

"*Moi ben, grazas.*"

"*Qué guapa es mi sobrina.*"

"*Boa noite.*"

"*Ponme un blanco.*"

"*Unha cervexa.*"

The talk is of jobs and unemployment, pretty nieces and good wine and local beer.

Six loud blasts are heard, the signal for the first bull to be released. We all rush outside. The bull appears, disappointingly but sensibly not running totally loose but tethered to ropes, skillfully managed by a team of men in white outfits. The crowd screams and the bull is chased by a posse of young men. I experience a fleeting sense of fear and awe and then almost immediately, complete empathy with the bull which is clearly scared out of its wits.

In truth, even Lee's little vignette at the Basque fiesta now leaves me more than a little cold on this damp and chilly evening.

I return to my rural escape. As I walk back across the Roman bridge, the daylight is fading silently into the night. Dark streaks of cloud are leeching the colour from a sky backlit by hues of blue, like the slipstream of jets they settle gently into the dying glow of the day's embers as the fire of the day extinguishes itself.

I guess I am no Hemingway and retire to my bed, consoled a touch by this thought.

7 June 2012, Allariz, Galicia

The whisper of the aspens is not drowned, And over lightless pane and footless road, Empty as sky, with every other sound Not ceasing, calls their ghosts from their abode.
– Edward Thomas in "Aspens", 1915

Edward Thomas spoke of "the ghostly world sharing the landscape with the living". Thomas, an English poet killed in the First World War just two years on from penning these lines, captures a sense of loss and mourning evoked by the Great War. As I head south to the aspen trees of Spain perhaps they will still whisper and call to the ghosts of Spain's own Great War, a war, brewing as Lee walked out oblivious to the culmination of decades, and centuries even, of conflict.

The words of Thomas fell on – and have been trampled into – the lush green old ways of Lee's England. But they resonate for me as I walk the paths of Spain, walking on and by the unconsecrated graves of the civil war fallen, ignored but not forgotten by the Spanish consciousness.

I walk alone but feel Lee's spirit present and feel comfortable in talking to him directly. I don't expect a direct response but I sense the presence of those who have walked before me.

Virginia Woolf wrote, "Is it not possible that things we have felt with great intensity have an existence independent of our minds: are in fact still in existence?"

Lee was following in the footsteps of the pioneers before him, who also charted the course of Spain's march through the early 20th century. V. S. Pritchett, Gerald Brenan and Ruth Anderson all saw, in Spain's absence from the Industrial Revolution, a pure unsullied society, a virgin undiscovered territory.

Lee came swiftly upon their heels, a romantic explorer.

Like him and the others before him, I am following a well-trodden path. Nietzsche talked of how most of us "are driven through surging waves of destiny, the most multifarious currents of the times and the nations, and yet always remain on top, bobbing like a cork." As I live through startling times – the end of the Cold War, the growth of China, the crisis in the Eurozone, the Arab Spring of 2011 – I want to learn from Lee's ability to immerse himself in the affairs of Spain and capture the essence of the times.

So as we head off down the long road to the south, I find myself still asking Lee why? Why did he really set off on that arduous trek, leaving behind all that he knew and loved? Had London's allure dimmed? Had the taste of city life, so sweet and sharp when first imbibed, turned sallow and dull? Years later he reflected of his life in London: "When I talk of home I still think of that damp green valley near Stroud… That is my home, and the image of it is still more real to me than the long years in this crowded capital city."

Was Lee marching on to better things, seeking out what lay beyond the horizon, or was he still out-running his past, fleeing from the comfort of hearth and home, striving still to shake loose the Slad-green pupa of his youth?

"The last days of my childhood were also the last days of the village… Old men in the pubs sang 'As I Walked Out', then walked out and never came back… As for me – for me, the grass grew longer and more sorrow-full, and the trees were surfaced like flesh."

We never quite manage to shake off the past, our formative years; perhaps it was harder for Lee to escape from his deep sided secret valley back in the mists of English time.

I am walking with the ghost of Lee to find the answers to these questions. I am hoping to get to know him, to gain his confidence. I am hoping he will allow me to get under his skin, to see the man enveloped in the velvet folds and linings of his trademark army officer's coat – his "British Warm" – and see what lies beneath that shy, secretive exterior.

I know though, that I may yet succumb to his honeyed prose and sticky-toffee charm, like all the rest, and lie prone at his feet at the end of the journey, tired and exhausted and none the wiser.

Maybe I am looking too hard. Perhaps after all he was just doing what all young men do: setting off on a journey to become a man, to find himself, to test himself in adversity. I say all young men, but it is something that passed me by. Lee may well ask the same of me now.

Why am I setting out to retrace his steps, to disturb his rest and stir up his soul? Am I, just like the descendants of all those who fell at the hands of Franco buried in unconsecrated mass graves, left to roam aimlessly in perpetuity? Do I, like them, sense a need to complete unfinished business, raise Lee from the dead, lay him out afresh?

It took Lee a long time to gather his thoughts and write about the time in Spain that changed him so much as a man. Perhaps, like Virginia Woolf, he had to wait for the right moment: "The past only comes back when the present runs so smoothly that it is like the sliding surface of a deep river. Then one sees through the surface to the depths."

All over Spain a new generation of young people are seeking to understand the lessons of the past. They want to break the pact of silence, *El Pacto de Olvido*, adopted by all sides in 1975 after the death of Franco and the advent of the new democracy. This new generation want to open up the warren of mass graves all over Spain. It is not, I think, that they want to finally expose the contamination of what we would now call ethnic cleansing to the pure air of democracy. The well of underground poison has long seeped into the Spanish body politic infusing it with toxicity and lacing it with venomous intent. I think they want to make people face up to the reality of a shameful past and ask themselves whether there are other skeletons, not hidden away in a closet, but hiding in full view masquerading as forces of good.

I do feel passionately about the injustice of the civil war, a sense of injustice first fuelled by Lee's account of life back in 1935 and his journey through Spain. It ignited a passion for Spain and fostered a sense that all was not well in my sheltered world. The passion, though cooled over time, is still there, just.

I am at a crossroads again in my life. I feel a need for reflection, a space, a pause in my life. I am not after stillness, solitude and retreat. I need to be on the move, I need to be moving forward. I need to walk out somewhere.

I need to find something other than loss.

*   *   *

I walk on down through the vineyards of Monterrei. They sit in the lee of the Sierra, which casts its rain-shadow over the vines, creating the dry conditions in which they flourish. As the afternoon wears on my own shadow lengthens as the sun bears down on the Cañado, the old drovers' road that is taking me towards the plain of Castile below me.

I pass yet another tiny pilgrim chapel nestling into the side of the road, at first sight more like a rustic barn housing oxen, but on closer inspection containing a tiny altar and a few bench pews. I pick up a small leaflet with an image of San Judas Tadeo, one of the twelve apostles, companion to Judas Iscariot and patron saint of desperate cases and lost causes. I tuck the leaflet away next to my St Christopher medal.

I spy a bright yellow shell symbol on a bright blue background, a Camino marker post. It is the first I have seen. British travel writer Robert Macfarlane writes, "walking, like faith, is a balm" and my spirits are raised by the sight of the religious way-marker. I am not alone in my walk. Macfarlane also talks of these ancient paths being associated with "time folding back on itself" and I do feel close to those who have passed this way before me.

My feet preoccupy me on this journey. They are holding up well so far, early on in my journey. I have invested in new boots. I am new to long distance walking and cautious about not overdoing the mileage until my boots are worn in. I wonder about Lee's boots. I doubt that they were made for walking across an alien country. More likely they were worn in by his months of labouring in London and still covered in the grime of the metropolis, with perhaps a sprinkling of chalk from the South Downs. I can visualise Lee, at this stage of his journey, his deceptive leggy gait, muscles hardened by a year on the building site, bouncing off the springy turfed sods, walking into a perfect storm of civil war.

I have a picture in my mind of A Pair of Shoes, the still life painting by Vincent Van Gogh. The story goes that Van Gogh bought a second-hand pair of boots from a Parisian flea market. Still considering them not to be assez ouvrières – not working class enough – he duly put them on and took them for a walk across the muddy woods of the capital. The resulting painting tells of feet battered into submission by unbending leather encased by a pointed ring of steel, held together by mean hobnails, stiff encrusted laces flapping helplessly. Not so much a work of craft than an instrument of torture.

A vision of the 207 Jarrow marchers in 1936 comes into my head, marching 300 miles from the slums of north-east England to parliament, protesting at the closure of the shipbuilding industry. They were led by their local labour MP, Ellen Wilkinson, known as "Red Ellen". She also accompanied a labour delegation, led by Clement Attlee, to Spain during the civil war. It is not known whether she met the similarly branded Dolores Ibarruri, the communist Republican leader. She was known as *La Pasionara*, famous for her banner *No Pasarán* (They Shall Not Pass) with which she greeted the Franco's fascist nationalist troops as they besieged Madrid.

Lee had mixed in communist circles in his months spent in London before setting off for Spain. On his arrival in the capital he was given shelter of a sort by the father of a striking young girl, Cleo. Lee had met both on a caravan site near Stroud. Lee was captivated by Cleo. She was smitten too, but only with the romance and drama of communism. The father was an impoverished but charismatic American communist who had fled the USA with his young well-to-do wife. Lee was unaware that, in the next few years, his life would be changed forever by another lifelong communist, this one the wealthy half of the partnership and his wife, the beautiful enigmatic driving force.

Cleo and her father were squatting in a semi-demolished part of a mansion, soon to be pulled down and converted into flats. The house lay on the edge of Putney Heath, by the Thames, with views stretching right across London to the Hampstead hills. Before making my own journey to Spain I had joined a writing group that met in a house on Parliament Hill, a stone's throw from Hampstead Heath. I would sit there, looking out over London across the river to Putney and think of Lee, climbing through young Cleo's bedroom window and into her bed. Her father had not been too impressed and had banished Lee from the house but found him a job in the demolition team to burn off all that youthful energy. In this unlikely setting Lee first inhaled the intoxicating fumes of revolution. There was a strike on the building site and for weeks anarchy ruled. Lee recalled, "I experienced hallucinations of communism, naïve and innocent as water, a physical sensation rather than an intellectual one." As always with Lee though, his vision of the revolution was a sugar-coated one, he dreamt of "a hint of free love shared with our prettier comrades." A young man, older than Lee, took on the role of the strike leader. His name was Fred Copeman and he was already a hard-bitten veteran of the Invergordan naval mutiny in which his leadership role was punished by expulsion from the Royal Navy. He made a stirring speech and was declared strike leader. The strike fizzled out but Lee had experienced the heady sense of revolution. He was not to know that he would soon meet Copeman again, this time on the battlefield in Spain. Copeman was by then an experienced International Brigade leader and Lee a raw recruit. According to Lee, Fred picked him out from the crowd: "When he recognised me, his hard eyes glittered with frosty warmth." And then he said, "The poet from the buildings, never thought you'd make it."

Walking and marching is still seen as a legitimate response to repression. The local paper that I glance at in a bar reports that the miners' strike in Asturias in the north of Spain is escalating and 240 miners from that region and Aragon, also in the north, are planning to walk to Madrid to protest at savage cuts to government subsidies. These cuts would, in effect, close the mines forever. In 1934 a strike by the same mining areas was brutally put down by a certain General Franco.

I arrive in Verin, my stop for the night, and ease off my dusty boots. I have a very simple meal in the only open café in town. The stew is salty and I need several beers to wash it down and take the taste of the salt away. The route to the south that I will take the following day is dotted with small lakes that were once a centre of salt production. Salt panning would once have been as productive and prosperous an occupation as gold prospecting once was in the Wild West in the USA. I contemplate my aching but satisfied feet and reflect that some inspirational walkers of the past did not have shoes and salt was once a symbol of oppression.

My grandfather once met with Pandit Nehru, the Prime Minister of India and the ideological and political heir to Mahatma Gandhi. The photograph of their meeting had looked down on me in my house in my previous life. I do not know what they spoke about, but my grandfather was a great walker so perhaps they touched on Gandhi's famous 24-day barefoot Dandi march. The so-called Salt Tax walk in 1930 – involving Ghandi and seventy-eight followers – struck a huge symbolic blow for the freedom of India from colonial rule. Although

Gandhi was a pacifist, when he walked into the sea off the Gujarat coast and picked up a lump of natural salt, he was, in effect, declaring war on the British administration. As I shake a few crystals of salt onto my hand and place them on my tongue, just for an instant as the sodium chloride explodes, I am back in a bitter world of recrimination and divisiveness.

Zamora-Toro

Into the White Heat of Castile

12 June 2012, Old Castile, Northern Spain

The morning brings a harsher, brighter, exposed Spain. The somnolent, shady green, green grass of Galicia is behind me. I have come down to the flatter, golden terrain of old Castile.

The fields of wheat stretch away from me, all the way to the blue-drenched horizon. The feverish Van Gogh-like scene is broken only by a single red poppy in the distance, an intruder, an anomaly of nature, a wild passionate creature going against the grain. I lie in the shade and consider this stranger for what seems like hours. As the sun's rays weaken, the proud, erect poppy – still nourished daily by the pointless sacrifices of the young in all those past, present and future battles for control of land – steadily empties its veins of its lifeblood until, as the sun sets, its shoulders sag, its spine droops. I call to mind the words of Homer in *The Iliad* describing the death of a soldier in battle: "And his head drooped, like a poppy in a spring garden weighed down with seeds and a heavy rain: so his head leaned to one side beneath the weight of his helmet."

I am left with an image of Lee, always one step ahead of me, a speck disappearing into the distance for another day.

That speck turns out to be Zamora, the first city I've encountered on the journey since Vigo. It sits high above the River Duero, a majestic river with dual Spanish/Portuguese nationality. It originates in the dry Castilian heartlands of Soria, home of one of Spain's most famous poets, Antonio Machado, and flows down into Portugal and empties itself into the Atlantic at Porto. It acts as a border between its Iberian neighbours and feeds the insatiable thirst of the vineyard roots in Porto to produce the light and subtle *vinho verde* (green wines) of the region. Unlike in the 1930s, the river looks healthy.

Machado was a walker too and wrote of the Castilian countryside. He was a member of the Generation of 98: a literary movement that reacted to Spain's loss of its last colony, Cuba, in 1898. As in Britain, the loss of an Empire inspired much soul searching. Machado, a Republican sympathiser, had talked of there being two Spains and the inevitability of the Spanish Civil War. He died from natural causes in 1939, three days before his mother, as they were finally pushed into exile in France by the nationalist advances.

Probably the best remembered line in Spanish poetry is Machado's *"No hay camino, se hace camino al andar"* (There are no roads, just paths made by walking).

Another dead poet lying by the roadside littered with so many as Franco turned the screw on his country.

Lee had no idea of the danger he was in as he descended into the heart of Spain. He was not a diehard ideological revolutionary, but something much more dangerous: a romantic, poetic drifter looking for a cause. He had seen the threat of Mosley and his Blackshirts prowling the streets of London. The rise of fascism in Europe was all around him. As we have seen with Bóveda in Orense, the nationalists distrusted and feared the poet.

He, however, had more important matters on his mind. He was too busy falling in love with Spain, a dangerous thing to do at this time. Like the young through the ages he was naïve in the face of seduction. He had been practising the art, himself, unconsciously perhaps: the solitary dreamy fair-haired poet, walking through old England, always on the cusp of adventure, never staying still; the unattainable object of desire. He felt he could control this art. But life is not art. It is people and emotions and hopes, and people get hurt. He had led a charmed life until crossing into Spain. No more those casual loves on Beacon Hill:

Now as we loose the knots of love,
Earth at our back and sky above,
Visible at last we gather
All that is, except each other.

At this point in his journey the only conflicts he was concerned about were those girls back home, fighting for his affections. He wrote of Patsy, Nell and Cleo, but didn't mention the others – such as Molly, who wrote to him of how he would send "flame after flame of moonlight through me". And there were others. Was he looking for new exotic loves? I expect so, but if so they were absent from his writings so far. Was Spain itself a big enough mistress for him?

Lee clearly had great charm, and wrote beautifully about this rare beast. A woman is charmed by what she hears, he thought. Was this, I wonder, a drawback for him? He had his looks, his music, his eyes, but his silver tongue was, for the moment, impotent. In England, it was often enough "to lie by one's sleeping love and to shield her eyes from the sun." In Spain perhaps a bit more was required?

His dalliance with Spain seemed to have quenched his search for love and passion, temporarily, at least.

As I walk I am listening to one of my favourite singers of the moment, Laura Marling, an English rose who seems to have Celtic blood coursing through her fingers on the guitar and the voice of someone so saddened by life and life in one so young. I love her song of a girl whose lover had gone to war 'What He Wrote'. She sings of the girl asking forgiveness from the Greek Gods, "He cut out my tongue, there is nothing to say." It sums up my feelings of helplessness and loneliness that are always there, even as I journey on in search of hope.

13 June, Zamora

Some objects do seem to retain the pulse of their making.
— Edmund De Waal, 2010

The city walls stand above me as I wait for the new day to begin. I am lying on a stretch of scorched grass beside the River Duero. Whether it's because I am beside water, I am not sure, but I feel for the scallop shell in my pocket. It retains a coolness to the touch. How old it is and where it has been I do not know. Shaped by the tide and the elements over time it has a reassuring feel. It seems to have the look of a charm, something that can take me back to better times.

The shell reminds me of the power of nature and the tendency of man to yield to its will and destiny. Lee refused to accept his fate of a village life and walked away from it. It is good to feel that I am also perhaps challenging the natural order of things and seeing what I can make of myself, even if late in the day.

I had passed a blacksmith the day before and paused to watch him work on a piece of iron. Using the four elements of life – fire, water, air and earth – he shaped nature into an object of his own making. An object that, in time, would disintegrate and be returned to nature. And yet I wonder if things and people ever die completely. Who has held this shell or that pot? Where has the shell washed up? What sun has bleached it white and what seas have worn it smooth? They say that ancient Chinese potters would write words in the mud before it became the body of the shape which became a pot. What happened to those words?

Ashes to ashes, dust to dust. I remember the annual ritual of the lead up to Easter, the period of Lent and fasting. This was the time I discovered, probably for the first time, the pleasure of giving something up, the long nights of desire, the gnawing feeling inside, the final release and ensuing indulgence, the discovery of real appetite. Lee wrote of the importance of preserving this sense: "It is the keenness of living; it is one of the senses that tell you that you are still curious to exist, that you still have an edge on your longings and want to bite into the world." I realise that I am slowly rediscovering this zest for life. I can still feel the dark smudge of ash pressed on to my forehead each Ash Wednesday by the thumb of Father Healy, the mark of eternal reincarnation.

As I sit in a Zamora square, under a cool canopy of plane trees and watch children pose for photos with two statues of medieval musicians, I can visualise Lee seeking out some companionship with Rudi, Heinrich and Artur, the German buskers that he linked up with so briefly. Did he see himself back in Slad with Sixpence the Tanner, Clergy Green and Boney, the gang of outlaws roaming the Cotswolds countryside looking for mischief? That night, Lee's only night in this city, he listened to the "choking rattle of Artur's breath and the sound of Heinrich weeping."

He must have thought of the childhood fevers that plagued him throughout his life: fevers that had him clinging on for life; fevers that so dominated family life that his sister, Frances, who watched over him as the "smiling black lanterns swung closer and closer" just slipped away and died in a corner.

That summer day back in 1935, Lee was unaware of the forthcoming conflagration, only a year away, one that would wipe out an entire Spanish generation. I doubt also that he was aware of the generation lost to Spain just 17 years before.

I had seen a plaque in the main square on the outside wall of the town hall. It honoured two young doctors from the town who had fought to contain the vicious outbreak of Spanish flu in 1918 that decimated Spain but hit Zamora the hardest. It affected the young the most and spared the old. This was a worldwide pandemic that died away after eighteen months as quickly as it flared up and spread, unlike the Spanish Civil War, the effect of which is still being felt nearly eighty years later.

I had recently, back in Cornwall, been invited to attend a Humanist naming ceremony for the newly born son, Ernesto, of a couple who are friends. I had only ever been to a Catholic christening before. I am godfather to three girls, all now in their late twenties and I take the role seriously. In the Humanist ceremony I was invited, along with all the other guests, to collectively pledge our commitment as "Ernesto's Village" to look after his well-being and support him as he grows up.

The ceremony had been a moving one and now the memory of it stirred a need to discover more about some of the young children and innocent villagers, struck down by this pestilence in Spain. I spent

41

the morning in the library and found an account of those times in the diary of a local family. I tried to imagine what life would have been like during those times.

26 October 1918, Zamora, Northern Spain

It's a cold autumnal day and I am wrapped up against the chill wind blowing in from the plain ruffling the surface of the River Duero below. Corowa is my name.

I stifle a cough and try not to catch the eye of my neighbour in the crowd assembled in front of the Convento de la Magdalena in the centre of the city. A cough at the moment is akin to the bells of the convent peeling out a death knell. Zamora, like all of Spain, is in the grip of a deadly flu virus that is decimating the community. Zamora, however, seems to be hit the hardest. For Father Tomas it is a sign from God that a sickness has been eating away at the congregation for too long: a tumescence of impurities; an overindulgence of carnal pleasures. We are receiving divine retribution. The masses gathered all around me have been summoned to prostrate themselves before the Virgen del Tránsito, the patron saint of Zamora, on her feast day.

I try not to think of the latent viruses circulating around the crowd, borne aloft above the weeping figure of the Virgin, floating on the cool thermal incubators of fetid air, transmitted from the feverish bodies huddling together for warmth whilst drawing their coats tightly in, both to suffocate any residue of creeping death and ward off any invading spores.

I see a child with a small Meiga doll clutched to her side. The Meiga is a pagan legacy of the past, from a time before the Reconquest and the Inquisition. She is a local sorceress willing and able to cleanse evil spirits from the body and mind, for a price. Father Tomás did not welcome the Meigas to his congregation but he knew they were there, lurking in the corner, still inhabiting the pueblos, the home villages of the city's community, spread out across the plain and visited on high days and feasts.

My fingers stray to my throat and trace a line down to the tip of my breasts and caress the two hard cold white stone pendants that lie there. Two white *Gotas de Leche*, Drops of Milk, agate stones

42

like mother of pearl. My mother gave them to me after the birth of my first child. "They will provide succour to your breasts and keep them full of God's milk," she said, "You cannot afford to bring more children into the world. If your breasts are full it is better."

The ladies of the city have their *Nodrizas*, their wet nurses. They can conserve their own milk and control the growth of their families within the rules of their faith. For the rest, we do our best, but Father Tomás prefers not to see the *Gotas de Leche*.

I am from Peru. My grandfather came to Spain to reclaim some of the fortune that the *reconquistadores del siglo xvi*, the Spanish explorers of Cortez and Pizarro, took from his land and brought back for the kings and queens of Spain. He retraced their steps on the Vía de la Plata to Zamora. My son has the name of his Harakmbut forefathers, Romeo.

My son is dead, killed by the Spanish virus, just four days ago. Four centuries on and Spain continues to wipe out my family.

La Señora Mendiri has also lost a young infant daughter. The day of her burial she was carried from the cathedral to the cemetery in La Carroza Funeraria, the Mendiri Family children's hearse. In the gloom of late afternoon two shod horses, black as night, pull the ornate open carriage through the streets of the city. The coachwork and wheels are painted in virgin white. The tiny coffin lies in a glass case, open to the elements. The driver sits on a white seat with a gold embossed wreath on its side. Below is inscribed a single word: Soledad. Alone; alone for all eternity.

Ana Mendiri, six years old, lies in her white, now redundant, Holy Communion dress. Her head on a soft white pillow, pale hollow cheeks, blue eyes closed and the tips of her toes pointing up towards heaven. Father Tomas leads the procession of mourners behind the solitary soul.

Romeo, he was buried quietly, no fuss.

The young of Spain are being killed off, a whole generation, for the virus has selected not the old and the weak but the young and virile.

I pray that we shall not see the likes of this again, not least in my lifetime.

I take off my necklace of white pearl stones and push it deep down into the pocket of my overcoat.

14 June 2012, Zamora, Northern Spain

Zamora is the first of many fortress cities in Castile. Here the modern foundations of Spain were laid. Castile was the homeland of the Catholic monarchs, Ferdinand and Isabella, who reconquered the country from 700 years of African Moorish rule. Spain, then and now, has half an ear to the siren strains emanating from across the strait of Gibraltar, the other half attuned to Europe. Just days after Franco's coup in July 1936, spearheaded by Spanish Moroccan elite shock troops, most of north-west Spain, including Zamora, had declared for the rebel nationalists.

Now Spain, once again, is at the heart of a European crisis with African overtones. The 2011 Arab Spring of uprisings against undemocratic regimes is still being played out, no more ruthlessly than in Syria. The cohesion of the European Union is under threat with the prosperous north increasingly in serious economic dispute with the underdeveloped south.

Zamora is traditionally an ultra-conservative city and instinctive supporter of all that Franco, the Church and the Army hold dear.

This is brought home to me twice over.

During my travels through Galicia I had seen posters and flyers for the latest *Las Huellas de La Barraca* 2012 tour. This is a tour that literally follows in the footsteps of *La Barraca*, a travelling theatre. *Barraca* means shed. In the 1930s much of the population of the rural areas of Spain was illiterate and disenfranchised. The Republican government had prioritised setting up educational programmes to deal with this issue. New schools were created, libraries set up and a rolling wave of culturally-based initiatives were created. *La Barraca* was spearheaded by Federico García Lorca. Images of the smiling poet in blue boiler suit overalls promoted the theatre. Golden Age playwrights like Lope De Vega and Calderón de la Barca, the Spanish equivalents to Shakespeare, had their works staged in sheds or on the back of trucks in small villages across the length and breadth of the country. The 2012 tribute educational tours were springing up all over Spain but not in Zamora. I feel the icy grip of local politics stifling grass root cultural growth. No books are being burned in the Plaza Mayor, but...

I flick through the programme of the *Teatro Principal* in Zamora and come across a concert staged in March 2012 – a follow-up to the previous year's staging of the same event which, by all accounts, was a sold-out success.

"*Música en la Guerra Civil Española*" (Music from the Spanish Civil War), reads the headline. I am more than a little taken aback. In all my 30 years and more of travelling to and living in Spain, I had never seen such a public concert advertised.

I read on: "As well as hymns like the celebrated *Cara al Sol* (Salute the Sun) of the Falange or *A las Barricadas* (To the Barricades) of the Anarchists, in this unusual programme you will get a feel for the romance of the era."

The hairs rise on the back of my neck. 'Salute the Sun' is the fascist call to arms, sung with right arm outstretched in Nazi-fashion. It is the anthem of the Falange, the only political movement allowed in Spain for the 36 years of Franco dictatorship. I cannot believe that this is democratic Spain in 2012. To my knowledge, the singing of this hymn is normally confined to a single celebration in public once a year by a small group of diehard Franco supporters at his tomb on the outskirts of Madrid on 20 November, the anniversary of Franco's death in 1975.

Reading on, it transpires that the whole event is a joint effort by the church choir and the army band, subsidised by the town hall.

This is possibly the loneliest I have felt on this journey to date.

Tracking the River Duero, the early afternoon sun glistens off the lazy meandering river's surface, resting up for the demanding stretch ahead, the descent into one of the many cavernous gorges on its passage to Portugal and into the Atlantic.

In the haze of the far distance, white flecks are moving and bobbing. A herd of sheep I fancy, being driven to market. But no, as I gain on the caravanserai, to my astonishment, I see a long line of small white cars, bumper to bumper, ascending the steep hill towards the town of Tordesillas. I move up a gear as the cavalcade winds its way around the twist in the river, like a giant caterpillar looking for shade.

When I catch my next glimpse, the parade has come to a halt. A stationary line of vintage Seat 600s – I have now identified the species – lies parked up on the verge, next to the approach to a small church tucked into the hillside.

The owners have decamped, en masse, to the church and I have an opportunity to inspect the vehicles. Their owners clearly look after them well. The Seat 600 is as emblematic of early 20th century Spanish motorcar production as the VW Beetle is of Germany and the Trabant is of East Germany in the old German Democratic Republic, the DDR.

I lean carefully against one of the cars and gulp down some local red wine from Zamora. I had drawn it straight from an old oak barrel from a *bodega* passed earlier in the day. It was stored in my other recent acquisition, my *bota*. The *bota* is a cream coloured stretched goatskin container with red piping all around the edges and a rather twee image of Don Quixote and Sancho Panza etched into its kidney shaped cover. I had bought it from a souvenir shop, partly out of nostalgia – I used to possess one when I first travelled across Spain as a young student in the 1970s with a Eurorail pass – and partly because it is still a hugely functional way to carry liquid on a walk.

I have not seen a Spanish person use one for many years and they are usually to be found only in souvenir shops or at flea markets like *El Rastro* in Madrid.

They were popular in the last century and were used in particular by the *campesinos*, the peasant farmers and workers, who toiled away in the heat and the cold of the huge land estates, in particular in the south of Spain in Andalusia. The custom was to share the *bota* around the group. The wine would be poured from above the head, a steady stream of red liquid being achieved by the holding of the container in both hands and squeezing the middle. In this fashion the neck of the *bota* did not need to touch the lips and thus avoided the spread of viruses and infection that could often lead to an early grave. This sort of wine pouring is still to be seen across Spain in certain wine producing regions like the *País Vasco*, the Basque country just to the west of the Pyrenees border with France, where the young, light white wine needs to be served frothy and full of air. Further to the west, the drinking of the local Asturian cider is afforded similar care and attention.

Lee would have observed the *bota* everywhere he went and no doubt shared in the ritual, though he does not mention it as far as I recall.

My *bota*, the Seat 600 – both are objects of nostalgia but both are practical still today.

The Seat 600 Club members, as they turn out to be, emerge in dribs and drabs from the church. The service has been to offer up thanks to San Cristóbal, St Christopher, for their safe passage. Instinctively I touch the simple St Christopher medal attached to my mobile phone, given to me by my anxious mother on my departure for Spain, on this – in her eyes – extremely ill-thought-out venture.

It was a nice touch and means a lot to me. The bearded saint, on one side of the medal, stands waist-deep in the sea. He is holding a staff in his right hand; the other arm cradles a baby boy. His robe and cloak are ruffled in the sea breeze. I imagine the monochrome scene brought to life in an El Greco painting, weeping purples contrasting with lime greens. On the reverse side, a modern aeroplane, boat and luxury motorcar (not a Seat 600) are set against the background of a soaring mountain range. It could be anywhere in the world, but I see the Guadarrama mountains, to the south of me, a cordillera sweeping across from east to west. Beyond them the capital city of Madrid and, further south again, the dusty orange tree-lined white road leading all the way to Seville.

A further novel aspect of the long line of cars is that several of them are sporting a variety of wheeled contraptions in tow. Some have early 1960 versions of trailer tents, some small boats, but my gaze is drawn to one car in particular that is towing a vivid blue farmer's cart. Two young lads are leaning against the cart and I engage them in conversation through the time-honoured fashion of offering them a swig from my *bota*.

"Hola, ¿te apetece un poco de vino?"

"Hombre, gracias, con gusto, las iglesias siempre me hacen seco."

They accept with the comment that churches always give them a thirst.

"¡Qué carro tan magnifico!"

"Sí, es de mi abuelo. ¿Que tal?, me llamo Pepe."

What a great cart, I say. It transpires it belongs to his grandfather.

The cart tells its own story: large black copperplate letters on the blue surface of its sides proclaim that it is "*La propiedad de Aladino Fernández.*" It belongs to Aladino, the grandfather of Pepe, my new friend.

Two bright red and white carnations flower at each end of the cart's side. In between stands a windmill and small church. There is

47

a white wooden board, nailed firmly in place. On it is stamped: "*SOGO. S. ZA. N42 AGRICOLA. LICENCIADO 'Rodaje de Carruajes'*."

It has the official seal of approval and is licensed to carry goods and chattels. Dotted around the side are further metallic licences of operation, updated annually: a bright yellow disc for 1959; a red triangle for 1960; a black square for 1962. It looks like it was off the road for 1961. Spanish bureaucracy may be as dull as anywhere else but at least it is more colourful and executed in style.

On the other side of the cart is a cartoon of an elderly gentleman with a bristling moustache; bald, save for a lush sprouting of black hair around the edges of one ear. He looks a bit lost, like the old cartoon figure Mr Magoo. Pepe assures me that this is not the local tax inspector.

The two cartwheels, one for each side, are enormous with large wooden spokes. It resembles more the wheels of a watermill.

Somehow the cart is hitched on to the car and Pepe, who has been regaling me with the history of the car while I am being smitten by the cart, offers me a lift to Tordesillas. His brother, Juan, hops into the cramped front seat of the car and Pepe and I sit on the tailgate, legs dangling in the slight breeze. Red dust clouds swirl around, clogging our throats and more wine is called for, to be streamed down from above. This demands good hand-to-eye co-ordination now that the jolting and bumping of the cart has to be factored into lines of trajectory. Enough of the wine hits the mark to enable conversation to take place.

"*Morcilla de Burgos, lo mejor, muy rico.*" He proffers a slice of greasy, fatty black pudding, raw; proclaiming it to be the best in the country, from Burgos.

"*No, gracias.*" It is cool, clear sparkling water I long for.

"*¿A Dónde va usted?*" (Where are you going?) he asks, adopting curiously the old-fashioned polite form of address, as he speaks in the pure as air accent of Valladolid.

"I'm not sure," I reply, truthfully, in my best Castilian Spanish accent, which I was proud of in Madrid, but rather ashamed of anywhere else. "I am looking for Laurie Lee."

At Pepe's blank look I give a general explanation, focussing more on the romantic and literary aspects of my quest and, perhaps unwisely, mentioning, "lost and troubled souls". It is the mention of the civil war, though, that hits home.

"I too am looking for lost souls, mi amigo, the souls of the dead and the living. Let me tell you about my grandfather. He was a proud man, a communist, a Red. He commanded a tank battalion during the defence of Madrid. He was a *madrileño*, brought up in Lavapies, a poor barrio in the south of the city. He fought at Jarama, the Ebro, he fought to the bitter end. *'No Pasarán,'* was the cry of *La Pasionara*, the talisman of the Reds. *'Madrid será la tumba del fascismo.'* 'They shall not pass, Madrid will bury fascism for good.' Of course it was not the case, Franco won and my grandfather was a marked man, there was a price on his head. Every Red who survived had a price on his head. One day I will take you to Almería where my grandfather was taken to be executed. He escaped and lived for three years underground. Literally, my friend, in a hole one metre square in his batman's garden in Madrid. He could only trust his batman not to betray him, even his brother – my great uncle – could betray him, he had kids to feed of his own."

He tells me this whilst we edge up hills and round corners, in a cloud of red dust rising from the crumbling pock-marked road, our hands gripping the side. Occasionally Pepe embellishes the story with internationally recognised gestures. One such crude gesture underscores his next point.

"He was a man: a Spanish man; a communist you know; red-blooded too – he had needs. Every so often he would risk discovery by slipping out in the night to have a shag, with his wife, you know, he had standards, well when he was *en casa* at least. No condoms or the pill then, my grandmother was regularly pregnant. As a consequence, she was taken locally to be a slag, a whore, it was common then. Ends had to be met by fair means or foul. A widow sleeping with the enemy. She wasn't tarred and feathered, but not far off."

Pepe pauses and takes a bite of raw blood and fat, belches and breaks wind. I stay quiet, not wanting to risk stemming this outpouring of living history.

"After three years he could stand it no more and disappeared into the Pyrenees and joined a gang of guerrillas tormenting the local *Guardia Civil* (Franco's hated quasi military police force). He came home again and took to smuggling. The Reds, the poor, the defeated;

we were starved into submission by Franco in those post-war years. My grandfather would go down to the south, to Andalusia, to the *dehesas* in the Sierra Aracena. This is the home of the black-footed Iberian pig, the king of all pigs. The pigs lived better than men. The *dehesas* were their heaven on earth: acorn-scented groves where the pigs snuffled to their heart's content and were fattened. They then met the same fate as the Reds: slaughter."

Pepe is quiet and takes a swig of wine from the *bota*. I take a slug and choke as the stream of red liquid hits the back of my parched throat.

"Now I look sometimes at the oak trees, at the time of the year when the bark is stripped back for conservation. Exposed is the shivering pink flesh of the tree, it speaks to me of rape and murder, the atrocities of the times. The land is prone to flash floods and sometimes you will find a bone, a human remain, floating on the surface, a reminder of a grisly past. The Dehesa is threatened by *El Gusano Bellota*, a parasitic worm that burrows into the acorn-bearing trees and sucks the life out of them. That's what they did to my grandfather."

Pepe turns around and points to a cool box in the cart filled with a variety of meat products, *embutido,* as he calls them: *chorizos* of all shape and sizes; hocks of *jamon Serrano*; *salchichones* (sausages); *morcilla* (black pudding); *orejas* (pig's ears).

"So, my grandfather and his friends return to Madrid with their booty of smuggled and illicit foodstuffs packed away into brown cardboard makeshift suitcases. They take a quiet night train. Imagine: it is dead of night, ten miles from Madrid. The train from Andalusia trundles through the countryside. It stops, as it always does, on the outskirts of a small village.

In an adjoining field, shadowy figures with baskets hover. They are the womenfolk of the Reds, they have walked from Madrid. My grandmother is there, my aunts and cousins. They wait expectantly and are soon rewarded. The night sky is suddenly filled with red and black and skin-white objects. They land on the earth with a thud. There are *chorizos, salchichones, jamones, orejas, morcilla*. The men know they will be searched on arrival in Madrid. To be found with smuggled goods is a death sentence.

This is how we lived, my friend, in those dark days. Now, once again, my people are being starved, many of my friends have no job.

I have two sons who have never worked. They want to know why!"

Before reaching the end of our journey, I lighten the conversation by telling Pepe the tale that Lee recounted when he was offered a lift in a farmer's cart to Segovia. It was a terrifying experience for Lee, an off-road nightmare, as the farmer dived down seemingly treacherous tracks at breakneck speeds and only stopped when the famous narrow aqueduct of Segovia came into view. The farmer boasted that he had driven a cart over the aqueduct in times past. Lee had timorously offered a view that that must have been quite difficult given the narrowness of the aqueduct. The farmer fixed him with an evil glint and replied, "I was driving a very small cart then."

Pepe drops me off at Tordesillas and I sadly wave goodbye to my new friends.

I do not linger in Tordesillas and move on rapidly to Valladolid.

Valladolid

A Club and a Candle

18 June 2012, Valladolid, The Lost Empire

Valladolid is a pleasant enough city in the evening dusk. I stroll through its main park, serenaded by love calls from all around. These come not from the young men and women from local families parading in all their finery, engaged in their evening *paseo* – the traditional Sunday walk through the streets; a custom that lingers on from earlier more repressed times when it was the one socially permitted public opportunity to flirt, from afar. No, these not so refined mating calls emanate from high above me in the trees.

Closer scrutiny confirms that the screeches of unrequited passion come from pairs of pheasants, practically indistinguishable from the dark branches that house them. Unlike their human cousins they seem determined to hide their colourful finery at this stage of affairs.

Even in the 1930s the courtship of the young in Spain could only be accommodated by a very regulated process, which became known as *Pedir la Conversación* (Requesting a Conversation). This offers a clue, perhaps, as to why Lee's amorous encounters in Spain were less frequent than back home in England, and often transactional in nature.

Even in those heady days of the 1930s, when the election of the left-wing Republican government ushered in a period of unfettered freedom in beliefs and sexual mores, the more rural and provincial areas of Spain were largely immune from or resistant to such fever.

If a single girl was so disposed she would respond to advances from a young man by signalling an appearance at a ground floor *reja* of her house, often late at night. This was a small grilled window where small talk would take place between the *novios* (the couple), the boys

52

earnestly pronouncing what they believed the girls wanted to hear, the girls giving blessings and dispensations through shy looks, signs of the cross and murmurings of approval. Touching was forbidden. It was a scene not dissimilar to one enacted every day inside the churches of the city as the priest hears daily confession.

Lee did not take to the city, he found it full of deformed beggars and conscripted soldiers, who, unaware of the imminent conflagration, were biding their time, playing at being at war and relieving their pent up frustrations with drink and the local whores down by the river.

He also had a violent, crazed landlord, El Borracho, the drunkard, who came to a sticky end at the hands of his long-suffering wife. Life, in the raw, was not that different from his home village of Slad, where often the village imposed its own justice rather than wait for that of the law.

Five hundred years ago Valladolid was the centre of the Spanish Empire. Ferdinand and Isabella, who were to be known forever as the Catholic monarchs who delivered Spain from 700 years of Moorish rule, were married in the city. Miguel de Cervantes lived here as he completed his masterpiece *Don Quixote* with his one good arm, the other having been crippled at the Battle of Lepanto against the Turks in 1572.

However, at the midpoint of the 16th century, Philip II condemned the city to relative obscurity for evermore. He took the decision to build the Escorial, a monastery and royal palace just 45km north-west of Madrid and to move the seat of power there. Valladolid never recovered. For Madrid it was just the beginning.

I approach the city along a *Cañada de Mesta*, an ancient trail dating from medieval times. The Mesta was a powerful body that oversaw the main industry of the day across the plains of Spain. Sheep rearing dominated the medieval economy: it was the chief form of agriculture, providing much needed food, and precious wool to sell at market to the Dutch cloth merchants. Sheep were herded to and fro across the spine of the country, seeking out fresh pastures. This nomadic existence served the nation well for centuries, but in the process impoverished the soil, created mass rural unemployment and, in so doing, created the foundations of the poor rural unequal society that still dogs Spain to the present day and undoubtedly contributed to the outbreak of the civil war.

Valladolid is still famed for two things. Chiefly, it is believed that the most pure form of Spanish (Castilian) is spoken here, and certainly you still notice the difference arriving, as I did, from Galicia and the north. It is revered also as the most pious of cities.

I had visited the city earlier in 2012, at Easter, during *Semana Santa* (Holy Week). It was cold and miserable and the traditional solemnity associated with the time of year seemed to hang heavily in the air. The visitor is never more a stranger in Spain than at a time of *fiesta*; even the visitor fluent in the language and customs.

The community plans the Holy Week processions all year, each parish with its own *Cofradía,* or brotherhood, preparing its own elaborate floats and forms of worship. Whole extended families take part in these preparations. News of the processions is communicated through word of mouth, and as I subsequently discover, through the dedicated radio network, Radio Maria, broadcasting on 95.5 FM.

Being back here brings that memory back to life. The Maundy Thursday processions had all been cancelled due to heavy rain. I console myself in a packed bar with a glass or two of the local *vino tinto* and *chorizo* cooked in cider, followed by a ripe, local *queso de oveja*, a sheep's cheese. It is called *Pata de Mulo*, mule trotter, and it has a kick.

Good Friday dawns dry but cold – very cold. The most important of Thursday's processions has been re-scheduled. I find this out by chance and discover that it will take place that evening starting at eight o'clock. This is *La Procesión de la Peregrinación del Silencio* (The Procession of the Silent Pilgrimage).

I take my place towards the end of the march at around 7.30pm, resigned to a long wait, but eager to secure a good pitch as the crowds swell. We wait and wait. The temperature drops and drops again. All around the city echoes the sound of silence; it is extraordinary. As ten o'clock approaches the crowds around me stir. The sporadic, whispered conversations die down and the procession appears from around the corner. Row upon row of white-clad worshippers walk slowly by: some made invisible, shrouded in full hooded outfits, with slits for eyes that stare blankly out. Seemingly immune to the cold, bare fingers hold up the emblems of their brotherhood. In the wake of the outriders on their march to Calvary trudge the very old, the young and able-bodied, male and female, young children, all pulling a pale bloodied figure of Christ. Police on horseback accompany the penitents. I stare in horror as I see some penitents hauling the floats behind them, their bare toes digging into the frozen street for purchase, sliding at times on the frosted surface. Some are no more than children.

I think back to my own childhood in England: Easter Sunday spent not in chocolate egg hunts in gardens full of daffodils but at Mass; the Stations of the Cross; enforced reflection; the quiet, the quiet.

As the procession winds on and the silence continue I find myself back in southern Ireland in the 1960s, a Catholic country, not dissimilar to 1930s Spain. On holiday in my father's childhood home, a cottage still without electricity and running water but awash with crosses and Madonnas.

I can take no more of the parade and, spying a break in the procession, I dart across the street to head for my hotel.

19 June 2012, Valladolid

To my surprise, as I awake, I hear the sound of flamenco from a nearby bar.

Lee recalled a vivid and intimate dance scene at an inn on the way to Valladolid in which the elderly innkeepers, husband and wife, were, for a night, roused by Lee's fiddle and the spirit of flamenco and experience a fleeting glimpse of their youth and a sense of pleasure denied them in their old age.

Lee had also written of being awoken by a beggar in Valladolid, a young boy, singing below in the street: "He sang with the whole of his body, his eyes tight-closed, his bare throat rippling in the sunlight, and his voice, a nasal wail that obliterated the city around him – the voice of Islam, aimed at the sky and pitched to an empty landscape."

Lee's writing struck a chord with his readers in getting close to capturing the soul of Spain with his rhythmic, lyrical and sparse prose.

Lorca attempted to define the core of Spanish humanity and coined the term *duende*. It is difficult to translate the meaning of this into English. My Welsh ancestors would talk about *Cynefyn*. Perhaps the nearest English can get to the meaning is to talk about a nation's "soul".

Lorca said that, "All that has dark sounds has *duende*." He spoke of *La Niña de los Peines* who sang flamenco with "a scorched throat, without voice, breath, colour, but with... *duende*."

I guess, whether consciously or sub-consciously, the search for *duende* is the reason why people continue to be attracted to Spain, the search for that indefinable spark of existence. Perhaps it is why I have been drawn back to Spain at a time of loss.

I hurry over to the dimly lit bar, where I find a small travelling group of dancers and singers from the Antonio Gades School. Gades is one of the finest dancers around in Spain. The room is dark, small, intimate. As I grow accustomed to the dark, I see that much of the audience is made up of young women, dressed for the occasion, straining forward at the front of the stage.

The stage is as black as night, pinpricks of red piercing the darkness. A crimson phosphorescent oval hovers above the centre of the stripped back stage: day leaching into the western night; dawn breaking in the east.

They take to the stage. There are four singers and two guitarists, all males, the bright yellow of their guitars cutting into the confined space. They are dressed simply but elegantly in black. Their hair is long, greasy. Some have beards – straggly, wild affairs. There is a hint of menace: these are outsiders, gypsies.

They start to play and one by one begin to sing. A dancer emerges from behind the curtain, he is tall and slight, a starved waif from the slums of Triana in Seville. He moves slowly in time to a solo singer picked out by the spotlight. His easy controlled movement is in contrast to the straining efforts of the singer, whose bulging blue and white veins ripple down his throat, popping like the buttons of his corseted black shirt, as he calls the faithful to prayer. The chant, from a long time ago, is torn from him and reborn, its bare pagan bones scattering on the hard surface. The staccato heels of the dancer stamp and fly in a swirling dance to the death. His arms arc through the air, the body erect and proud, the eyes are dark and all seeing. The black outfit snakes over his frame, accentuating each point of reference, marbling long white fingers splay through the air.

The young female audience scarcely dares breathe.

* * *

Sitting outside the *Palacio de los Vivero,* where King Ferdinand and Queen Isabella were married on 18 October 1469, nothing is stirring in the midday heat. Ferdinand and Isabella were 17 and 18 years old respectively, and through their marriage created a unified Spain by bringing together the kingdoms of Castile and Aragon. They set in train a crusade of reconquest to expel the alien occupiers of their new kingdom, the Moors. In time they would also attempt to rid the country of its Jewish element.

As Lee was making his way through Spain, the right-wing nationalist factions were drawing up their plans to overthrow the government. In time Franco would use the very terms *Reconquista* and *Cruzada* to justify the need for a coup. He would declare war on democrats, socialists, communists, anarchists, republicans, liberals, Freemasons and Jews. Ironically, his two main allies would be his Islamic Moroccan troops (self-styled *Novios de la Muerte,* Bridegrooms of Death, who had no expectation other than death in action) and his Protestant German Nazi allies.

Lee had encountered deeply entrenched anti-clerical feelings in the rural areas of his travels. Over centuries the Church had become almost as one with the ruling power. It was a universal landlord, a credit-provider, customer, employer and alms giver. It also had a stranglehold on the education system. The Second Republic reform programme threatened this elemental force, aligned as it was with the status quo and the rich establishment.

Lee clearly had communist sympathies, though how deeply they were held is a matter of conjecture. Certainly for a large part of the rural underclass in 1930s Spain, communism filled a void left by the decline of trust and faith in a Church that was deemed to have betrayed its core values of a gospel, of brotherhood and social justice. A priest of the times who taught at a seminary said to his students: "Had not the Spanish people always followed their clergy with a candle or a club in its hands." On being asked by his students why the Church had always been on the side of the right, he had responded, "Because the left has always kicked and beaten the church to the right." There was clearly no agreement on this issue and I am sure similar sentiments are still expressed today all over Spain.

As I prepare to head south from Valladolid, like Lee, I am not particularly sad to leave the city. For him it meant escaping from

El Borracho and from soldiers very much on the edge. For me, the memories of my previous visit and the evidence of the hold that the Spanish Church still exerts over its people overshadow the glimpse of *duende* provided by the flamenco.

Segovia

Cliff of Crows

22 June 2012, Segovia

"Have a nice day."

I had reached Segovia and encountered my first American voice since arriving in Spain. Segovia – like Canterbury, Salisbury or Oxford – is a fixture on the overseas tourist circuit. It broke the spell and alerted me that I was very much coming back to the realities of modern-day Spain.

The Americanism had intruded into my reflections of a long ago Spain: a Spain that had faced another crisis in the early 19th century. I had been standing in front of the Alcázar of Segovia, a strategically placed fortress that had protected the city over the years. It looked over the plains below. Adjacent to the Alcázar was the Museum of the Artillery Academy which had housed a Research Centre for Chemistry in the 18th century.

In front of me is a large stone monument erected in honour of Louis Proust, an eminent French chemist who had spent time in Segovia as a researcher. Like many artists and intellectuals in Spain, he was hounded out as a result of a war. This was not a civil war but the Peninsular War when Napoleon invaded Spain in 1802. He burned Proust's laboratory and repatriated him. Proust died a few years later.

The inscription on the monument reads:

In the hands of man, metal oxidation is a process subject to the laws of definite proportion and the law of nature itself, and incapable of influence by the human will.

Whilst not professing to understand the pure science of the statement, I think it profound in the sense that – as much as he might like to – man cannot force change upon the ancient laws of nature.

However much Franco repressed the citizens of the country over which he ruled for 36 years, he could not quench the thirst for individual freedom in his nation. Lee had felt the hot breath of the regime on his collar and he had responded instinctively by allying himself with the forces of natural justice, just as Pepe's grandfather had done.

Lee did not stay long in Segovia but he did return many years later. In August 1969, having written *As I Walked Out*, he went to Spain with the BBC to film a promotional piece for the book. It was there that his priceless 1935-1937 Spanish diaries were stolen from a car. There was suspicion that they had been stolen by the Spanish secret police. In 1955 Lee had published a book on Spain, *A Rose for Winter*, which whilst being non-controversial, would have brought him to the attention of the authorities. It would have been known that a BBC crew was filming. Gerald Brenan, who wrote several books on Spain in the 1950s and lived and travelled in Spain, had testified that he was under constant surveillance from the police and informers.

I pass another plaque which tells me that the 17th century writer Quevedo had set the beginning of his famous work *El Buscón* in the city. A sort of early Spanish version of *Oliver Twist*, it tells the story of a *Pícaro*, Don Pablos, a thief who lived off his wits.

I am not sure Lee would have appreciated the irony.

Segovia is renowned as being a city of storks. Lee wrote of "the storks roosting gravely on the chimney-pots, gazing across the valley like bony Arabs." I saw none on my brief stay in the city.

I did want to see the tiny church that Lee visited just outside the city walls. It was located down below the Alcázar. The *Iglesia de la Virgen de Fencisla* was the church dedicated to the patron saint of the city. It stood at the foot of *La Peña Grajera*, the Cliff of Crows. Lee told the legend of how the church had come to be built. Most Spanish cities have a dark place in their consciousness, a place in which atrocities have been routinely committed throughout their history. For Segovia, the Cliff of Crows was such a place. Heretics, thieves and adulteresses would be routinely thrown off the top of the cliff to their certain death.

The 13th century legend told of an alleged Jewish adulteress, María del Salto, who was tried and sentenced to death. She was in mid-flight when she prayed to her namesake for mercy; she was granted reprieve and floated gently to the ground. It was hailed as a miracle, and the church was built to commemorate it.

Lee was much affected by this macabre place. I wondered how many Republican bodies had been picked over by the crows in the years following Lee's visit.

I sit in the church as Lee did. It is quiet apart from the shuffling feet of an elderly man, dressed all in black, as he approaches the altar. Like an off-licence on a rough English estate, the sacrificial slab is protected by a tall heavy black grill gate. The priest reaches into the inner recesses of his black garment and extracts a large bunch of medieval-looking keys. One by one he unlocks and pushes open with both hands each of the iron gates.

As if on cue, a coach party enters the church and a tape of mournful mood music is activated. At a stroke any likelihood of a transfer of souls or prospect of communion with oneself or a higher order is suspended, perhaps forever.

I love the tranquillity, coolness and peace of a church of any denomination. However, my education at the hands of Our Lady of Fidelity nuns, De La Salle Brothers and Jesuit priests managed to instil in me a deep-seated aversion to religion, along with a lifelong fascination with its visceral attraction to the human person.

Each row of seats has a white carnation posy placed at its end, together with a spray of young buds with a string of white ribbon cascading down. Colourful tableaux line the walls. I relax for a moment but then catch sight of the forbidding dreaded confessional box in the corner. Distracted, I investigate the tableaux and, with a sickening feeling in the pit of my stomach, read about the great honour that Franco had bestowed upon the local Virgin Mary patron saint at the end of the civil war. To commemorate the fact that the city had been protected from serious damage when "taken" by the victorious nationalist rebels, Franco had pronounced that the Virgin would become, in perpetuity, the head of the local armed forces of the city. And she still is, to this day; paraded every year to celebrate the victory of a fascist dictator.

Like Lee, I depart with the cackle of the crows ringing in my ears.

I head south to Madrid via the strange anomaly of La Granja: a village, almost a suburb of Segovia, consisting of a royal palace neglected for centuries, with sad gardens and dry fountains. The fountains are activated a twice a year. Nobody seems to know why and when. It has changed little since Lee passed through and since my first visit in 1977 as a student on a field trip. I had been abandoned, with a fellow student, by our Linguistics professor. Our remit was to record the local dialect. We were left to fend for ourselves. My companion was a serious young woman. She had been brought up in some sort of strict religious sect and was just beginning to find out about life and make her own way. Accommodation was tight and we could only find a double room to share, offered to us by the proprietor with a knowing smile. We took it and somehow made the arrangement work. In truth I was probably more embarrassed than she was.

25 June 2012, Madrid

Crossing the Guadarrama mountains was a rite of passage for Lee. It was the first real landmark on his quest to find the real Spain of Andalusia.

Like Lee, I can feel the change in the atmosphere as the foothills of the Sierra give way to the lower slopes of the mountain. It is greener and fresher. Lee talked of being "Never so alive and so alone again." He felt euphoric at arriving at what must have seemed like the highest point in Spain with Madrid laid out below him. It was a turning point in his journey, after so long on the road with himself for company, he was about to plunge into one of the greatest European cities and yet he had no companion with whom to share this joy. A bitter-sweet moment indeed. As for me, I just felt alone.

I am catching a train from El Espinar up to Cercadilla where a narrow-gauge electric mountain train takes you to the top of El Puerto de Navacerrada, from where it is downhill all the way to Madrid. The train was inaugurated in 1923 but Lee makes no mention of whether he hitched a lift. Today it is only travelling halfway to the now-deserted ski resort, from where I will have to walk.

It is very early in the morning. The station of El Espinar is semi-abandoned and has a feel of decline about it. Odd bits of track are overgrown with weeds. Clumps of wild red poppies add a touch of colour to the grey scene.

There is a stork nesting on top of a railway pylon and another on a chimney stack of a factory building next to the station; refugees from Segovia perhaps.

The Guadarrama range looms up ahead, its peaks obscured by low-lying early morning mist.

The train arrives at Cercadilla and soon we are off again. It chugs out of the small station and begins its winding ascent up the mountain. We pass through the mist. The train is shadowed all the way up by tall pine trees that tip tap on the window for attention.

We arrive soon enough at the deserted ski slope and my fellow passengers and I quickly melt into the green foliage, following a well-trodden path that leads up to the top of the pass. Fairly quickly the memories of the never-ending burning golden wheat fields of the north fade, and are replaced by lung-bursting mint-flavoured gasps for air as I approach the top of the 6,000-foot pass. Lee described reaching this milestone in his journey as "one of those sudden jerky advances in life, which once made closes, the past for ever."

I sit down and look back. The air whistles past me, carrying faint sounds of life below. Juggernaut lorries crawl up the pass like ants. The word juggernaut has a Hindu origin: Lord of the Universe – any mighty force demanding a huge level of self-sacrifice.

Franco's impressive war machine comes to mind, so many soldiers demanding of others that they sacrifice their lives for a less than noble cause, the preservation of a deeply unjust ruling status quo of state, army, Church and aristocracy.

It is still early as the reddish sun warms away the mist hugging the contours of the lake below. It begins to work on the matted cotton wool covering the high slopes of the mountain to the west.

My eyes begin to water; it is as if the shifting sands of North Africa have settled overnight in the folds of the hills. Great seas of Saharan sand shimmer and ripple in the breeze. Gradually, as the morning wears on, the full majesty of the Sierra reveals itself, its serrated edges breaking through the brittle early morning crust and scattering the sands to the four winds.

It suits me to be up on high. The rhythm of walking keeps the mind moving along. Interrupting this rhythm seems to obstruct the flow of positive thoughts and allow regrets and small demons an element of purchase. The crisp clean air accelerates the passage. The filter of selective memory has not yet kicked in, the hurt still too raw. Memory is still acting as a fixative, rather than a solvent on those black and white negatives that haven't yet faded away. The tears stream down to join the racing brook of clear water down below me.

The sun is warming up the large granite rock on which I perch. My legs are grazed from brushes with the bright yellow bramble thorns typical of this wild landscape: the *Zarzamora* is an unforgiving defender of the range. A *buitre negro*, a black vulture, cruises lazily above the peaks. He hovers on the warming morning thermals waiting for his moment. He is serenely alone, his flight path bisecting the turning-blue sky.

Then a darker scene impressed itself upon me. Decades before, a similar scene had played out in the skies above Spain. This time it was not the silence of the graceful wing flight of a black vulture that stood out – it was the low mesmeric hum of a plane's engine that disturbed the peace of an early April day in 1937 in the Basque region of Spain. It announced the presence of the Luftwaffe, the German air force sent by Hitler. It was the elite Condor division as it prepared to experiment with a new and terrifying war tactic: the carpet bombing of civilian populations. The assault lasted for over three hours and it concentrated on the strafing of the exposed village residents, mainly women and children, cutting them down as they fled for safety. There were no military targets; this was a calculated act. Over 4,000 Basque children were subsequently evacuated to Britain. Those that could, returned after the war, to parents or grandparents.

I feel a cold wave of anger at this memory though it is comforting to acknowledge to myself that I am capable of such feelings in my numbed state.

In the certainty that Lee must have seen the same plain that unfolded below me and descended the same hilly terrain, leaving behind a trail of scattered words and a dust cloud of musical notes, I feel the ground beneath me must connect me in some way to him; it must hold a memory of his passing that will be retained long after Lee's stories and recordings and the memories of his contemporaries have gone.

At this moment I have to believe that.

At this point Lee headed straight to the centre of Madrid. I have to make a slight detour to a place that did not exist when Lee made his original journey. I am not sure if he ever did visit this place. If he did, I am sure he would not have liked it at all.

I take no pleasure in visiting this location. Many of my Spanish friends have never set foot in this place and never will whilst the current occupants remain.

As you approach the *Valle de los Caídos*, the Valley of the Fallen, up a long drive, you get glimpses, between the immaculately kept pine trees, of a sombre stone cross. Intimidating rather than majestic, the cross is of mammoth proportions and dominates the whole valley. It has been driven into the bare rock. Inside, the rock has been hollowed out to create a giant crypt.

The bunker-like basilica below the cross is officially presented as a shrine to the fallen of both sides of the civil war. Indeed it does contain bodies from both sides of the conflict. In reality it is a monument to the nationalist martyrs of the war killed by the Republican Reds. Above all, it is the final statement of Franco himself, who saw the whole obscene project as his memorial to rival the imposing palace of the Escorial just down the road. The Escorial is home to the tombs of most of the Spanish monarchy over the centuries. The overwhelming majority of those buried in the Valley of the Fallen are nationalists. The cross and basilica were built over 19 years by Republican prisoners-of-war; effectively slaves. It now contains only two marked gravestones which have pride of place in front of the altar, those of José Antonio Primo de Rivera and General Franco.

Primo de Rivera was the founder of the Falange movement which came to be Franco's only authorised political party during 36 years of dictatorship. He was killed by Republicans in November 1936. Franco was buried there in November 1975.

I have been here once before, in 1974, when Franco was terminally ill but still being propped up by the regime. He was still powerful and had recently caused worldwide horror and protest by executing a young Catalan terrorist, José Luis Cerveto. He was garrotted, seen as the worst of all execution methods. It was the manner of the sentence being carried out as much as the execution itself that seemed to resonate so much in the rest of the western world. I disliked the place then and still do. I need, however, to see and smell the last bastion of the Franco legacy. It is an anomaly. Opened in 1959, the building is run by Benedictine monks, officially owned and funded by the state through its *Patrimonio Nacional* department – a Spanish version of English Heritage. And yet the basilica is nowhere listed as an official state monument. The official guides on sale within the basilica make scarce mention of how the monument was built or the number of Republican prisoners that died in the process.

I decide to join a commercial guided tour. The other participants come from all over the world: Americans, Australians, a mix of Europeans, and several Spanish family groups. The tour is conducted in Spanish and English.

Our guide is a well-educated, articulate historian called Pilar. She warms us up by explaining that the monument is dedicated to the fallen of both sides of the conflict. Primo de Rivera was apparently a gentle idealist who got caught up with the wrong crowd: the extreme right wing. She omits to mention that the Falange doctrine was based on, and rooted in, the ideals of Hitler and Mussolini. Franco is only really mentioned in passing but allusions are made to his many good points that tended to be overlooked. I am getting more and more angry. Pilar finishes the tour and asks for questions. I can bite my tongue no longer. I approach her and take her to one side.

"Pilar, thank you for that. I did feel though that your version of events was a somewhat sanitised one."

She scarcely blinks. "I am sorry but I do not agree. I gave a factual account and acknowledged that there were issues and opinions on both sides. This is natural in a civil war."

"But it is generally agreed by the international community that Franco was a war criminal, is it not?"

"I do not come to a site of religious veneration to walk on the grave of a national statesman and insult his memory."

"You made no mention of the prisoners who died building this memorial?"

"There is no proof of that. Look, I was brought up under Franco, I know what happened then. I am a historian. I have no opinion on Franco and if I had, I would talk of it only in my own home with my family. Now, excuse me."

The independent, objective commentator, employed by a commercial tour guide company, with no state links, goes on her way.

I walk back and stand on Franco's smooth white marble tombstone and marvel that this man still rules from his grave: his grip on the national psyche still intact.

The autumn of 1975, I was studying in Granada in the south of Spain and Franco was finally in his last death throes. The whole painful long drawn out process had become a soap opera. The young Spanish students I mixed with had a different macabre Franco joke each day of October and November. He finally died on 20 November 1975 and was buried in the Valley of the Fallen. King Juan Carlos, his anointed successor, broke down and cried at the funeral.

It is cold in the basilica and I shiver, even though outside the temperature is soaring. To misquote Lorca, I decide that Franco is never more alive than when dead. King Juan Carlos, who had introduced democracy to his country, still keeps the candle of Franco's ideals alive and flickering. I feel a deep sense that the memory of Lee and his fellow Republicans is still being betrayed by Spanish society.

I manage to find lodgings at the Universidad Complutense de Madrid (UCM). As I walk through the park to my residence I realise that the two large bunkers in front of me are monuments to the Siege of Madrid during the civil war. The University campus is on a large area of land to the west of the city centre, gifted to the University by King Alfonso XIII in the 1920s. For much of the civil war, the University was a front line battleground.

The International Brigade had its headquarters in the School of Philosophy and fighting took place from building to building, at times even from floor to floor.

After the nationalists, as Pepe had told me, succeeded in starving Madrid into submission, Franco took his revenge on the University and purged the staff of radicals, replacing them with party officials.

I notice that the campus still has a preponderance of cypress trees. These were planted en masse on the direct orders of Franco. In Spain the cypress symbolises death, and most cemeteries are ringed by cypress trees. Every cypress that was planted at the University represented a nationalist martyr.

Lee loved Madrid. It was second only in his affections to Andalusia. In 1935, on his first visit, the University was flourishing. The cream of

European intelligentsia of the time had flocked to its colleges during the 1930s, when, for a brief period, democratic Spain offered a haven from the terror of fascism that was sweeping across the continent.

Many of the students at the University are funded by the Erasmus European Union (EU). I am delighted to be told by a journalist in Madrid, over a late night *copa*, that the best compliment he had heard about such EU schemes had come from a well-known European academic and bestselling writer. He had said that Erasmus was uniquely responsible, in the main, for successful European integration, as the scheme allowed regular congress to take place between Europe's finest young male and female intellectuals, thus ensuring a steady crop of like-minded perfectly formed new baby citizens.

Pepe had told me how his grandfather and his fellow communists had felt betrayed by their leader, Santiago Carrillo. Carrillo, along with several other leading figures in the movement, had escaped from Spain by air just before Franco secured his final victory. They took with them the party's assets and gold reserves and left Pepe and his comrades to deal with the reprisals of the victorious army. As I walk around the campus I cannot fail to see the graffiti spray-painted in bright colours everywhere I look. All the messages are on the same theme: *Muerte al Rector* (Death to the Rector). I enquire as to the identity of the Rector and am told it is a Señor Carrillo, a son of the very same former leader of the Spanish Communists. I am sure Pepe would not be first in the queue for a graffiti clean-up at the campus.

Photographs of the period show the centre of Madrid that Lee encountered in 1935 was a busy one, with the main streets full of black "Keystone Cop" cars, threading their way around the trams, like dodgem cars at a fair. The trams were like the open-ended cable cars that can still be seen in San Francisco. Large advertising hoardings running along the length of the tram cars promoted the fashionable drinks of the time, like *Martini Rossi* and *Rhum Negrita*. Lowry-esque stick figures rushed to and fro. Three years later, in 1938, it was a very different scene with the city, a Republican stronghold, under siege from an unremitting aerial bombardment and hand to hand fighting on the front line encircling the city.

Lee was to return to Madrid 18 months later to undertake some radio propaganda work for the Republicans. He was billeted in the centre of the city, near the Puerta de Sol. Lee took particular delight in the proximity he had to the young militia girls with their "small jungly bodies, split olive eyes, and voices like laser beams." They wore "blue baggy overalls, but so tightly belted at the waist, and deeply slashed at the throat, they appeared to have arisen half-naked from tumbled beds."

He talked of the experience of being bombed and the sounds of the shells: "Curiously these sounds then seemed to fall back on themselves, receding in waves of silence, shouts, running feet and finally in distant cries."

I recalled that Lee had also spoken of being told of a gracious gesture from a bomber pilot just before Christmas. Flying over the city, late one afternoon, the pilot dropped a fine, fat Serrano ham. This was then a rare delicacy. The ham fell on a man and tore off his arm.

For Lee, during this brief period of intoxication with Spain and its cause, love and passion and death seemed to merge as one.

*　　*　　*

I walk all around Madrid revisiting Lee's haunts; all the familiar street names are there, many of the bars are still trading. Lee loved to descend into the cool of Madrid's cellar bars and talked of the vast array of fresh seafood available from late morning – oysters, lobsters, crayfish, crabs: "Passenger trains all over the country have been halted or shunted into sidings in order that the crustaceans from Biscay, Vigo and Malaga may be rushed still alive to the city." So that in Madrid "hundreds of miles from any ocean, the inheritors of Cristóbal Colón drink, pause, break the crust from a prawn and smell again the salt seas of past glories."

I love the idea of people living in the capital city of Spain, in the middle of this sun stroked peninsula, being able to sniff the sea air. I am from London where as Ackroyd said in his giant biography of the city: "If you were to touch the plinth upon which the equestrian statue of King Charles I is placed, at Charing Cross, your fingers might rest upon the projecting fossils of sea lilies, starfish or sea urchins."

Madrid in the summer of 2012 is all heat and noise. University City is full of plane trees as well as cypresses. The plane trees are shedding their bark. The dry bark skin lies in chunks all over the pavements. As passers-by saunter along, the bark is scrunched underfoot and large black metallic beetles scuttle through the detritus of the street. Like the current financial contagion of the Eurozone, in which Spain is at the centre, there is a deadly disease sweeping Europe that is killing off the plane trees altogether. Like the financial crisis it had originated in Greece. I wonder whether once again Spain would soon be in the eye of this particular storm too.

I cannot escape from the past in Madrid. It is the 75th anniversary of the bombing of Guernica, so I have to visit the Reina Sofía gallery where Picasso's depiction of the atrocity is now on permanent display. The disturbing but compelling tableau of screaming women, dismembered bodies, crazed animals and dead children is always on display in the same room.

It is a powerful image but the picture I will take away from the exhibition is that of a little boy of about seven who sits in front of the Guernica painting, paper and pencils to hand, absorbed in recreating aspects of the painting.

I am also drawn to another exhibition of Edward Hopper, the 20th century American artist. He is famous for haunting pictures of American society and in particular for the depiction of solitary women in hotel rooms or bars, waiting for something or someone. The light in the pictures is exquisite and the viewer observes the paintings as an outsider, often on the street, looking into the private lives of individuals. As I walk around the gallery, I see the loneliness of individuals, the emptiness of dying marriages and the intrusion of the growing urban sprawl. Lee would empathise with the latter. For all his abandoned lovers, it would no doubt be like looking into a mirror with regard to the former.

It is 2.30am and I am in the Puerta del Sol square, just round the corner from where Lee stayed in 1938. I am one amongst several thousand who have been waiting patiently for hours. The miners have been on strike and had walked all the way to Madrid from the northern Cantabrian coast shadowing my own descent from the north. They are now marching as a group into the heart of the capital itself and are expected any time. I am anxious to be there when they reach the end of their journey. Their protest march has not been well covered in the media in England or Spain. It is as if there exists a conspiracy of silence.

The square is packed and not just with the committed left-wing regulars. There are families with children, elderly couples, and visitors like myself. There is a Frank Sinatra look-alike dressed all in silver, standing still on a plinth: the modern equivalent of Lee busking with his fiddle. Representatives of the miners sport t-shirts with the caption *"quiren acabar con todo"* (they want to kill us off for good). There are echoes of the violent year long miners' strike in Britain in the 1980s. Arthur Scargill, the miners' leader, had taken on Mrs Thatcher, the prime minister. He had declared it was a struggle for the very soul of mining: she had countered that it was simply a matter of cutting capacity. He would be roundly defeated but he was proved right. Twenty-five years on there is scarcely a coal mine still operational in the land, and whole communities have still to recover from this. This is the fear of the miners in Spain.

The police are keeping a low profile. The firemen seem to be in charge of security, working closely with the miners. At last the miners arrive to a huge roar, much singing and not a few tears. The miners are men and women of all ages. Each wears a lamp on their head. The lamps are lit, like beacons of hope in the darkness.

I am humbled by their dignity. These are men and women fighting for their working lives and their communities, but there are no signs of aggression and violence. There is passion and determination, and speeches and shaking of fists. At the end the miners sit down on the square and are led in an emotional rendition of the hymn *"Santa Barbara Bendita"*, the Blessed Saint Barbara. She is the patron saint of Asturian miners.

Traigo la camisa roxa
Trailarai larai, trailarai
Traigo la camisa roxa
Trailarai larai, trailarai
De sangre d'un compañeru
Mirái, mirái Maruxina, mirái
mirái como vengo yo.

My shirt has turned red
Trailarai larai, trailarai
My shirt has turned red
Trailarai larai, trailarai
Stained with the blood of a fellow miner
Look, look Maruxina, look
look how I'm coming home.

This provides the emotional climax to the evening and everyone heads off home in an orderly fashion. All the trains and buses stopped running a long time ago so I walk home to my halls of residence three miles away. My head is spinning with the euphoria of the welcome for the miners to the capital. I am confused by my response to the miners' act of faith in singing the hymn of their patron, which I found moving.

I doubt that the march will achieve the objectives of the miners. I doubt that other workers will strike in sympathy. The establishment is a tough opponent and I admire the spirit of the miners who are still standing up for their communities.

I reach my hall, La Residencia de Santa Teresa, a former convent building. I retire to bed contentedly, thinking about Santa Barbara showing the way for the miners to follow with their helmet flashlights, and myself, safe in the crook of Saint Christopher's arm and watched over as I sleep by Santa Teresa.

Perhaps Spain is getting to me more than I know.

Madrid

In Search of *Duende*

July 2012

Much as Lee enjoyed his time in Madrid, his goal had always been to reach the sunlit plains of Andalusia, beyond the arid *meseta* of Don Quixote's La Mancha. A land bathed by the waters of the Rio Guadalquivir, whose own golden syllables conjure up a dusky world of 700 years of Moorish rule: shady frescoed patios with fountains trickling snow-melted waters; haremed-silk *haiks* wafting on the occasional breeze; nightingale song damping down the fever of the midday sun.

I want to see what Madrid can offer me in preparation for the trip to the holy land of the south.

I walk through the Plaza de Santa Ana and pass a statue of Federico García Lorca, the poet whose prose cut to the very quick of the Spanish soul and who lived, breathed and died at the altar of his beloved Granada, a city that Lee grew to love. A city that reeks still of winter melancholy, and yet cultured from its spring-green African soft running waterfalls, pearls of such brilliance that spoke for and inhabited the spirit of Spain.

Lorca was one such pearl. I am on my way to one of Madrid's cultural institutions, the Zarzuela Theatre, to acquaint myself with another Granadino pearl in preparation for my journey south, deep into the inner soul of this passionate country and into that of a more cold-blooded temperate English creature.

The Zarzuela celebrates the best of Spanish classical music, folksong and opera, and tonight in its *Ay Amor* production, it is paying tribute to Manuel de Falla, one of Spain's greatest composers. He was a Granadino, though an adopted one, as originally he was from Cadiz. He looked for inspiration in the gypsy roots of the country. Tonight two works are being highlighted: *La Vida Breve (Fleeting Life)*, which premiered in this very theatre back in 1914, the year of Lee's birth, and the more well-known *El Amor Brujo (Love The Magician)*. Both focus on the mystical roots of two forms of Spanish song, *El Cante Jondo* (Deep Song) and flamenco. *El Amor Brujo* deals with a couple, each haunted by ghosts of past loves and lovers. Lorca and Falla were friends, though Lorca was executed by the nationalists and Falla composed a martial hymn in their honour before living out his life in exile in Argentina, rebuffing the overtures of Franco to return.

The following day I go to a place in Madrid that I had only read about before. It is the nearest thing that exists to a shrine to a generation of writers and artists that caught the mood of Spain in the 1930s, the Generation of 27. Many of them studied at the University of Madrid. Unlike me, they had stayed in a residence in the heart of the city. *La Residencia de Estudiantes* is now a centre of literary study for Spanish students and writers and visiting writers from abroad. It was where Lorca, Buñuel and Dalí all studied and lived together back in the 1920s and where Falla would pay many a visit.

Lee, though knowing nothing of such academic subjects as the Generation of 27 in 1935, was to become fascinated by Lorca and be influenced heavily by his writing. On his first return to Almuñecar in the early 1950s, the small village on the Mediterranean where he was to end his long journey, Lee had written of an early morning scene from his balcony, "The stars snapped shut, the sky bled green, vermilion tides ran over the water, the hills around took on the colour of firebrick, and the great sun drew himself at last raw and dripping from the waves."

I wanted to know more of Lorca who had clearly been the inspiration for Lee's words, and who had written in *Bodas de Sangre (Blood Wedding)*, one of his great dramatic tragedies:

¡Ay luna sola! ¡Luna de las verdes hojas! ¡Llena de
     jazmines de sangre!

*Oh solitary moon, translucent leaf-green, a blood-crimson
     heart of jasmine!*

74

The Residencia, now a green oasis amidst the urban sprawl, was, when founded in 1910, on the outskirts of the city with views stretching to the Guadarrama mountains. Back in 1935, the eyes of the Spanish intelligentsia might well have picked out Lee stumbling over the pass and descending into Madrid.

The Residencia was the heartbeat of a living experiment to drag Spain back into the mainstream of European thinking. The 1920s and 1930s were its heyday before the reactionary forces of the right snuffed out much of its light in the years following the civil war.

Unashamedly based on the English Oxford and Cambridge tradition of clusters of residential study rooms set in congenial surroundings, it was designed to foster intellectual interaction between academic disciplines. It was biased towards middle and upper class aspirational families and its feel was that of a slice of Andalusia transported to Madrid. As such, Lee would have loved it, as demonstrated by the influence that Lorca and other Spanish artists had on his writing as he matured and grew in confidence as a poet. Lee, in his later life, might have loved the lifestyle of the Residencia, might have adopted it, as he did with the Chelsea Arts Club in London, another liberal bohemian haunt. He might have struggled with the Residencia's ban on alcohol on the premises, though judging from Lorca's letters home to his parents, this was a ban routinely circumvented.

I have been invited to the Residencia to attend a seminar about the poet Gerardo Diego, one of Lorca's Generation of twenty-seven contemporaries, and a son of Santander where I spent some years in my youth. I wander around the grounds of the college. Box hedges from the Escorial Palace line the route, interspersed with red and white oleanders and poplar trees. What was once a bare Castilian hillside is now a flowering of colour. The college buildings were inspired by the Moorish architects of the 16th century, who combined African elegance with the modern Christian style. The birthplace of modern Spanish thinking, its verdant trees glisten with silver droplets cascading from imaginary Moorish fountains conjured up by the perfumed scent of the flora wafting in the breeze that ruffles the treetops of the *Colina de los Chopos* (Poplar Hill).

As I stroll through the Garden of the Poets I feel the presence of Lee. He would have been comfortable here in a way that I don't think he would ever have been in the Oxford or Cambridge of his time.

Did he ever come here? I don't know, but I would like to think that he had put his ear to the ground and listened for the strains of Falla's songlines and the chink of bone china as Lorca took tea with lemon.

Einstein would have strolled here, Stravinsky came here, Ravel, Debussy, and John Maynard Keynes all dropped by to pay their respects. Whilst Lee flirted with the early skirmishes of the civil war and returned to a Madrid under siege, the life of the Residencia went on. A student of the time, Jose Moreno Villa, wrote of studying while aerial dogfights played out above him. It is a description that could have been lifted straight from contemporary accounts of the Battle of Britain fought out over the rolling Kent countryside just a few years later and witnessed by Lee.

Across the entrance to the Residencia a giant white canvas sheet printed with the image of the college's late-1920s poster boys hangs limply. They are dressed up to the nines; Dalí in tennis whites; Buñuel, centre stage, red carnation in an Al Capone suit; Lorca dressed in sober black, a guest perhaps at his own *Bodas de Sangre*. Lorca was in love with Dalí at this time, but it is not Dalí who embraces him fondly in the image; Dalí is on the edge of the group.

The "*Ultraístas*", as the Generation of twenty-seven were known, despised sentimentality, embraced the modern age of new technology and delved into the surreal. At the time, the moon was considered the symbol of Romanticism and Generation 27 considered their purpose to "hurl a stone at the eye of the moon". The gravitational pull of the moon was polarising opinion dangerously and unleashing foaming white horse tides of opinion, outriders of dark forces that lay in waiting under the surface.

I pass in front of the Transatlantic building, so-called because the wooden balustraded balcony that runs its full length is reminiscent of a 1920s ocean liner. Etched into the glass frontage of the lower floor are the names of past students and residents. I recognise some: Paul Preston, the most eminent of modern historians of civil war Spain; Stockhausen; Antonio Muñoz Molina, a leading contemporary novelist. The college is still working its alchemy.

Visitors can see a typical student room, laid out in the style of the 1920s. It could be anyone's room, but hanging on its wall is a copy of Dalí's 1924 still life painting that he had gifted to Lorca. The room has a comfortable cluttered feel. It is brightly but simply furnished:

cream walls offset by a russet throw over the couch, a white porcelain washing bowl and jug, a teapot, a tennis racket in its frame hanging on the wall and brightly coloured cushions spread about. Like an Edward Hopper painting, you cannot enter the room, just observe from the outside looking in, a snapshot of 1920s life viewed from the future.

The façade of the building opposite is reflected in the window-pane, a row of full-length second floor windows looking out from austere cells just like this one. The mirror on the wall picks out Dalí's cubist work opposite. Dalí has written of how even some of his enlightened contemporary fellow students would mock his early surreal work. It is all so easy to picture Lorca and his literary set sitting on the couch, a cup of tea on a saucer in one hand, poems in the other, someone picking at a guitar and an artist in the corner sketching the scene for posterity. Lee, meanwhile, on his first visit to Madrid was staying in a "cell without any windows with bedbugs as big as beetles. Lying down was to be ridden, racked and eaten, to scratch and fight for breath."

Earlier in the summer I had gone to a production at the *Teatro Real*, the Opera House in Madrid's Plaza del Oriente. The opera was a reworking of Lorca's play *Mariana Pineda* and a celebration of his collaboration with Margarita Xirgu, an actress who played many Lorca roles. It is a tragedy, a story of martyrdom, exile, repression and the strength of the human spirit, staying alive in the face of a state determined to extinguish every last dying ember. It is the story of all civil wars, and Spain's civil war in particular, and an insight into Lee's motivation to fight for the cause of freedom in a foreign land. In a way, it spoke to me, too, of Lee's exile from his beloved Spain. Did he stay away from a Spain while it was in the grip of a fascist dictator? Although he didn't foot in Spain from 1938 to 1953, it continued to dominate his life, his thinking and his work.

The Plaza de Oriente has always been synonymous with Franco, both in my mind and that of many Spaniards of my age. On this hot summer evening the square is quiet and calm with just a few late night strollers passing through. The last time I had stood in this square was 1 October 1975. I was crushed amongst a frenzied crowd of 300,000 people. The crowd was being controlled and closely watched by Franco's storm troopers, the Guardia Civil. They were standing, each with their right arm held stiffly aloft in a Nazi-style salute. I was tense and wondering if it was like this in Nuremberg in the 1930s at the

Reichsparteitag Rallies of the Third Reich, when Hitler was making his entrance past lit torches cascading up ominous clouds of smoke, dwarfed by giant eagle statues, Nazi flags and stone carved symbols of oppression hammered into the wall. Hitler, twitching with vigour and passion, face consumed by hatred, spitting out his ode to glory.

Here, when the crowd grew quiet and allowed the stage performance to begin, an old man shuffled to the front of the balcony, flesh drooping on a skeletal frame, a palsied right hand at half-mast, a voice that warbled a sad old tune. This was General Franco, the most powerful man in Spain and these were the death throes of his regime. It was his last public appearance before a drawn out painful death seven weeks later. In the background, the King of Spain stood quietly awaiting his turn to be crowned ruler of Spain. Even further in the background, in the obscure corners of the balcony, invisible to the eye, were the kingmaker politicians. Franco was dressed all in black with a scarlet sash across his waist. I felt wretched wondering whether another civil war loomed ahead. I was a student in Spain for a year and my tutors were already drawing up plans to pull me out if things began to turn really nasty.

In the end, Franco's death and the restoration of the monarchy passed over relatively peacefully. Spain was not ready for more conflict. It turned a blind eye to the newly constituted democracy's ruling governments that bore an uncanny resemblance to the rank and file of Franco's puppet governments of before. The King was dead, long live the King.

I shake off the memory, returning to 2012. I am due to meet some friends in the Café de Oriente in the square. Now, it is well known for its avant-garde cuisine and excellent coffee selection, in 1924 it was where Lorca first met Dalí and fell in love.

I am meeting Javi, a young student friend with the air of a saint, a kind and generous soul who is entranced by the Celtic mists and legends of Ireland in a similar fashion to the way both Lee and myself fell for the passion and colour of Spain. He reminds me of a young Irish Merlin who has hung over the edge of Blarney Castle and kissed the stone. He has learned to play the *bodhran*, the traditional Irish drum, and marches to its beat

Javi is sitting in the corner with Miguel, a friend of his who I have not met before. I am introduced and we chat happily for a while. There is something about Miguel that intrigues me, he has an angular thin face, a prominent but weak jaw and a pair of delicate metallic glasses perched over his gaunt nose. He reminds me of a priest, the sort of priest that Lee encountered on his journey. Lee had talked of visiting a village outside Segovia, "whose streets were black with priests". In Spain today they are not so common.

We have wine and break bread. I watch Miguel scuttle across to the bar, his undernourished frame covered by a layer of dry skin, sapped of its goodness by the futility of fighting against a dying flame of faith, a spirit drained of any vestige of holiness, in truth a broken sacramental body and blood reduced to a dried up husk.

We drink some more and Miguel becomes more animated, hyperactive even. I can contain myself no longer and confess that I am harbouring a strong feeling he is connected to the church and wonder if he might be a priest. A look of panic, followed quickly by one of incredulity passes between Javi and Miguel.

Miguel turns and looks right at me. "I am asked this question a lot and yet I continue to be surprised at hearing it. I am not a priest, but there was a time when I thought I was, when I thought I was a priest operating at the highest levels of the Vatican."

A tale unfolds that shocks me, not so much for its content, but for its confirmation of my first impression. He had gone to Italy on a form of personal retreat, to seek redemption at a difficult time. He had immersed himself in the idolatry of the Catholic faith, he had worshipped at the feet of wooden Madonnas, basked in the glow from sunlit cathedral stained glass, worn his fingers down by continually threading rosary beads, knelt prostrate before scenes of crucifixion. He had been blessed by the Pope in St Peter's Square, on Good Friday. On the plane home to Madrid, he had had a breakdown. He had thought he was the Pope himself, he closed his eyes and saw an *Escudo de Popa*, an escutcheon.

"Apparently," said Miguel, "all I could do was repeat the Second Commandment from the Book of Exodus like a mantra, 'You shall not make a carved image, or any likeness of anything that is in heaven above, or that is in the earth beneath, or that is in the water under the earth.' I had become an iconoclast."

He goes on to tell me that his family had looked after him and he had recovered and was able to take up his life again. I congratulate him on his recovery and we laugh, a trifle nervously on my part, at my assumption that he had been ordained. I ask him what he is doing now, assuming that like Javi he is a student.

"Oh no, I work in a bookshop now, it's run by the St Paul's Society." As he says this, he looks at Javi out of the corner of his eye and dares him to comment.

Afterwards, on my way home, I remember that the St Paul's Society run a bookshop in London in Westminster, next to the Catholic cathedral. It sells exclusively religious books and idols, statues, rosaries, crucifixes. I shiver in the warm night stillness and walk that little bit quicker.

I later meet Javi in his favourite Spanish Irish bar, La Elisa on Calle Santa Maria. He wants me to hear some traditional Irish music, drums, flute and fiddle. How can I refuse? He arrives alone.

While we listen to Blanca and Chuchi from Burgos playing their version of Irish/Spanish folk fusion, Javi talks about his love for Ireland. He has visited several times and is as fascinated by Ireland's culture and history as I am by Spain's. He tells me the story of his visit to the Garden of Remembrance in Dublin and how he came across a poem written in large golden letters near the site of the Sons of Lir statue that symbolises resurrection and rebirth. He quotes me the words of the poem written by Liam Mac Uistin:

We planted the tree of valour and it blossomed
In the winter of bondage we saw a vision
We melted the snow of lethargy and the river
Of resurrection flowed from it.
We sent our vision aswim like a swan on the river.
The vision became a reality.

Javi pauses, then says, "These words sent a shiver down my spine when I first read them. Firstly, the beautiful setting – all we have to remember the fallen is Franco's grotesque mausoleum in the Valley of the Fallen. Secondly, I thought, where is our vision, Spain's vision? It's 37 years on from Franco's death and we have not moved on, I see the country disintegrating around me and we are scared."

He is not the first young Spaniard to talk like this: many people I have met on my journey are saying the same thing. Parents and grandparents who had never discussed the war before have began to express concerns about the direction of travel that Spain and Greece seem set on and how it echoes with their memories of the 1930s.

Javi wants to hear about my father growing up in Ireland against the background of the Irish uprisings of the 1920s. I tell him the little I know. Like many, my father had been silent on such matters. The Irish in London, where I grew up in the 1970s when the Irish Republican Army was at its strongest, were not popular, so tongues were stifled. I knew enough to sense that my father was an Irish patriot who was uneasy with the English then. He had moved to England, settled and raised a family. He played no part in the future Irish struggle, was not called up, as an Irish national, in the Second World War – he saw out the war in Liverpool as a medical officer. I recall no delight expressed at the signing of the Good Friday Agreement in 1998.

I recall that Laurie Lee had visited Ireland in the 1960s and made no mention of the Troubles but was clearly taken with the country and its people. He wrote of The Burren, a barren moonscape of a place where "3,000-year-old legends grow like lichen on the rocks, and a dog may scratch up the crowns of kings." He told of the "forty kinds of green, fired or damped by every shade of weather, from an electric brilliance to something deep and cold as the eyes of a witch's cat." It brings to mind the man in the Spanish bar who Lee had quoted on the significance of the colour to the Asturian region of Spain, "There are in Asturias three greens: the clear green of water; the dark green of the night; and the pallid green of a dead virgin."

As we leave the bar, Blanca and Chuchi are ending their set with a traditional folk song from Burgos, Pititón:

Se ufana Melitón, un vago del lugar,
de jamás anís catar,mas cuando no lo ven,
perejil, don don, perejil don don, el remolón,
se toma sin chistar un frasco de Chinchón.

Boasts Meliton, a lad from the village,
that not a drop of anis has ever passed his lips,
but when eyes are fixed elsewhere,
Mister n'eer do well, Mister n'eer do well,
he steals away with a bottle of Chinchón.

As we walk away I am humming the refrain, *"perejil don don, un frasco de Chinchón."*

Javi turns to me and asks, "Have you ever been to Chinchón?"

I haven't.

*   *   *

It is a shame that Lorca and Lee never met. Lorca was dead days after Lee returned to England after the outbreak of the civil war. Lee grew to love Lorca's home city of Granada and wrote about it at length in *A Rose for Winter*, an account of his visit to Andalusia in 1955.

I lived in Granada for a year in 1975, the year of Franco's death and, like Lee and Lorca before him, I loved to walk up into the hills above the city, to the Alhambra palace, the gypsy quarter of Sacromonte, the old Moorish district of the Albaizín. Much has changed, but not the views of the Sierra Nevada high above the Alhambra. Lee described the scene on All Souls Day in January 1955.

Lee had walked up high above the city to the cemetery, where earlier there had been a steady stream of visitors to pay their respects on this day of holiness for the dead: "As the sun sank, the bright paper landscape crumpled and contorted with savage shadows. The bare furrowed foothills of the Sierras writhed and dimpled like brains. And the snows, from the vivid incandescence of daylight, turned pink, mauve, purple, cold as slate, like the dying face of a dying man slowly drained of his blood."

Lee would have been well aware that this was precisely the spot where many Republicans were executed by nationalist forces and at the time would have had no reason to doubt that Lorca himself may have met his fate here. In fact, we now know that this was not the case.

Even in 1955, Lorca's death in 1936 was a taboo subject, but Lee was clearly interested to discover more about the mysterious circumstances surrounding his death. He spent many weeks trying to penetrate the wall of silence that had been erected and eventually a meeting with 'friends' of the dead poet was arranged by a journalist called Horsehead who had links with the Falange, essentially Franco's political party front. The 'friends' were happy to talk for hours about their dear friend, but clammed up when Lee mentioned his death.

82

They prevaricated and postulated, "It was an accident, it was a private murder, it was a case of mistaken identity, it was a blunder by a Civil Guard who has since been punished." Every story was different, except in its effort to prove that the killing was not political.

The truth is that Lorca was a marked man; he wrote provocative plays about repression and dictatorship. He wrote verses to traditional tunes which anyone could sing, they were sung by anti-Franco factions, and he was considered a Red poet.

Lorca loved the concept of *duende*, the soul of the Spanish people that defined a concept as elusive as running water. What Falla captured in his *Nocturno del Generalife* score, Lorca nailed down in prose. I am fascinated by his words. I think Laurie Lee was seduced, like me, by Spain's *duende* and came closest to expressing it in English. I had experienced the sound of pure flamenco in Valladolid. A sound that, in Lorca's words, originated not in the throat, but that "climbs up inside you, from the soles of the feet." Lorca wrote that "all that has black sounds has *duende*." He spoke of the "moon-frozen heads painted by Zurburán" in Seville, El Greco's "butter yellow and lightening yellow" paintings in Toledo and the "innumerable rites of Good Friday... the popular triumph of Spanish death" which I had witnessed in Valladolid.

Lorca saw the roots of *duende* in a music that predated flamenco and *Cante Jondo* (Deep Song).

In words eerily prescient of the civil war to come, he said that the *siguiriya* begins "with a terrible scream that divides the landscape into two ideal hemispheres. It is the scream of dead generations, a poignant eulogy for lost centuries, the pathetic evocation of love under other moons and other winds." In words that would have infuriated his right-wing critics who espoused a vision of Spain as a nation cleansed of inferior races by the Christian Crusades, Lorca went on to say, "the transcendence... of deep song comes from remote races and crosses the graveyard of the years and the fronds of parched winds. It comes from the first sob and the first kiss."

I have been in Madrid for too long and am eager to leave for Toledo. On my last day I decide to visit a few more of Madrid's cafes with long-standing literary connections. While Paris is famous for its Left Bank drinking dens and Vienna is renowned for its coffee houses, Madrid is not so well known for its historic cafes frequented by its writers and artists down the centuries. I have an additional motive in seeking out some of the places that Lee visited. Lee recounted his last night in Madrid which had began in Calle Echegarray, near Puerta de Sol, a street of café brothels at the heart of the red light district, where sex was sold as erotica laced with blood, sand, bulls and death.

Lee had ended his night at Bar Chicote on the Gran Vía and I make my way there to pay my respects. Now the bar is legendary and very much promoted as the place to see and be seen, with whole walls taken up with black and white photographs of film stars, writers, politicians and bullfighters. It is garish and expensive and I don't linger.

Lee had been rather drunk by the end of his evening here, and had flirted with a pretty young girl who begged him to take her with her on his travels. Lee wrote, "Another drink and I was imagining this girl barefooted, walking beside me, rolled in my blanket at night." Before Lee could respond, a minor bullfighter made his entrance and she was gone. He had left the bar, gone home and been seduced by Concha.

Concha was a young widow with whom Lee lodged in the working class area in the south of the city. She had a boyfriend who was away a lot and a young child. She liked to take the sun in the courtyard of the inn while Lee ran his fingers through her hair. He would massage in fish oil to condition her hair as she pressed in against him. They ignored the comments of the carters as they went by. It was, apparently, initially a platonic relationship; Lee was in awe of this mature creature well beyond his reach. On this last night he had returned to the inn and ascended the stairs unsteadily.

He was intercepted by Concha who led him, unresisting, to her bed. Pausing briefly to feed the baby some jam, ease off his boots and then to make the sign of the cross, she joined him.

I have a date too this evening, but it is with a 75-year-old from Leeds. Stephen Drake-Jones is his name and he is a Madrid institution. Resident in Spain for decades, he is an expert in the Spanish/French Peninsular Wars, President of the Wellington Society and an expert on Hemingway's Madrid. We meet in Bar Alemana in Plaza Santa Ana, where we sit in Hemingway's corner with a framed photo of the great man above our heads. Stephen loves Spain, India, curries and Leeds United Football Club, and anything you ever wanted to know about Wellington's Scorched Earth Military Strategy is in his head. He ran tours of Madrid: Civil War Years Madrid; Hemingway's

Madrid; George Borrow's Madrid (takers to date over the past ten years for this one – nil).

I am here to talk about Lee, but Hemingway is Stephen's passion. He talks about Hemingway's thirst for knowledge, about bullfighting, and how he would visit the old abattoir, down by the River Manzanares. Back in the 1930s it was a poor district, and the place where Lee spent the most time in during his stay. The American would visit at dawn to see the young raw hungry toreadors practise the art of killing cattle, "the old women standing in line… to drink the supposedly nutritious blood of the freshly killed cattle."

All evening Stephen has been exchanging nods of welcome with other customers and after we had been talking of blood and sand, a middle-aged lady sitting behind Stephen turns and taps him on the shoulder, "Stephen, it is you! How good to see you. Please let me introduce my friends." A handsome couple in their 40s are duly introduced. Tom is very English and an engineer, Cruz is an artist and absolutely stunning. It transpires that Cruz's family are from Huelva right down in the south-west of Spain near Portugal, and they have links to the aristocracy as well as connections to bullfighting. Her father had been killed in the ring. I am fascinated and want to learn more. Cruz is reluctant to talk of the family business, but tells me all about contemporary art.

It is time to go and on parting I am invited to visit their summer house outside the city the following weekend when there is a fiesta in the *pueblo*. The highlight of the fiesta is a bullfight in the village square, which is to be transformed into a bullring for the weekend. It is a ring in which her father had fought. The name of the *pueblo*: Chinchón.

I would soon leave the capital in search of Lorca's *duende* in its spiritual home of Andalusia, the place where Lee above all longed to be.

Lee had left Madrid on a fiercely hot day and headed south to Toledo, where his head would soon be swooning and his eyes swimming in a sea of medieval colour from El Greco's frescoes and portraits. He was also to meet a beautiful English rose married to a South African poet. The meeting was the first in a chain of coincidences that would change his life forever.

First of all though I had to make a slight detour to Chinchón, home to sweet *anís* and sweeter Cruz.

4 July 2013, Chinchón

I am late, a day late. The *corrida* took place the day before. The main square of Chinchón is still laid out as a bullring, its floor of sand seemingly not dotted with recently spilt crimson blood. But still, the previous day it had hosted an ancient ritual of slaughter that seems to have a hold still on the national psyche in certain parts of the country and a continuing fascination for certain people.

For Tom and Cruz it is a bolthole from Madrid, a place to wind down. The town has a proud history and there must be a heartbeat fluttering somewhere, but quite where it is difficult to fathom. Most houses seem deserted, even though it is a holiday weekend. The folk that are here, dotted about, have the air of Madrileños on a fleeting visit. Perhaps now the highlight of the weekend, the Saturday bullfight, has passed, the rest have just drifted away.

It is a market town, but times are hard and its traditional role as Madrid's orchard, outside larder and storehouse has long since died away. It is a town of memories: well-known bullfighters, like Cruz's father, had fought in the ring, some had perished. The town sits on a maze of subterranean passages and caves that in long hot summers past had kept produce fresh until demand from Madrid had summoned it. Each holiday home seemed to have, in its cellar, a row of giant rust-red terracotta Ali Baba jars. They had stored a precious commodity, olive oil. They have been dry for centuries. They are, like Chinchón itself, just for show now.

Tom and Cruz, Tom's sister Lucy, myself, and a family friend from Huelva, Pilar, have all been invited to lunch in the neighbouring village of Colmenar de Oreja. Our hosts are Tom's neighbours in Chinchón, three families who are also Madrileños with holiday homes in Chinchón. The meal is superb, *Pochas*, a broth with green beans and tender ox tail, Japanese style tempura vegetables and a goat's milk mousse for dessert which, to my surprise, is delicious. I tell a tale of eating goat paella in Mallorca some years back. This is received with shock: goat's cheese is a delicacy but it is not done to eat the meat in this part of Spain. The local red wine is fresh and fruity and has travelled well from the *bodega* across the road. The gentlemen light up big fat Havana cigars. Rum soaked swirls of smoke drift up to the ceiling passing the *"No Fumar"* notices on the way.

Luis invites us back for coffee and liquors. I am beginning to drift off into an alcoholic stupor, hoping that a stray spark from the cigars hitting the haze will not result in a conflagration. I speak more with Cruz about her surreal art. She quotes a definition from the French philosopher Jean Baudrillard, "the simulation of something which never really existed." She goes on to describe her art as a false reality, a convincing illusion based on a simulation of reality. Actually Cruz can talk to me about anything she likes.

Pilar turns down a glass of Chinchón anís, saying that the sweet confection is fit only for northeners and that she craves a sharp dry *aguardiente* from Huelva on Spain's south-west border with Portugal. Pilar has the air of a Spanish Miss Marple, nicely plump and angelic in profile. She has the measure of the group and slips in tart observations like a matador in his prime, inserting a stiletto into the neck severing the spinal cord. Death and social discomfort is instant. I feel her gaze turn on me when I ask if she had been present for Cruz's father's *corrida* in Chinchón in 1964. She fixes me with her ice blue eyes and says, "No, I was not, firstly because I was not around at the time of his debut and secondly because it was not a *corrida*. Our bullring is too small, we can only host the baby bulls, *los novillos*."

I risk a follow-up, which is in retrospect, foolish, "Ah, they don't kill those then."

"Of course they do, it is an honour for them to die in the ring and they taste very good."

Pilar and Cruz are childhood friends; they were brought up in Andalusia together. They take me home to Cruz's house so I can sleep off the lunch. The room is lined with her paintings, digital impressions of analogue subjects, colours enhanced, curves straightened. Cruz places a blanket over me and leaves me be. The last thing I remember, as she slips away, is her eyes sparkling with early morning stars in the late afternoon of this summer.

I sleep and dream of a country like Spain, a democratic, fair, just society with an even more golden past of halcyon days of law and order, people in their place, incense-drenched smiling congregations, confessional boxes dusty and cobwebbed. I awake in the early morning, but it is a false dawn and Cruz is gone.

Toledo

Weeping Purples, Lime Greens and Bitter Yellows

7 July 2012, The Road to Toledo

The citadel of Toledo towers over me far off in the distance, I am on the road again on my way to El Greco's home city, a fairy tale, once-upon-time city, perched above the River Tagus.

I am in a sombre mood and need some light relief. The roads on which I have travelled to Toledo have taken me across one of the killing fields of the Spanish Civil War. The intersection of the Tagus and Jarama rivers was, in February 1937, the scene of one of the bloodiest battles of the war. The Republicans were trying to hold the Madrid to Valencia front line, with Franco's army intent on penetrating its defences to lay siege to Madrid. The International Brigade corps was pitched into battle with Franco's crack troops from Morocco who know how to exploit the flat, open terrain of the river valley. A combination of inexperience, faulty weaponry and incompetence resulted in a bloodbath for the international troops. A late Republican rally retrieved the situation, but only at a great cost. The Battle of Jarama attained a mythical status for the cause. Somewhere up above me is the hill of slaughter, known by the survivors as Suicide Hill.

Lee was by then back in England, licking his wounds, but his old comrade-in-arms Fred Copeman was still in Spain. He recalled the Moroccan troops advancing towards their lines, with "flowing cloaks lined in red and red berets or turbans". Orwell was on the Aragon front and Hemingway dropped in to chew the fat, but left before the fighting. Cyril Connolly, an English journalist, also reported from the front. He would later launch Lee's career as a poet by covering his early poetry in his literary review.

As I walk along on this quiet July day, a weak sun breaks through the olive trees and orange groves. I breathe in menthol from the pine trees and disappear into the sombre shadows of the cypresses.

I cross the Tagus River and begin the climb up to the centre of Toledo. There is an escalator built into the side of the cliff on which the city has been built. The moving walkways carry me up into the heart of the city and deposit me, reassuringly, into a spider's web of intricate narrow streets. The early morning sun warms the walls, the cladding softening the urgent peal of Sunday morning bells.

I emerge into the light of the *Plaza de Zocodover*, Toledo's Plaza Mayor. The square is surrounded by bars, cafes and shops. The shops sell mainly swords, daggers and shields all forged from Toledo steel, a reminder of the city's turbulent past in medieval times. The city played host to the Spanish Inquisition in an early attempt to purify the religious and racial make-up of Spanish society. It was a process that successions of Spanish rulers were to continue, culminating in the civil war of the 1930s. Curiously, the other main commodity sold by the shops is marzipan. A fairytale city in its truest sense, Toledo is a place where the harsh reality of life is sugar-coated with a dusting of romantic make-believe.

On 31 July 1935, Lee took up a busking pitch in the square, weary and sunburnt from the journey from Madrid. It was a day that would change his life forever.

I know the date because it was the feast day of St Ignatius. In the crowd of revellers that day in the plaza was Roy Campbell, a South African poet, and his wife, Mary, and family. Both Roy and Mary had recently converted to the Catholic faith and he had chosen Ignatius Loyola as his confirmation name, while Mary had chosen Mary Magdalene. Loyola was the founder of the Society of Jesus, the Jesuits, at the time when the Spanish Inquisition was at the height of its powers. They were celebrating Roy's saint's day with coffee and cakes and he invited Laurie over for a drink. Lee was charmed by Roy and entranced by Mary. She was one of the infamous Garman sisters, a social set of London society that rivalled Virginia Woolf's Bloomsbury set. The two sets were in fact linked, at times in an intimate fashion.

The Campbells invited Lee back to their rented house for lunch and then to stay. The house nestled in the shadows of the cathedral walls and belonged to a cardinal. I seek out the house, now a well-appointed small hotel, *Casa de Cisneros*. It has changed little over the last century. It now has a roof over the central patio area where Lee wrote of the Campbell's five-year-old daughter Anna, "She danced like a firefly, floating over the flagstones with a precocious, iridescent skill." Roy would read his poems to Lee and talk of El Greco, while Mary attended to her devotions.

Despite growing up in the repressed early years of the 20th century, Mary, like her six sisters and two brothers, had led a life up until then of non- conformity and hedonism. In the early 1920s she had achieved a certain notoriety in London society by not wearing a hat outside on the street. Up until this point only prostitutes strolled hatless down the avenues of London town.

While Mary's sexuality is still a matter of conjecture, she was happily married to Roy who would entertain Lee, Mary looking on, with tales of their youthful courtship, "We never grew tired of it, did we girl? We must have broken half the beds in the town." Mary would murmur touching her lavender lips, "I'm sure he doesn't want to hear all that."

Mary had several affairs with women throughout her life. The longest and deepest, and most commented on in polite society as well as elsewhere, was her relationship with Vita Sackville-West, who was married to Harold Nicholson. Both were prominent members of literary life of the time. Sackville-West was also involved amorously with Virginia Woolf.

The prodigious sexual appetite of Sackville-West was the subject of much speculation at the time. It is said that Roy Campbell became aware of the affair and tolerated it for a while, exclaiming at the sight of cuts and grazes on the inner thighs of his wife, "For God's sake, I don't mind what the two of you get up to but remind Vita to take her earrings off first."

But in Toledo in 1935, Mary had been reborn: she was now chaste, devoted, and living up to her chosen confirmation name of Mary Magdalene. She was in the habit of attending mass every day and had become a Carmelite tertiary, which involved renouncing earthly temptations such as fine clothes and jewellery. She had taken to wearing a brown scapular and regularly fasted. Lee described her as wearing dazzling white on the day he met her, so perhaps she had retained a little bit of her former self.

I walk down the hill from the house to the Carmelite Church of Santa Teresa and imagine Mary barefoot, scapular draped over her like a schoolgirl's convent uniform, strolling down to the church in the musky dusk of a summer evening.

The sign outside the church reads *Carmelitas Descalzas*, Barefoot Order of Carmelites. It was founded in 1569 by Saint Teresa, the mystical writer who spent her days writing devotions here high above the river gorge. Four hundred years later, Laurie Lee would publish his own account of a nomadic, often barefoot pilgrimage across a nation still suffering from the legacy of the national crusade against the Moors and the harsh repression of the Inquisition.

Lee had written of spending hours with Mary as she spoke to him of her faith and chided him for his louche lifestyle. Lee confessed to feeling an empathy with her state of grace and becoming dangerously close to being seduced into a life of abstinence and earthly austerity in return for celestial rewards in the next life. It was a dangerous time for Lee, as at that time, he had yet to feel the heat from the all-consuming fires of human love and passion. Lust, he had known, but earthly ecstasy was a state of knowledge so far denied him. Meeting Mary was to change all that.

Lee was clearly fixated with Mary for a brief while. She, however, was unattainable, immune to his easy charm, come-to-bed eyes and quicksilver tongue.

Mary, however, was a Garman and she had six sisters back in England, not cocooned in an ethereal, enlightened, eternal aura, but slithering around the gardens of Eden, their darting tongues of sweet poison awaiting the next rosy-cheeked apple to drop by.

*   *   *

El Greco used a visual language that ignored classical balance and proportion, rational space and harmonious colours – all for one purpose only: to express his devotion to God.

As I walk around Toledo, paintings of El Greco hang seemingly in every little church I come across. Just as Lee did, I visit the house El Greco was said to have lived in (the Spanish government now admit that they have no idea whether it was actually his house or not) and lose myself in, as Lee wrote, "Colours I had never seen before, weeping purples, lime greens, bitter yellows; the long skulls of the saints and their sunken eyelids." All the apostles are lined up like the Stations of the Cross on the way to Calvary. Saint Peter who denied; Saint Judas, my saint of the lost cause; the ghostly figure of Saint Thomas who doubted.

The sun is hot and I am battling with the flies. I recall that Lee had suffered sunstroke and hallucinations after walking to Toledo and I start to imagine how he would have felt in this mystical city, dehydrated by the sun, new blisters forming over old, beset by fever, having his brow wiped by Mary, all on one stifling hot day back in 1935.

20 July 1935, Toledo

I lie, an Englishman abroad, in a sun-induced stupor in the courtyard of an old muleteers' inn. My brow still burning from the heat of a day that has been left behind, a day that has galloped into a long night, perfumed by malt-brewed extract that lulls the brain into a false dawn, the side of my face resting on a cold metal fountain that drips solace during fitful snatches of sleep.

I am walking down a marzipan street, sweat dripping down my elongated face, weeping coloured pigments, a blood-red trail forming behind me. Bells are ringing all around me, oranges and lemons say the bells of St Clement's, the sounds muffled by fog, sparks fly off the cobbled surface as carriages thunder by, furnaces light up the sky, six of loam and three of sand, hair of goat, cauldron bubble, is that my father I see? I lie low, cowering. Pauper lunatics pose for the Greek, Mary Magdalene perfumes her flesh with forbidden unguent, seven devils rise into the sky, nine beauties dance on the altar of a burned-out church. I lie with Mary above the silver city, an angel of the stories flies overhead through skies rent with naked blue and dead-virgin green, the cold white moon floats above, its pull exciting the foaming waters below, its push turning wrong into right, he who is without sin, my skull is taut, my skin stretched, an isotopic movement: falling, falling, falling from Grace.

Roy finds me, sweet, gentle Roy.

In a matter of months, Roy Campbell would give sanctuary to Carmelite monks as Republican troops rampage through the city, watching helplessly by as 17 more are executed in reprisal killings, risking his and his family's lives by taking in for safe keeping the personal papers of Saint John of the Cross. Sweet Roy, who says of the Jews that they are, "A race that is intellectually subversive as far as we are concerned: that has none of our visual sense, but a wonderful dim-sighted instinct for dissolving, softening, undermining and vulgarising." This was the man who seemed to have offered Lee a fatherly hand on the shoulder, a hand that Lee was only too grateful to have.

8 July, 2013

I escape for the day and visit the city's iconic building, the Alcazar. A large fortress, it towers over the main square and dominates the skyline. It was destroyed during the civil war and has now been rebuilt and houses the National Museum of the Army. During Lee's visit it stood majestically and housed an elite group of young army officers, including, I discover, my old landlord from Santander, Milans del Bosch, who was a young cadet at the time. Years later, in 1981, after the death of Franco, he would go on to be one of the leaders of the plot to unseat the newly-elected democratic government, possibly with the implicit support of the king. The plot failed and the king's authority was strengthened.

Early on in the civil war, Franco's troops were on the brink of capturing Madrid from the Republicans. Franco made the decision to divert troops away from the Madrid assault southwards to Toledo. He had become aware of the actions of local nationalist, Colonel Moscardo. He had seized the Alcazar fortress and had been under siege, with the rest of the city under Republican control, for three months.

Franco did not take this decision on humanitarian grounds, but on grounds of self-interest and long-term strategy. Franco understood the symbolic value – and, therefore, the propaganda value – of recapturing the Alcazar and rescuing the small band of heroes that had held out against all odds in the face of starvation and superior forces. The location of Toledo too was hugely significant. For the hard-line right wing of the military, Toledo had been the scene of their greatest triumph centuries earlier when it became the first city to be retaken in the Christian crusade against the occupying Moors.

From the outset, Franco was not interested in winning a quick war: he had his eye on the long game. His goal was to win the peace after the war and to ensure the absolute subjugation of the post-war Spanish nation; both the winners and the losers. He was determined to extinguish any flickering light of liberalism. This needed a long drawn out war and the crushing of the enemy. To this end reprisals were savage, surrender often meant death and slaughter was commonplace.

I am reminded of another bloody civil war fought out 75 years earlier in the USA. In winning the war, President Lincoln abolished the great injustice of slavery and desired the Union of States to "cohere". Along with the hard-line rebel stance of white supremacy over black, there were some more genteel examples of Confederate propaganda. At one point the rebels sought to gain advantage and raise morale by flying a hot air balloon purportedly sewn together from the dresses of southern ladies, in an attempt to honour, in their eyes, their fine white upstanding men. Franco, on the other hand, was not interested in cohesion and he brought back slavery for the defeated Republican army.

Colonel Jose Moscardo Ituarte was not the most senior officer in Toledo, but when the coup started – the planning and plotting of which Moscardo had been completely ignorant – it was the summer vacation for Spain's top military officer corps training academy and Moscardo was, as it were, left holding the fort. His sympathies were with the rebels and he immediately occupied the Alcazar and refused all orders from his Republican government chiefs to send the large supplies of ammunition to the front. The precise number of the occupying force in the Alcazar has never been precisely established, but it included a good section of the local police force, the Guardia Civil and many women and children family members. The Colonel himself had a teenage son hiding in the city from the enemy.

I had expected to find a restored fortress left very much as it was in the 1930s, but actually find an ultra-modern new Museum of the Spanish Army superimposed onto the shell of the old fortress. Original brick is set against shiny new steel structures. I admire it but I don't love it.

At the entrance a quote from 1936 by Gregorio Marañon is written in large letters above the door:

Cada uno de sus sillares está transido de quimeras de España: y a la larga, son las quimeras las que hacen que los hombres y los pueblos sean perdurables. Una vez más también rescicitara de sus encombros y seguirá elevándose bajo el cielo de Castilla. Una ruina es siempre una circunstancia y El Alcazar representa algo que está por encima de las circunstancias. Es a saber, la continuidad de la historia y la eternidad de España.

Each one of its building blocks is infused with the elixir of promised lands to come for Spain; the very stuff that ensures its people and nation will live on forever. Once more the phoenix will rise from its ashes and soar upwards into the Castillian sky. The ruin of a building is a mere mortal detail, and the Alcazar has but disdain for earthly matters. It is Spain, a land that goes on and endures for all time.

Once again I am struck by the emotional weight of good propaganda. The Alcazar symbolically lives on in the beating heart of the old regime, the triumph of a fascist dictatorial power still being celebrated and yet I love the sound of the words, the cadence of the phrasing and the sense of a lost place that it evokes. I have to admit to myself that I have always wanted to come here to feel, touch and smell a place of myth and legend. The Alcazar has a story, a myth that has endured down the years. Its truth is hard to verify, but its tale is plausible.

A priest was sent in to talk to Moscardo and make a plea to surrender or release the women and children. On returning he said, "My words fell on deaf ears, but I bore no arms and carried only in my hand, a crucifix."

It is said that later the Colonel took a phone call from his Republican opposite number, the Colonel-in-Chief. Moscardo was informed that his 17 year-old son Luis was under arrest and would be shot if Moscardo did not surrender in the next ten minutes. Luis was brought to the phone to speak to his father.

"Papa, how are you?"

"Well son, what's up with you then?"

"Nothing important; they say they are going to shoot me if you do not surrender, but don't worry on my account."

"Look son; yes they will shoot you, offer your soul up to the Almighty, cry out for Christ the King and Long Live Spain! Die like a hero and martyr. Goodbye my son, I send you a loving kiss."

"Goodbye Papa, a loving kiss too."

Luis handed back the phone.

"How say you?"

"The Alcazar will never surrender, forget the ten minutes, get it over with."

Luis was shot, but only several weeks later.

Lee must have heard the story; back in England it was big news. I wonder if, at that point, Lee thought about whether he could ever betray a child of his own?

The story reminds me of a phone call almost 20 years ago that had put me on the spot and given me a life-changing decision to make. I had fewer than ten minutes to decide. I was in Ireland on my way home from a business trip. I had rung my girlfriend to say I was on my way back home. She said that she had a six-year-old beside her who had something important to ask me.

"Hello," the young voice came crystal clear down the line, followed by a short pause and an intake of breath. "Will you be my daddy?"

I had just left my dad, now living back in Ireland in his home town. I had waved goodbye to him as he stood in his doorway, diminished and holding onto the door, tears in his blue eyes. He looked up at me and I wondered if he saw what I saw and heard what I heard: a little lost boy, hands over his ears.

The little girl, waiting patiently for an answer, coughed and the 39-year-old little lost boy swallowed and managed a strangled, "Of course I will."

There is a range of exhibits in the museum. I come across the old mill grinder and the motorcycle used to power it. It ground the flour from which the rebels made bread that saved them from starving. There is also an Enigma code machine, one of fifteen that the Germans donated to the rebels during the war. I had seen the machine before at Bletchley, the secret intelligence base in Buckinghamshire, from where the English and their allies had cracked the secret German Enigma code and changed the path of the Second World War.

Later in the civil war, Lee would be accused of being a spy for the fascists, of being in Morocco in the period leading up to the war. It almost cost him his life.

I go to leave, disappointed that they have not kept the Colonel's office intact, the scene of the phone call. I mention this to the attendant who looks surprised and directs me down a maze of corridors and doors and there it is. I step into the room and back in time to 1936.

The sign above the door reads No Exit.

The sun is streaming in through full-length windows, dark heavy shutters open. Two pools of dappled light form on the brown wooden herringbone patterned floor, like spotlights on the stage of history. A carefully choreographed drama still taking place every day in the museum. A black Bakelite telephone with its dialling circle stuck in time, spinning no more, sits on a small table under the portrait of an army officer. Perhaps it is Moscardo himself, a hero of his times, no sacrifice too great for his country. The phone sits inside a transparent glass case, like a sweaty cheese on a board, sleepy flies secreting over the gauze cover. The wallpaper is peeling behind the Colonel who sits upright behind a glass table, staring ahead, eyes fixed on the row of predecessors parading across the wall in front of him. They stare back at him from within their glass frames. They see each other, but there is no connection. The plasterwork is crumbling, the chandelier hovers above, just waiting – you think – to crash down and splinter into a thousand pieces. We are all waiting for the phone to ring, to sound its death knell, to call us to arms.

Outside the shelling has ceased, the snipers are reloading, the occupying forces driving the siege are lighting cigarettes and chatting behind the bullet-pocked sandbags. A man in a black cloak, crucifix in hand, walks slowly back through no-man's-land.

Still the phone is silent as drops of sweat trickle down its black shiny body, coagulating into a red pool staining the splintered oak table. The instrument of terror, a prisoner in the case; time melting away in the July heat on that oppressive day; all that is missing is a rotting apple, its peel coiled like a serpent, the ultimate symbol of betrayal, of Jesus by mankind, sons of fathers and fathers of sons.

Lee learnt early in his life about parental betrayal: "I was never recalled to my mother's bed again. It was my first betrayal, my first dose of ageing hardness, my first lesson in the gentle, merciless rejection of women."

The phone stays silent and I leave the room.

10 July 2012, Toledo

I am due to leave the city soon and head further south across the plains of La Mancha, the hunting ground of Sancho Panza and Don Quixote.

Unusually for Lee, he had someone to send him on his way from Toledo. Roy Campbell walked with him to the city walls.

He came with Lee as far as the bridge, but he didn't cross over it. This would be their point of farewell. Conversation had dried up as they approached the waterside. The breeze was drifting off the river, coming from the north and blowing Lee towards the south.

Roy wanted to embrace Lee and mark the parting, but all he could do was shake his hand, look him in the eye and push him on his way. Lee's step faltered as he walked over the water. When he reached the opposite bank, he looked back. Roy was backing away, home to Mary, doffing his brown hat, bidding Lee farewell.

By the time Lee and Roy next met, a war had been and gone. Lee looked at Roy noting that he looked older, though he was still sporting the same hat. Perhaps time had just passed more slowly for Lee and it just seemed that he ought to be older. Roy greeted him as if it was just the previous week that they had parted, not three years of a war of partition; a war in which they had lined up on opposing sides, not just of a slow moving river, but of a schism of a nation. A nation that neither of them had been born into. The River Tagus still drifted along but at a slower tempo, silted up by the blood and guts spilt on both banks.

Back in Toledo, before the war, in that previous world, they had only known each other for a week; a week longer than Lee had ever known his father for.

It's a sunny morning as I take my leave of Toledo. Valdepeñas is my next port of call and I head there with a heavy heart. For all that Lee was taken with Mary and the hours spent discussing doubt and faith, carnal knowledge or spiritual peace, for all that he wrestled with Mary's vision of life eternal for the pure of mind and body, he was always going to be tempted by the sins of the flesh: he was young, he was a poet.

Sooner or later he would betray the promises he had made to Mary of steering a straighter path as he went on his way.

I head out across the plains of La Mancha to Valladolid. This is Don Quixote territory and I wish I had the wise companionship of a Sancho Panza as I continue on my quest.

I set off on the road to Andalusia with Lorca's ominous words being whispered into my ear, "an endless road... the road where the first bird died and the first arrow grew rusty."

Valdepeñas

Knots in my Flesh

Do we know exactly who we are? The more urgently we
quest for our authentic selves, the more they tend to recede.
– Harold Bloom, introduction to Edith Grossman's translation
of *Don Quixote*, 2003

2 August 2012

I am walking south from Toledo through La Mancha, the setting for
the fictional adventures of Don Quixote. Miguel de Cervantes finished
his epic novel *Don Quixote* in 1615. He died a year later on 23 April
1616, the same day exactly that William Shakespeare passed away.

The landscape I am now crossing bears little resemblance to
Stratford-upon-Avon, not so far from Lee's Cotswolds home. It is
not the Avon bubbling up in the valley around me but the Guadiana,
another of Spain's great rivers that carries on through La Mancha,
through Extremadura – the birthplace of so many of Spain's
conquistadores. The river slips in and out of Portugal and finally
meets the Mediterranean at Huelva, the home city of my friend Pilar
who I met in Chinchón. It was from Huelva province that Christopher
Columbus set sail on the Santa Maria in August 1492 to seek the New
World.

I am walking through the *Lagunas de Ruidera* Natural Park,
made up of sixteen interconnected lakes. Legend has it that they take
their name from a story in Don Quixote. The presence of water is a
pleasant change from the dry terrain that has dominated the landscape
from Toledo. I can smell wood smoke as I walk through small hamlets

and I am transported back to my mother's Oxfordshire village and its oasis of green and cool breezes, the very thought of which soothes my increasingly fevered brain.

I do not have the bulky volume of my favourite translation of Don Quixote by Edith Grossman with me, but I did pick up a copy of Graham Greene's delightful *Monsignor Quixote* in a small bookshop in Toledo, which is lighter, in both senses of the word, than Grossman's 940-page tome. Greene's short novel imagines a similar journey through 1980s Spain by a kindly Catholic priest and a communist mayor: a contemporary Don Quixote and Sancho Panza. It is a lovely companion on a journey through La Mancha. The introduction to the book talks of its theme, and the interplay between the two protagonists as being a meeting point of two minds, "They are, in their different ways, both men of faith, and doubt is the place that they meet."

Doubt is not something that lingers too long in the long hot summer days of La Mancha, there is no space for it between the two constants of light and shade: burning sun in the open, exposed plain, or the cooling cover of a line of poplar trees, or simply the passing of a god-given cloud.

Doubt, though, comes to you in the night. I am no Don Quixote and neither was Lee, but we are wanderers on a quest with no Sancho Panza by our side, just the haze of the heat of the day or the early morning mist rising from the lakes to play tricks with the mind.

For some time now I have been beset with concerns about the purpose of my walk. My grief is not lifting and has intensified ever since my ascent into the rarefied air above Madrid. I still have the sense of being an outsider, seeing into the inner world of my lifelong hero, and glimpsing only a bare Edward Hopper-esque world of sadness, loneliness and despair. The betrayal of a soldier's son in Toledo, the knowledge that Lee would go on himself to betray his firstborn, nightmares of Lee hallucinating, the insight into Lee's father figure of Roy Campbell, a figure that resembled far too closely the reality of my own father. And always the dread of the approaching town of Valdepeñas where Lee would cross a line, the strains of Mary Campbell's softly spoken words consigned to the past. Was I searching for a poet or the spectre of the sort of man that my father so wanted me to be?

As I walk through another small village the squawking of the birds intermingles with the shrieks coming from the school playground, a cacophony that breaks the silence of the still waters all around me. Further on I pass a watermill and again the stillness is broken by the rush of water from the sluice gates.

The dry crumbling surface of the central plains sits above a water system whose vascular tendrils stretch far and wide, seeking out new springs at source to quench their never-ending thirst. Dried up men tread on the surface crust, dried up men who were once themselves vessels of liquidity, but somehow the sharp trebles of racing mountain streams have slowed to the flat dull drip of a rusty tap.

Alder trees line the lakes, their roots holding the banks fast against the volume of water pushing against it, guarding against further erosion of these once magical lands. We all need to be tended, watered.

An old man looks out at me through his kitchen window. The glass is streaked with oil and dirt and his face is flattened, his eyes vacant. A moment later he is gone.

The bells ring out for evening service as I look up to see the August sun dipping into the waters of the black lake.

The Guadiana River is one of the longest in Spain, but it is the least visited, remotest and hardest to find of them all. Often, when it disappears under the ground for long stretches, it seems to be hiding away, seeking protection from the harsh terrain and climate.

Followers of transcendental meditation say there are two bodies, the physical and the subtle, and talk of the human body having a literal truth and a poetic truth; one is visible and the other is not, one is composed of flesh and blood and bone and the other of energy and memory and faith. Virginia Woolf wrote of moments "when the self empties or eddies away". I had also read Saint Teresa of Avila the mystic, Mary Campbell's mentor, describing entering meditative trances so deep that her fellow nuns couldn't feel her pulse anymore. Once upon a time I would have been sceptical of such claims. However, I have had my own experience of witnessing a state of "near death". Ten years ago, I visited my father in a nursing home. He was not well and we were wondering how long he had left. We chatted for a few minutes until there came a point when he appeared to enter a trance-like state. He was not asleep and was breathing easily, but he was not there. His eyes turned to glass, unseeing and blank. This seemed to last for minutes, but was probably only seconds. I was beginning to panic when he suddenly came to, looked at me and began to talk again. I left, reassured. 24 hours later he was dead.

Lee's presence feels less real now. The more I seek him out the further away he appears.

Don Quixote said, as he lay dying, in response to his good man Sancho Panza's exhortations not to die on him, "let us go slowly, for there are no birds today in yesterday's nests." This seems to make as much sense as anything else I have read on the meaning and manner of death.

I am heading for Valdepeñas, a town embraced by succulent green vines pouring forth a steady stream of light red wine. It is sited on a tributary of the Guadiana River, the Jabalon. My body aches but my head aches more, the river alongside me looks threatening as the heat of the day threatens to implode.

The road into the centre is lined with huge Ali Baba terracotta pots. I have to cross the main Madrid-Cadiz railway line. On a deserted platform lies a dead bird. I look ahead to the south through barbed wire, the train tracks stretching away, wasteland on both sides. "No immigrantes" says the graffiti on a wall. I walk down from the enclosed overhead bridge. It is like passing through a cage to be released onto the streets. On a rusted bridge support is the outline of a haunted black figure, her head not encased in a black burka but bound by a black rope wound tightly around it and tied at the side. Just two black dots stare out from a narrow slit. I slow down and take a good look around before proceeding.

I reach the main square, bright blue and white apartments set around the edges. Lee described the town as graceful and friendly, but now, apart from these splashes of colour, it seems drab and distinctly unwelcoming.

I walk back from the centre into the outskirts of the town, as Lee had done accompanied by his new friends, three Spanish teenagers as they made their way to *La Casa de Putas* (the town brothel). I wonder what that experience would be like: I have never been to a brothel. As an adolescent I would walk the streets of Soho, regaled by bright lights, red lights, the flashing neon lights and walk on quickly by. I often wondered what a prostitute looked like. I expect I thought of "older" women, well beyond their prime, (which at that age meant anyone over 35!). On the eve of going down to Portsmouth to study for my first degree, I can remember my godfather visiting me, a lovely man. He wished me well, put his arm around me and said, "Mind you keep away from the dock area, The Hard, as it's known. There are too many sailors on the razzle looking for those naughty ladies of the night."

Spanish society, even when under the strictest of moral guardians at various times through its history, be it the Spanish Inquisition or the Franco dictatorship, has always had an ambivalent approach to the black market of sexual goods and exchanges. When I was first in Spain at the end of the Franco regime, I can recall the Spanish students whispering about houses where the girls would "tocar la flauta" (play the flute) – and they were not musical academies. In Madrid there were girls known as "Pajaristas", literally "strawmakers", who would, for a small fee in a shadowy corner of the Retiro park, relieve you of your pent up stress with their magical fingers. For a little extra they would softly sing sweet nothings into your ear.

The nearest I got to a "close encounter" was sitting in the Tuileries Gardens in Paris, awaiting my "gap year" train to Madrid and realising that the nice young French postman sitting next to me and chatting away, was actually offering me after hours service with guaranteed delivery.

Lee wrote often of wandering through the streets and parks of London "picking up servant girls from the last great houses... round(ing) off the evening in a Soho café smoking coal-black Mexican cigars... surrounded by soft-tongued Greeks."

I have no idea where Lee's brothel was, so I follow a sad, graffiti-sprayed sculpture trail called *La Batalla de los Molinos* (The Battle of the Windmills). Don Quixote famously fought with windmills, confusing them for an imaginary enemy force. The windmills are depicted by rods of iron fanned into giant windmill blades standing on round metal rusted blocks, which are embedded in a stream running through the town centre. A plaque lies under dirty rainwater in a sunken square cut out of the pavement. It is shrouded by a tissue of faded red leaves which have fallen on odd letters of the message, obscuring the full text. It is like a gravestone, and indeed, Cervantes's name is one of the few words I can read, but it is not his final resting place, for that is still unknown.

I carry on walking, the streets becoming more and more rundown, on turning a corner, I am surprised to see the façade of a brand new brick and glass building surrounded by small terraced houses all boarded up. I move closer and read the proud letters *Museo del Vino* (The Museum of Wine). It is early evening now, but I can see a shape moving inside. I knock and hear the jangling of heavy keys and the unbolting of doors. An elderly man peers at me and waves me in.

"Are you open?" I ask.

"Yes, of course. Do you want to see the museum, or are you just buying in the shop?"

I express a wish to look around if I can and he sighs and takes my money and informs me that he will have to go ahead of me while he opens up the exhibit rooms and switches the lights on. It is clear I am not just a late visitor today, but the only one; perhaps the only one this summer.

I learn much of vine roots and diseases and see the whole production process from start to finish. Eminent Spanish politicians, philosophers and writers praise the modest local wine on large, wine-coloured boards. My favourite quote is from Luis Buñuel, the famous surrealist film director who tested the patience of Franco's censors and guardians of the national conscience, more than once.

"If I had a final wish before breathing my last, high on my list would be a glass of red. I have a great fondness for a glass of Valdepeñas, drunk cold, straight from a goatskin flask."

I am struck most by a series of black and white photographs showing the daily routines of the workers: men and women working side by side, thigh deep in vats of grapes with shovels to hand; a blacksmith forging the steel bands around the barrel rims; young girls dancing together arm in arm; and a shady-looking character, cigarette in hand, smart jacket, the tip of a folded handkerchief just peering out from his breast pocket, a jaunty hat worn at an angle, the very image of a boss standing outside his office. Guitars are being played, two pale hands hold up two glasses of thin red liquid suffused through with the dark shadows playing in the foreground.

I sit outside in the square of the old *bodega* in which the museum is sited, whitewashed walls face out onto a sand floor. In the middle is a round water well.

At the end of my tour I am offered a complimentary drink from a dusty bottle. I sip the cold glass of Valdepeñas, pour a drop of wine onto my scallop shell, long since dried out from the Atlantic spray, and slurp the wine down as if it were a fleshy oyster. Bathed in the curious evening light, the shell takes on a delicate light blue tinge as if there were a blue pearl secreted in its innermost recess.

I imagine the *bodega* back in the 1930s, not so grand and not so clean, a pervading smell of yeast and fermentation. Perhaps there was a boarding house here, attached for the workers and the cart drivers. As night fell it would have been frequented by drinkers, men, perhaps later still, will o' the wisp sprites emerged from the shadows to practice their ancient craft. Was Laurie Lee here that September night in 1935? Watching, hanging back in the shadows as his three friends, Antonio, Amistad and Julio, approached the door of a dark house, "kicked it delicately with their pointed shoes and made low-pitched animal cries... the door was opened at last by a girl in a dressing gown, sleepily eating chips."

I lean back in the square, looking up at a full pale moon, remembering how Lee described that scene in the book when he slept with a prostitute, a mere slip of a girl. No money changed hands for Lee was a troubadour and had sung for his supper. Lee described the encounter, "The girl's wandering finger, tipped with precocious cunning, seemed the only thing left alive in the world, and moved absently about me, loosening knots in my flesh, then tying them up again."

The velvety smooth words had slipped down the throat of this adolescent reader when first read a lifetime ago. I wondered, what it had really been like?

September 1935 – A Brothel in Valdepeñas

There is a soft knock on the door. She wakes him, El Abuelo, her grandfather. He coughs, spits, shuffles across on his board, strong gnarled wrists propelling him along, reaches up high, slips the latch and lets the three young men inside. The first three are regulars, the fourth, a blonde-haired young man, is not. She greets them, sweat running down her hot cheeks, mixing in with the raw, garlic-infused spittle lying in pools on the straw-laden floor. The liquid globules react in what air there is in the barn with the wine vapours seeping in through every pore of the thin walls.

Sugars, grape skin and seeds, ground together in the threshing machine, create a thin fluid soon to turn into nectar, a miracle no less than the church-blessed wine turning into the blood of Christ. Mama had spoken to her of the angel's share, the wine goodness that evaporated into thin air as the alchemy took place. She breathes in that goodness with huge gulps before it hits the stale stench of male perspiration and semen-soaked waves of nausea permeate the room and leave her choking and gasping for breath.

The lads help themselves to greasy titbits, provided by Him; fried sparrows on a spit, fatty chorizo soaked in cider, glasses of the local red wine famed throughout Spain, nothing is too good for the three kings and the prince from England, Lorenzo. She yawns and examines her nails. There was a time when she had been a princess, virgin-pressed, a Grand cru, a first growth, a flowering young maiden, a bright red rose. She had been sold, one summer evening, to Don Gonzalo, director of the *bodega*. She had taken his eye during the grape harvest dance, she in her checked blouse and faded dungarees, Chinese coolie sun hat, roped sandals encasing her pretty ankles. It was a good harvest that year and as the girls had danced in the courtyard, her grandfather had crooked his bony finger and sent her up to the Don's room.

The Don's skin was smooth, his smell, oh so fine, but he was rough, like all the rest when it came to it. He had taken her innocence that night, just the first of many thieves in her many nights. He left her bruised, skin split, seeds swimming in a translucent film, a red stain spreading outwards. From the beginning of time man has crushed the grape and the fair sex.

Don Gonzalo had buttoned up his long white pants, paid his dues and left. The Don had not remembered her Mama, taken by him too in her prime: Mama, long driven-out by Him, the girl's grandfather. Like the black rot that can lay waste to a harvest, she had contracted the pox and had been exiled, sent north to the factories.

He summons her to accommodate Julio, one of the three

kings. She lies, mute but not unresponsive, examining her hands and feet, scratched by the rough vine roots. Round and round goes the wine press mangle, squeezing, crushing, draining the skin, till finally leaving it lifeless, limp, spent.

She goes to Lorenzo, the English boy. He asks her name, and she tells him, "Encarnación". It is quick. She likes him for that.

The candle has burned to the stub, the customers have gone. She waits for the scrape on the ground, the pumping of thin, wiry wrists. She waits for Him to come for her as she knows He will.

I cannot get the image of Lee and this young girl out of my mind.

I am somewhere in La Mancha and cannot think straight anymore, perhaps my melancholy is down to the flatness, the dryness, the sheer monotony of the terrain, perhaps it is the heat or the wind from the north. After all Don Quixote, the knight of the sorrowful countenance "is mad only north-northwest and when the wind blows from the south he is as canny as Hamlet, Shakespeare and Cervantes."

I had always loved playing with the definitions of *duende*, seeing the concept in romantic terms, for the first time I recalled a darker description of it by Lorca, a view of life that could have been conjured up by a man sunk into the deepest of clinical depressions: "Where is the *duende*? Through the empty arch comes a wind, a mental wind blowing relentlessly over the heads of the dead, in search of new landscapes and unknown accents; a wind that smells of baby's spittle, crushed glass, and jellyfish veil, announcing the constant baptism of newly created things."

I had embarked on this journey to reawaken some of the senses that seemed to have deserted me. I had felt numb for so long, not trusting my ability to deal with complex, deep emotion. I had gradually allowed myself to begin to feel a sense of hope that all could be well again, anger at what I was seeing in Spain, an attraction to a woman. I had been damaged by the rejection of my wife, the sudden ending of a career. Other people had lost faith in me. Now, I faced the real prospect that I had lost faith in myself, with the values I had lived my life by. The writer who had been my hero ever since I can remember was diminishing in front of me. All of a sudden, like Don Quixote and Sancho Panza, I was being faced with doubt about my beliefs. I had once suffered from a very severe anxiety-related form of depression.

I doubted everything about life, what I might do to others, what others might do to me; everything closed in on me.

I do not feel like that now, but the re-emergence of a very elemental form of doubt is enough to spook me. I am alone in a foreign land and I am not sure any more why I began this strange journey and what will happen if I complete the journey and find nothing has changed. A fear of failure or even more likely a fear of success I suppose is what people will say and they would be right.

I resolve to sleep on it but deep down I know.

The next day I catch a train back to Madrid and head home. I cannot go any further on this journey. I leave Lee behind sleeping off his drink-fuelled night on the stained straw-covered floor of the inn, my own insides consumed by the twisted and tangled tightening knots in my flesh.

The Lizard, England

Her Chanel-Scented Bed

There is nothing, either good or bad,
but thinking makes it so.

– William Shakespeare, *Hamlet*

August 2012, St Helen's, Ireland

It is good to be back in a familiar place and on my own. I can't face yet the return home to friends and family. I am not ready for those expectant eyes, the welcoming but pitying eyes, the eyes that would seek out mine and fail.

The house had changed little since the days when, as a child, I had visited regularly in the summer. My father grew up here, a small village on the coast.

I planned to stay here for a few days and then return to England. I am not yet sure why I have abandoned my journey across Spain.

I have come to Ireland partly to defer the return back to Oxford. I am not ready for that yet.

Cill Eillean, this tiny hamlet on the southern Irish coast in County Wexford, is also a place that I have avoided coming back to for many years but somewhere that I always knew would draw me back one day. This seemed like the right moment.

My feelings are still raw from Spain, I have little idea still of why I had to leave Spain and give up on my journey, perhaps the heat of the summer had got to me, or I was getting too close to Lee's ghost, getting too close to my own demons that lay in waiting under the protective covers of my adolescent crush on Lee.

The fine particles of the cold sand on this Irish strand slip through my fingers. I had last been here ten years ago when my father was lain to rest or at least his ashes were buried in the family cemetery just outside the nearby village of Kilrane. I am staying in the old coastguard cottages that belonged to my godfather, Jack, and are still owned by the family. They lie on a cliff top overlooking the Irish Sea and the Tuskar Rock lighthouse. The cliffs are crumbling, eroded by the sea.

My father grew up in Kilrane, a village a few miles away, inland. His family ran the village shop. He left eventually to go to England and become a doctor. Jack was the only other brother to leave Ireland, he too went to England. My father left five brothers in Ireland. He had a sister who had died tragically young from tuberculosis at the age of 18.

My father spent much of his adult and later life wracked with guilt. He kept a secret from his five sons: that there was a sixth son, born to another woman. In the early 1960s, my mother had five children between one and ten, and employed a series of au pair girls to help her. They never stayed long. I was fond of the last one, Friedericke from Munich, who brought me chocolate and let me stay up to watch football games on the TV. She stayed longer than most. She was in her early 20s when it happened. My father took advantage of this young woman away from home. I am told he could be charming; in his 40s he still had a masculine allure and presence. I have a picture of him from this time, probably taken just down the road at the harbour's edge. His hair is tousled, a roll-your-own cigarette dangling from lips, the smoke rising up through a willow reed hedge-layed moustache. He is wearing a shaggy pullover and is holding up a large sea bass, two nicotine-stained fingers inserted into its gills.

He groomed Friedericke carefully, loved her carelessly and two became three. As they were both devout Catholics, the baby, Christopher, was born quietly in Southampton on Spike Island where Jack lived. Another boy, a ruined marriage, a young woman lost to a spinner of tales, a charmer, an alchemist who turned shining gold into base metal.

I finger the medal still hanging around my neck, my protective guardian, my new brother named after him.

When we brought his ashes for burial in the family plot we stayed in the old family home above the shop. It is now a guesthouse and we placed his ashes in his old room, just down the corridor from the music room where a tiger skin rug lurked and where my dad would play the piano and sing "Danny Boy".

He loved music; his favourite opera was "Cavalleria Rusticana", a tale of lust and adultery and death. It is a beautiful opera and I am listening to it now with tears streaming down my face.

I had lain my father to rest but the hurt had never gone. It stayed quietly in the background as I got on with my life.

It was my father, though, that I had come to make peace with, back in his home, the only place, I thought, he ever felt safe.

Lee had talked of the Irish and their land, "They seem to inhabit its surfaces as birds ride on the sea, coming and going with wind-blown cries."

Lee lived in a similar small village and grew up without a father. I only ever found one reference to Lee's father in his memoirs and that was when Lee was in London as a young man, prowling around its inner districts, whiling away the time before he set sail for Spain. He was in the old city, where he knew his father worked. He was walking along and suddenly paused. I imagine him shrinking into the sides of a dark alley: "It made me uneasy. I always expected to run into my father," he wrote.

The wind is howling, the seas surging, overtopping waves batter the harbour walls that I walked on as a child. I sit on the cliff top above the raging seas, in a lee, a small oasis of calm on this dark night. The intermittent light of Tuskar Rock lighthouse pierces the darkness, still guarding the ships' passage, showing them the way around the point and south, south-west to the Atlantic, Spain and the New World.

I cradle an Irish green scarred stone in my hands, rescued from the beach earlier. This stone has a body that has been washed almost clean over the years on this Wexford beach. Given time perhaps the greenness will fade into opaque colourless nothing.

Down below on the beach, as a child, I learnt how to swim and met strange-talking Irish girl cousins. Close by, or so I had been told, my uncle Kevin had driven the family car over the cliff top, full of other uncles and no doubt their girls, after a drunken night at the Lobster Pot pub.

I think of betrayal, of my mother by my father, my own betrayal by my wife, Lee's betrayal of his daughter, of the young prostitute. I think of loss, loss of innocence, loss of childhood, loss of a hero but most of all loss of my father who I so wanted to love. I think of the vivid dream from the night before, my first night back in this family home since my long ago childhood, a dark dream of strangeness and feelings shut away in a cupboard.

*   *   *

Grey waves mourn the loss of yet another day, another year, in Ireland. I turn the corner and see two figures approaching. As the shapes take on a recognisable form, they reveal themselves as my cousin Declan and a companion. He is draped over her, one arm holding her close, the other cradling an infant. She is younger, much younger. The child, like her mother, has blue eyes, dark, curly hair and a smile that lights up the gloomy dusk. The last time I saw Declan, he had been a Catholic priest.

They slip on by and I carry on up to the house.

An old coastguard cottage, it keeps watch over the treacherous seas exposed on the cliff top, defiant in the face of the encroaching sea that inches ever closer. The onslaught of the waves is remorseless: the corrosive salty venom, mined from its ocean depths, eats away at the soft tissue of the cliff.

I look out from the cottage towards the lighthouse, just as generations of keepers have done before me: unable or unwilling to escape from the unremitting light shining deep into troubled souls. They understood the lore and law of the sea: for every life they saved, the sea would demand another. A message repeated by the ceaseless chatter of the armada of gulls ever circling above. One faltering step along the way and they are in, tearing apart any exposed underbelly or unattended soul.

The house has been updated: the light is no longer provided by oil lamps and candles; running water has been installed, negating the need for the dawn run, braving waist-high sodden stinging nettles, down to the well. The bare floor of the kitchen leads to a larder. The separating door provides a glimpse into a dark interior through a square window of black gauze. Echoes of whispered and hurried confessions linger in the damp air, clouds of incense constrict my throat, a worn leather strap hangs on a rusty hook.

I am in a bedroom. My bony fingers trace a path across the familiar whitewashed walls, the surface rough and naked save for the single metallic cross: the Messiah nailed firmly into place; He is keeping watch over me. My fingers touch the betrayal oozing from his wounds, wipe the pity from his eyes. He looks down on a high brass bed, a large white porcelain bowl and jug, an open fireplace.

I slip into the lounge. The ever-changing skyline charts the moods of the elements framing the floor-to-ceiling picture window. Dusk continues to fall and the sweeping arc of the lighthouse beam cuts through the dusty layers of now and streams into the recesses of the distant then.

The shaft of light picks out a small boy in the adjoining bedroom. He is lying in bed, trapped in the no-man's-land between sleep and wakefulness. I know it is the child in me. He comes to, shivers and looks around him. He is alone. He can see outside the outline of a formation of dark-winged geese, gathered off Spanish Point. A clutch of harpies, they screech past and swoop down onto Lady's Island; a black mass of robed, faceless clerics chanting, "Forgive us our sins, forgive us our sins." He thinks of putting on his trousers over his pyjamas and braving the cold to go outside. He considers carefully the noise he would make: the pulling back of the bolt, the creaking of the door's heavy hinges, the inrush of wind and rain. He opts for the chamber pot. Even then the sound of hot liquid hitting cold shiny surface and the ensuing escaping hiss of steam shreds his nerves. He gets back into bed, straining for the slightest noise. He tries to shut out the fetid air in the room by burying his head under the covers. The deadweight of sleep drags him down in the end.

It is the shortest day of the year, the winter solstice. It has been dark for hours. Declan, again, by himself, walking down to the sea. Moving closer, I hover at his shoulder. An old weathered red and blue striped boat emerges from the low-lying sea mist, a scene bathed in a strange ethereal shade of white. Silhouettes appear, hauling a net encasing a body. We creep closer, Declan and I, and see the body of a young girl dressed in a long white dress, a red sash tied to the waist. The scene is lit up by a wreath of blazing candles on her "moon-frozen" head, revealing a face of white marble flickering in and out of view. Declan kneels in front of the prostrate form and blesses her. Santa Lucia Encoronada, the bringer of light.

The shining face of a young boy, the sweet transient taste of innocence lingering but fleetingly on his lips; the radiant clear eyes of the young priest, a certainty that over time would leach away to reveal the opacity of doubt.

I walk back down to the harbour, abandoned long ago by the fishermen. It is silted up and covered in layers of cracked, rotting seaweed choking off memories of times past. The outline of the derelict church tower stands out, behind me, against the full moon. The Church of Storms it is called. The tower is silent, its bells drowned long ago.

I still hear those muffled bells tolling for me, a boy stranded on the sandbanks, my cries borne away by the wind, lost in the suck and spit of the rolling sea. Nobody comes. Nobody comes.

A man of grace stands to one side, he has no name, his nose frost-bitten away, his one arm hanging loose, a hand long gone. His stone body is wracked with cold and damp and riddled with yellow mushrooming spores. He braves the elements and watches over still the small once-white slab of stone that lies sheltered in the lee of the wind. It once had shiny black lettering etched into its surface. Now it fades steadily away, sinking inexorably into the earth, into the darkness, into the emptiness below.

The grey waves roll on.

*   *   *

That was just a dream but I recognise, in my conscious state, its clear message.

I shiver as the very real wind whips in off the sea. Declan is indeed my cousin and he became a priest at a young age and knew little of life other than school, seminary, church and parish. I had empathy with his schooling: I was also raised by nuns, Christian Brothers and Jesuits. Like him, I was asked by my father, at the age of seventeen, on my birthday, whether I felt I had a vocation for the priesthood. However, I had said no and escaped his fate.

I had recently been to a talk in London given by a famous literary son of Wexford, the Irish writer Colm Toibin. He was speaking on how his writing was influenced by the dramatic setting and musical tempo of the operatic form. He is the same age as me and went to a boys-only Catholic boarding school in Wexford Town, St Peters. Wexford also hosts an international festival of, mainly obscure and rarely performed operas. In an evocative short story called The Pearl Fishers, Toibin describes how at the age of sixteen he discovered opera and his latent sexuality at around the same time and brings the opera narrative and the story of his ever closer friendship with a classmate to a shattering crescendo at the same time. The burning funeral pyre, lovers fleeing, savage cries renting the night air, balanced by the urgent adolescent cut and thrust coupling in a dark empty classroom, punctuated by smothered gasps of exultation and the coming to a head of the exchange with the outpouring of lemony scented sperm, greedily palmed up and swallowed down as the panting died away. The black-robed Christian Brother on duty that night, hearing the strange animal cries echoing down the long corridors, arriving too late to catch the boys in the act. They had come and gone, the birds had flown.

As for Declan, in middle age, he fell in love, left the Church, had two children and became a house husband.

I had dreamed of Lady's Island located just around the headland, a place of pilgrimage for many centuries. The island had an air of mystery at times, a low mist hanging just above the early morning light, a latticed spider-web of grey filaments shrouding the still waters, woven and taut across the lake, a tensile strength that could dissolve with the merest puff of wind from the grey seas just beyond.

The Ireland of my father is a foreign land to me, its ways and customs so alien to my English-born sensibilities. My father could never quite escape its clutches and spent his last years back on home soil.

My godfather, Uncle Jack, who would go on to become an eminent psychiatrist in the British Army, would sit in the back garden of the family home and lob glass lemonade bottles over the wall at the passing occupying Black and Tan British Forces.

My father, as a boy, when in trouble would run and hide under the voluminous skirts of Bridy, the kitchen cook, and listen as she put Granny off the scent and sent her off into the garden, past the greyhounds resting up for their next race at Enniscorthy and Martin the Gardner, tending to his tomato plants that reached high into the sky filling the air with a luscious smell that lives with me to this day. Martin who died one afternoon in the garden, crashing through the tomato canes, just like Don Corleone in the film *The Godfather*. My uncle Fintan had a farm up the road and I am often reminded by my younger brother of the time that I lifted him into the pig sty and left him there to be rescued by my uncle who feared the pigs would eat the little mite up. It was one small slice of Laurie Lee village life and humour that I could boast from my urban London sprawl childhood.

The weak sun of the day had dipped into the Irish Sea. I reflected on my childhood and my journey to Spain, both cut short. I had been reminded that even heroes have feet of clay, history is written by the victors and writers and fathers don't always tell the truth.

In the desk in the lounge, underneath the grainy black and white photo of my father's sister taking the air outside an alpine sanatorium, is my father's old black rosary. I imagine him, as a young man, praying for his sister, praying for a miracle that didn't happen. The diseased spores were resistant to the rarefied air and she died. The rosary recital follows a set of mysteries grouped into three sets: the Joyful mysteries; the Sorrowful mysteries; and the Glorious mysteries. In 2002, Pope John Paul 11 announced a set of new optional mysteries called the Luminous mysteries. Would the light shone by the Luminous mysteries have saved my aunt? I doubt it.

I had come to know that I had never really said goodbye to my father; I had followed Lee across Spain and came to know the man rather than the legend; I had begun to feel more at ease with my real self. But more than that, I had realised that I was not just searching for Lee, a man I knew only through his words, I was searching also for a man who really shaped my life – my father.

I feel now, sitting above the Irish Sea, that I have found him, forgiven him, forgiven myself and found some semblance of peace.

I feel able to go home, to the only place that feels like home at the moment, to Oxfordshire and the wise, searching eyes of my mother, who was not expecting me home until I had completed my journey.

I feel I have the strength to return to England and consider my next steps.

21 August 2012

I go back to London, still wary of venturing to Oxfordshire. London is where I was brought up and where Lee spent much of his life, feeling like an exile:

"I come from generations of Cotswold farmers. I have inherited instincts that are tuned to pastoral rhythms, to the moods of the earth, to seedtime and harvest, and the great cycle of the seasons. London cannot fulfil those instincts, and I for my part cannot lose them."

He was for a long time though unable to return to the suffocating narrowness of the Slad Valley.

I take the ferry from Rosslare to Fishguard and the train to London. I may have cut short my journey across Spain but I still feel the need to follow Lee's trail, to understand more about his life. I had been once to his grave but now I hasten to the final resting place of his legacy to his fellow man. The British Library, just round the corner from St Pancras Station, is where his diaries and notebooks and letters are buried under the ebb and flow of traffic on the Euston Road.

I am looking for more of him there and to unearth many of his original writings. I own a signed first edition of his book of poems, *A Many-Coated Man*, but holding and reading his original manuscripts, deciphering his handwriting and seeing his stories evolve from conception to print via a process as messy as life itself is fascinating.

It is perhaps fitting that the body of his creative life's work was laid to rest in London, his adopted home.

I walk into the British Library and take a seat on a bench. The bench is a sculpture of a book randomly opened at a page, weighted down with a giant chain and ball.

Lee died in 1997. I never met him. I wonder now why I never did; I had several opportunities. The Lee Estate gifted his papers and drawings to the library soon after.

The archives are clean, dust free and cool.

I come across fragments of his past: faded hand-written messages, shopping lists, bills, love letters, plenty of those...

> After you had gone, I walked out to sea, fully half a mile, with
> a solitary seagull to keep me company. I bless that bird too,
> Laurie, because I would like to keep your friendship if you think
> mine worthwhile.

I don't know whether to call you a cool bastard or beg you to come back. We had an unforgettable winter together and I'm letting you go that easily. I still adore you mon chère... I feel very depressed on this bleak wet Thursday afternoon at the prospect of the future without you. Don't forget, I shan't, your adoring girl still, R x

In addition there are letters from his mother addressed to Laurence Edward Alan Lee, Socorro Rojo (Red Cross) Albacete, Spain in early 1938,an index card plan for *As I Walked Out One Midsummer Morning*, a loose torn leaf from a 1935 diary recording snatches of conversation.

The notes are scrawled on odd pages in old red exercise books, all stamped with Gloucestershire County Council Education Service. Most of the pages are blank.

* * *

I often meet a writer, John Simmons, here in the coffee shop of the British Library. He feels at home here having grown up in the streets of King's Cross. We meet today. He is good to me on this occasion and doesn't ask specific questions about Spain and journeys. He does though turn the conversation around to a tale of his own very personal link to the Spanish Civil War and a small act of humanity on behalf of his parents.

"My mum and dad – Jessie and Frank – married in 1936. They were an idealistic young couple, growing up in a politically-charged period. In London they were active campaigners against fascism. When the Spanish Civil War started in the year of their marriage, they wanted to do something. In April 1937 they were horrified by Franco's bombing of the Basque town of Guernica. A month later, 4000 Spanish children from the Basque country set sail from Bilbao on a ship called the *Habana*. They were refugees from the war, whose parents were on the Republican side and desperate for their children to find safety.

When they arrived at Southampton, the children were dispersed to all parts of the country – to camps, to convents, to institutions and to the homes of ordinary families who volunteered to take them. Jessie and Frank took in a Spanish boy called Jesús (pronounced Hay-zus). The war ended a year or so later, with the wrong side winning. My dad had not joined the International Brigade to go and fight alongside many young Englishmen including George Orwell – otherwise I might not be here now. But he fought in the Second World War.

By then Jesus had returned to his family in Spain, leaving only memories and a couple of photos that have passed down to me. Here is Jesús's friend and fellow refugee angel."

John shows me a photograph of a young boy wearing a Grandfather coat.

"On the backs of the photographs the boys had written their words of thanks to Jessie and Frank."

Another photograph shows Jessie, a young woman of 25, with some of the Spanish refugee boys at a camp in Kent.

"I've always been proud of my mum for her political commitment – she was a fighter for causes she believed in. As long as Franco was in power, my family could not visit Spain. Jesús could not travel from Spain and we never saw him after his time as a refugee. The memories died when Jessie and Frank died. Except that one memory remains, and it means that we can never forget this story."

John takes out another black and white image. It is of a ordinary wooden desk, covered in toys and with a picture of an angel leaning against the wall of the room.

"Jesús's father was a carpenter (is that why his son was named Jesús?) When Jesús returned to Bilbao, his father made a small desk and had it shipped to Jessie and Frank in London. It was his way of saying thank you. The desk is solidly made but it's not a work of art – it's a functional piece of furniture. It was used first by my brother Dave as he grew up, and then by me. When Dave died, it became mine, and I passed it on to my son Matt who would sit and do his homework at it – sometimes my daughter Jessie too. Now Matt has it in his house, and it's used by Aimee and Ada, my grandchildren. Objects have extraordinary emotive power, you know. They contain stories, and those stories and objects pass on from generation to generation," John concludes.

I still have that sea shell in my pocket and I sit for a while, as John takes his leave, lost in thought.

I go back to Lee's papers and make a startling discovery which will send me off to a Celtic land, this time not Galicia, but Cornwall – another of my safe havens since being cast adrift by Elizabeth. I have spent a lot of time in Cornwall over the past two years, dividing my time between there and Oxfordshire. I would stay in Falmouth, a busy fishing small port, perhaps my version of Almuñecar, where Lee would hole up for the winter after his journey.

Falmouth is not far from The Lizard, a beautiful wild spit of land jutting out into the Atlantic. It was here that I would reconnect with the Lee that I thought I knew, but who had got lost in recent weeks.

23 August 2012, Gunwalloe, Cornwall

Girl of green waters, liquid as lies,
Cool as the calloused snow,
From my attic brain and prisoned eyes
Draw me and drown me now.

— Laurie Lee in "Song by the Sea", 1955

I am drawn to a small cove on the Lizard Peninsula on a bright August morning: Church Cove, Gunwalloe. It is hidden away behind a maze of high-hedged approach roads, even the perpendicular telegraph poles wrapped around with purple and white-flecked wild flowers. The Lizard is the most southerly point on the English mainland, with France and Spain between here and North Africa. It sits proudly above the wild sea that defies any attempt to corral its spirit. Named from the Celtic *lys ardh*, high point, it stands watch over the wild Cornish dunes.

Orange-tipped butterflies nuzzle at the pink-tipped lady's smock flowers. A small water bird, a spotted crake, flies by; its blue-grey breast flashing in the light, its whiplash wings moving smoothly through the air. It has come all the way from Africa and will go back there.

This is a rocky and dangerous part of the coast and many lives have been shipwrecked and lie buried in the surrounding Halzephron Cliff.

The remains of many ships have been washed up on these shores. The little church, wedged into the cliff behind the cove, St Winwaloe, the "Church of the Storms", as it is known, lists its trophy collection of wrecks over the years: San Salvador, Lady Lucy, Fancy, Betsey, Nellie Harding. They could so easily be a list of Lee's past lovers.

I am not here by chance. According to my discovery in the papers in the British Museum, on this day 75 years ago two star-crossed lovers met for the first time. One of them was Lee.

I still have my scallop shell with me, my link to Lee and his past. I dip the shell into the Cornish Atlantic waters, trace my fingers across its reflective eye ridges and conjure up the moment that was about to change Lee's life forever.

23 August 1937, Gunwalloe, Cornwall

Laurie Lee perches on the rocks, listening to the Atlantic Ocean driving into the shore.

Sucking up the hard English grey stones, it retreats and then comes again, to fling the stones back up onto the strand. He has his violin, but any sound of bow across strings is lost in the roar of the waves. His thoughts are fixed hundreds of miles south, across the Bay of Biscay, where his adopted countrymen are fighting for their lives and country in Spain: The light, fresh, green-tinted Cornish waves close to the shore grow a darker serpentine-green colour as the sea edges away into the distance and drops over the horizon into Spanish waters.

Across the cove, Lee's eye is caught by a flash of blue against the pale green and white of the sea's outlying riders. The blue shape shifts in the breeze. Lee wipes the morning sleep from his eyes, softened by the salt-encrusted spray from the ocean. He walks across the strand towards the blur of blue, lost momentarily in the mustard cliffs facing him.

Lorna, legs covered in the surf, is aware of the shore urchin with the violin long before her cool blue eyes meet his. She flicks a stray wisp of jet-black dampened hair back over her ear with her right hand, beckons him to her with the fingers of her left and bids him play for her. He does and continues to play to her tune for the rest of his days.

She would bring him moments of ecstasy and she would bring him to the edge of despair and madness. Lee wrote the following words in his

1944 poem, "At Night" , almost certainly about Lorna at a time when he was tormented by her betrayal of him:

> *I think at night my hands are mad,*
> *For they follow the irritant texture of darkness*
> *Continually carving the sad leaf of your mouth*
> *In the black bark of sleep.*

After Cornwall the initial affair was a torrid and passionate one carried out across England and France, in luxury hotels and Chanel-scented beds, in long abandoned huts on windswept deserted beaches as Lee inched his way back to the French border with Spain, fighting his conscience at deserting his Spanish comrades, perhaps wanting to impress his lover with his moral fibre- he had not yet realised the futility of this line of attack – or perhaps he had and simply wanted to show his credentials as a man of action, a lover prepared to fight for a cause.

The affair lasted for over six years; Lee would leave Lorna almost instantly to return to Spain and the civil war. On his return she would bear him a child, Yasmin, who she took with her when she eventually returned to her husband, Ernest Wishart, or Wish, as he was known. Wish was always there waiting and she always returned. Wish was not a weak man but he understood his wife. Lee learnt the hard way what it was to love and be rejected. It was new to him and something he never really recovered from. It was the losing of Lorna that almost destroyed him. As for Yasmin, he seemed able to cope with this loss. In the 1930s the stigma of being a child born out of wedlock was still great and Lee and Yasmin owed a great debt to Wish and his tolerance.

It was another man who brought about the end of Lee and Lorna's affair, not Wish, but a young bisexual artist, Lucian Freud. He was a tormented man who, when Lorna rejected Lee and took up with him, seemed to both repel and attract her.

Lee and Lorna would both refer forever more to their initial meeting on the Cornish beach as "the final enchantment" of their lives, and yet just six years later, on the anniversary of their meeting in 1943, Lorna would bring Freud to the same spot and make sure that Lee knew of this act of casual treachery. It was almost too much for Lee who documented in his diary that he was close to taking his own life.

Freud liked to draw life and death in the raw; at about this time he had drawn the body of a dead puffin. I had been to see the picture and others at the Tate after my visit to the British Library. I wanted to get the measure of this man who had brought Lee to the edge of despair. I wondered if what I was actually looking at was a trophy picture of Lee, vanquished and lifeless and at the mercy of Freud's savage pen.

Lee, however, was not finished and a year later was still expressing publicly his love for Lorna when he dedicated his new volume of poetry to her, an account of his last decade entitled *The Sun My Monument*. Given the nature of the period covered, the witnessing at close hand of a country being consumed by a civil war and the playing out at a sustained pitch of passion of a private war, a love match, that produced ecstasy but ended in hell, it was apt that a proof copy of the book was cut and scarred by fragments from a bomb blast during a raid on London by the Germans. Lee and Lorna had carried out much of their affair over the preceding years in the open air of the South Downs and had come to know the sight and feel of thin strips of metal strewn in the grass and thistledown, not fragments of shrapnel, but 'dupel' materiel dropped by German planes to interfere with radar systems.

Later that year Lee recorded in his diary that he had thought of killing Lorna, in his poem "My Many-coated Man" he writes of a man "hooded by a smile" who "commits/his private murder in the mind."

The paths of Lee and Freud were to follow similar lines over the next few years once Lorna inevitably discarded Freud and went back to Wish and Yasmin and her other neglected children.

Lee and Freud would both go on to marry a Garman sister's niece: Kathy for Lee and Kitty for Freud. Lee also managed to sleep with Kitty before Freud came on the scene.

It was Kathy though that intrigued me at this point. Lee, after grieving for Lorna, took up with three Garman nieces, one after the other, all in their late teens or early twenties. Esther and Kitty were true Garmans in their dreamy approach to life, caught up in the drama of being gay young things, perhaps trying a bit too hard. They were agreeable to Lee, but he had tasted the real thing. Kathy was different: she was down to earth. Lee had known her since she was a child, and she had a crush on him that lingered. It was at a party, hosted by Roy and Mary Campbell, that Lorna pointed Kathy out to Lee and suggested that she might be the girl for him.

I was beginning to realise, sitting on a narrow bench in the shelter of the Church of the Storms, just above the cove, that life back in the 1930s in the non-conformist areas of London that I never knew, was a different place indeed with a set of values of its own. Lee had courted Kathy from the age of 14 (an age that according to Lee was the perfect age for a girl), and had probably slept with her once she reached the age of sixteen. He was twice her age but this was no short-lived fling. On the 17 May 1950, Lee married Kathy and stayed with her for the rest of his life. He would continue to stray and have affairs, but like Wish with Lorna, Kathy knew what she had taken on and gave Lee what he needed: a solid base.

However, to the day he died, Lee never took off the signet ring that Lorna had given him.

I sit there at the cove, not wanting to move from the place that changed Lee's life forever. But I must return to Oxfordshire and face the music, though I am beginning to dare to think about going back to Spain and fulfilling my quest. I realise that there is still much to learn from heroes, even those that have slipped from their pedestal, deities made mortal and none the worse for it. First though I have a date with my own daughter in Herefordshire, where she is appearing at a folk festival.

August 2012, Herefordshire

I have not seen Daniella since leaving for Spain, and I am looking forward to meeting up with her and seeing her perform at the festival. She has been following her own path as a singer/songwriter for a few years now, and is starting to attract more attention, but it is a tough career choice. She is, though, doing what she wants to do and I am proud of her – and a little envious: I did not have the courage to do the same when I was that age.

It is a typical New Age festival with Romany caravans, horses, dogs and young children mixing in with the festival-goers. The sun is beginning to set behind the Malvern Hills in the distance as Daniella begins her set of acoustic country/folk/blues fusion. Her mellow laid-back approach is in stark contrast to the raw sound of the balding seadog drifter Pete, who had preceded her on stage. He came from Preston in Lancashire but played his sawn-off guitar, attached to an old paraffin can, like an old hand from Tennessee. Pete had introduced the set and talked of his life roaming the festival scene around England and Wales. He made no mention of his earlier life, although it was clear that Texas and the Deep South had claimed him at some point. I couldn't help but think of Lee on his walk to London all those years ago being taken under the wing of Alf, the old tramp, one of many who took to the roads in the depression between the two world wars. Alf looked out for him for a few days before sending him off to London.

Daniella plays a short set of songs that I know well. "My Friend Becky", a song about her childhood friend, followed by "Tiredly in Love", which usually leaves at least one audience member in tears.

I lie back on the grass, a makeshift log fire burning beside me, a stillness in the valley hollow below, the words and music playing gently over the dark waters of the lake.

Perhaps it is the dampness of the grass or the smell of harvest-time in the air or perhaps I just cannot shake the "final enchantment" of the meeting between Lee and Lorna at Gunwalloe Cove from my mind. Lorna, in the later years of her childhood, had lived in an old black and white half-timbered farmhouse in deepest Herefordshire in the Welsh Marches. She was fourteen when her brother Douglas brought a friend, Ernest Wishart, down to the house. Lorna took a liking to this older man of twenty-four. Lorna was a wild child; she and her sister Ruth had an exuberant "Roaring Twenties", lifestyle of parties, frequently being picked up by young men and driven in their motor cars to village hops. Ernest didn't stand much of a chance, I thought as I pictured the scene as Lorna plotted his seduction.

Summer 1925, Herefordshire

It was the summer of 1925. Lorna Garman was fourteen and as wild as the flowers growing all around the remote Herefordshire farm that she shared with her mother and sister.

They had moved there not long after her father died. On hearing the news of his death she had jumped for joy, literally, over the tennis court net. She was free at last from the one restraint that could have curbed the latent restless energy that drove her.

She was a beautiful creature, thought Ernest, as he lay against her in the field at the edge of the forest. He was still more comfortable in the ivy-clad Oxford quad than in the wilds of the Herefordshire countryside to where he had been lured by the dazzling blue-eyed temptress beside him, but he seemed powerless to resist. Four years at Oxford and still an innocent in so many ways.

He was a deep thinker and increasingly interested in the news of the new creed of communism spreading west from Russia: this, despite the family fortune that in due course he would inherit.

Lorna enjoyed the freedom of the Welsh borderlands but had already inhaled the intoxicating air of London society and craved for more.

All around the field were bundles of sheaved and stooked wheat. They would soon be taken in and flailed. The goodness kept and the chaff disposed of.

Lorna's fingers played with a long single golden stalk and her mind played with that of Ernest's.

Ernest was aware of her impulsive and unpredictable bent, so different from his calm and stoic persona, but not blind to the cool, calculating strain that ran through her. He understood that she knew that money was the root of all evil and... pleasure.

Lorna chewed on the stalk, softening it up, plaited it between her fingers, twisting it languidly to and fro and, taking Earnest's wrist, wrapped the stalk cord around it.

She pulled him to his feet and tugged him towards the forest.

September 2012

Daniella is coming to the end of her performance. She pauses after a song, fiddles with a guitar string, and announces that she is going to perform a new song tonight, one she wrote for her father who is on a journey and needs a keepsake. It is called, she says, "A Stone-Shaped Locket", and it goes like this:

127

I left, too many seas, too many seas, too many seas,
I had, too many dreams, to many dreams, too many
I swept, across the floor, to be with me, to be with me,
My help, was not with me, too many shores, too many shores

I found you in my pocket
I prayed to my Stone-Shaped Locket
I gave up all my pastures
I took all the gold from my masters

I left, too many shores, too many shores, as before,
I gave, up all my dreams, and took them back, to get some
   more,
I kept, you with me, along with me, we sailed the seas,
A cat, in a tin boat, it could not float, without me

I found you in my pocket
I prayed to my Stone-Shaped Locket
I gave up all my pastures
I took all the gold from my masters

Dream, I still can dream,
can still let my eyes light up, can still feel the glory,
is part of me, is part of me, is part of me,
is part of me, me, me, me, me

I found you in my pocket
I prayed to my Stone-Shaped Locket
I gave you to me
I swayed into the sea.

At the end, she seeks me out and hands me a locket and a beautifully hand-written set of lyrics, gives me a kiss and disappears off with her friends. She doesn't ask me why I have come back, or where I am going next. I understand. For many years she has been teaching me about the wisdom of listening, stifling that urge to act, solve, plan... Just listen, she would say, listen...

I look at the lyrics and see all the hope, loss and guilt that had gone into the song, we all take the gold from our masters and some of us never give any of it back...

I go down to the lake and look into the water. Are there relics of the past hidden down there, in the mud? I take the scallop shell out of my pocket and for a second I am tempted to hurl it out into the lake. In the end I keep it and it nestles down alongside my stone-shaped locket with my daughter inside.

August 2012, Dorchester-On-Thames

The apples are falling, green Granny Smiths and red Worcesters. I spend an afternoon raking them up and taking them away. It is a favour for my mother's neighbour who has an apple orchard of a garden but is now too elderly to retrieve the fallen fruit herself. Connie is her name and she has lived in the village most of her life, she is in her eighties now. Over a coffee and homemade cake, my reward, I tell her of my journey through Spain and my quest for Lee. She seems to understand, she had been talking before of the village's links with famous writers. It turns out that Iris Murdoch had lived just up the path in a small thatched cottage, John Masefield down on the Abingdon Road, Agatha Christie born in Wallingford a few miles away in Wallingford and George Orwell, buried under his original name of Eric Blair, in Sutton Courtney towards Oxford.

She takes a sip of her coffee and then says, "Of course there was also Rosamond Lehmann down at Little Wittenham Manor, she moved there in 1946, stayed for years. I bought her fridge when she left."

I pick up at this. Rosamond Lehmann was a good friend of Lee's and he would stay with her when he was in trouble.

I walk back home, and go straight to my library of Lee books and papers. It does not take long to find out that Lee had indeed been a visitor to Little Wittenham Manor in 1946. I know the property; I have walked past it every time I ascend up to the top of The Clumps, and I had gazed down upon it from the top when deciding whether to set off for Spain earlier that year. Not only had Nash painted The Clumps, it now seemed more than likely that Lee had walked them while thinking of Lorna and Yasmin and Spain.

My mother, in the end, had asked few questions on my return, just looked at me with a quizzical eye and offered tea.

Since I came back from Spain, I have felt even more rootless. I have travelled back in time to my childhood in Ireland, folded back the pages of time, finding traces of Lee in the creases, in the British Library, lost myself but found Lee again in the Celtic mists and slipped back into the groove of his footprints, with my ear to the ground picking out once again his songline on the gentle hills of Oxfordshire.

I walk down to the old watermill on the Hurst meadow and sit on an old wooden bench, the sun is going down, a chill in the autumnal air. The sluice gates are still churning the water out and sending it off into the distance, a maelstrom of emotions gradually settling down into a smooth motion of travel.

It is a week later now and I am on board a ferry taking me from Plymouth to Santander in the north of Spain. I am on my way back to the real heart of Spain to Andalusia and like Lee, I "already I saw myself there, brown as an apostle, walking the white dust roads through the orange groves".

Córdoba

Breathing In and Breathing Out
and In Between the Making

September 2012

I am back on the road again, walking south on the road to Andalusia, where Lee always felt most at ease in his adopted country. It is a region on the edge, a place where European straight lines taper away into the swirls of African calligraphy, the cradle of the Spanish essence, the *duende*, its soul. The light is sharp and the heat of the day dry and unsparing. It is like I have just woken up from a long sleep: a deep English summer snooze that has refreshed both myself and my purpose.

Following in Lee's footsteps once again, I am looking eagerly, as I descend into the foothills of the Sierra Morena, for signs of one of Spain's great rivers, the Guadalquivir, that passes through Córdoba, Seville and spills into the Atlantic. I hope to find more than Lee found. He wrote of his first sighting, "Rinsed sweat from the bare Sierras, courses a curled furrow in the dust, a sun-dazed wanderer staggering to the sea."

I walk on down to the white village clinging to the side of a hill. From afar the dry landscape of olive trees dotted amongst the brown and red earth vegetable allotments produce a picture not unlike the early cave drawings found deep underground in this ancient land, coloured pigments of mottled shapes dulled by centuries of darkness and now revealed again to modern man.

My first sight of the great river is impressive as it bisects the city of Cordoba. Night falls suddenly at this time of year in the immense Spanish plains, like a black cloak smothering the fading light in one throw. A harvest moon lights the way in a sky not yet done for the day, its paler tones contrasting the 5 o'clock shadow cloud formation that lies like charcoal pen shading on a broad canvas, smudges of smaller grey cloud applied elsewhere, single pinpricks of light from stars thousands of miles apart set the scene.

I am staying with Pilar and Antonio, friends of a good friend of mine with whom I had studied Spanish. Pilar has recently retired from teaching English and Antonio is a 6th form teacher of philosophy. They take me under their wing for a few days and introduce me into their lives in Córdoba.

Lee passed through Córdoba but did not write much about it. He revisited whilst wintering in Almuñecar in the spring of 1936 and wrote a poem, "Music in a Spanish Town" which he subsequently included in the volume dedicated to Lorna:

In the streets I take my stand
With my fiddle like a gun against my shoulder
And the hot strings under my trigger hand
Shooting an old dance at the evening wall.

Lee was beginning to hear more rumours of a civil war in the offing.

Pilar and Antonio know little of Lee but are in the midst of celebrations for another poet, Luis de Góngora, a contemporary of Cervantes and Shakespeare and a son of Córdoba. It is the 450th anniversary of his birth this year. Antonio has co-authored a book, *A la luz de Góngora*, a tribute to the poet. He takes me to an exhibition about the poet and I learn of a revival of interest in him almost a century ago led by the Generation of 27, the literary set of which Lorca was a key part. I wonder if Lee, such an admirer of Lorca, had heard of Góngora.

I am struck by a poster of a classic film by Jean Cocteau, *La belle et la bête, Beauty and the Beast,* and discover that Góngora was fascinated by the Greek legend myth of the monster Polyphemus falling in love with the beautiful Galatea, the one-eyed cyclopic monster caught up in a love triangle.

Antonio and a group of dedicated followers and I follow a Góngora trail around the city, pausing every now and then to quote from his poems. The weather is unseasonal, cold and very wet, the rain lashing down. I notice a mosaic featuring Polyphemus and Galatea in the Plaza de La Corredera. I can't help asking myself which of us presents the stranger sight: this group quoting 16th century baroque poetry in a 21st century rainstorm, or a middle-aged Englishman following in the footsteps of a poet who walked the length of a country soon to be at war with itself eighty years ago.

I quite like the image forming in my mind of a Nostradamus-like Góngora anticipating a 20th century one-eyed monster laying siege to a fair, beautiful country and ruling it for over forty years.

We retire to a bar and I listen to tales of the middle class in a modern Spanish city of the south. Francisco talks of his three daughters, all grown up now in their twenties, all graduates, all with Masters degrees and all unemployed. He is considering moving the family to Germany to seek work, and says he has many friends in the same position.

Meanwhile, we eat and drink and laugh. There is plenty on offer, including *boquerones,* fried anchovies dusted in flour, that are sweet as a nut washed down with glasses of cold sherry. I am politely admonished for not grasping the glass by its elegant stem, any higher and the drink is warmed by the touch. I also enjoy *berenjenas a la miel*, aubergines dipped in honey cooked tempura-style, which are delicious and something I have never eaten before. I am told they are only to be found in bars. When I ask why, the reply is simple: "*Es la ley*", literally, that's the law.

Góngora was at the height of his powers, Antonio tells me, at the beginning of the 17th century, a time in Spain of great economic crisis, a succession of wars and endless pandemics. Not even the gold and silver from the South American colonization from the century before could staunch the bleeding economy. Not much has changed, I think, as I look around a country once again on its knees.

Lee, later in his career, wrote a highly regarded radio play *The Voyage of Magellan,* about the navigator who first circumnavigated the world in 1519.

Lee, I think, was fascinated by explorers, by the new world, by the instinct to seek out new horizons and beyond. He visited many places and wrote beautifully of them in his underrated book, *I Can't Stay Long*, including Warsaw, Ireland, Trinidad and Tobago, Mexico and Tuscany. He wrote movingly of visiting Aberfan, a Welsh valley village hit by a man-made disaster in 1966 when a slag heap built over a natural spring collapsed and demolished a primary school, wiping out a generation of children. I remember that day as an eleven-year-old boy.

Lee came from an English generation of wanderers, of lost souls, he was perhaps at the Romantic end of the spectrum seeing walking as a voyage of discovery, but others, stretching back to the era of the guild culture were accustomed to job commissions that were reached by walking to them. The breakdown of this system and the end of the Great War saw a whole generation of men walking the roads of England out of habit and more likely desperation. For generations in England, whole populations had remained static, dug in and grown roots now they were on the move, stepping out. Dwelling was out and displacement was in. The country was on the move.

Much as I loved the writings and poetry of the open road and sense of places, I had become fascinated also by the artists of place and time. Paul Nash drew my spiritual home in Oxfordshire throughout his life and it was one of his pupils, Eric Ravilious, whose drawings of the South Downs chalk landscapes in the 1930s caught, for me, a visual essence of Lee's writing about place. It was in the Downs that Lee would roam with Lorna while the war raged over their heads. Ravilious's pictures seem to shimmer in a summer haze, on the edge of another world, images that frame a truth but at a detached and distracted slant. Ravilious was wary of relationships and personal intimacy. I could see a similar pattern in Lee's life, a reluctance to give too much of himself to others. Certainly this was there after Lorna, but perhaps it was always there, a legacy of the desertion of his father, something that all the love of a mother and doting sisters could never quite erase. I know that feeling too. Some philosophers think that there is only really one form of unhappiness, the grief of bereavement, of being abandoned. The cycle starts at birth and is a part of growing up.

Antonio invites me to attend one of his 6th form classes to see Spanish education at close hand. I agree and as he sets up for the class, I am the subject of great interest from the assembled class of young adults. They are quiet and well behaved which surprises me as, beforehand in the corridor, it was noisy and chaotic. Antonio later explains that in Spain, students are encouraged to let off steam outside the class, but in lessons silence and decorum is expected and received – the inference being that this is where the British have gone wrong. Perhaps he is right. Antonio introduces me as a guest, speaks briefly about my journey and then, much to my surprise, invites me to take the class and discuss my view of Spain observed through my journey. I get up and start speaking off the cuff in my best Spanish. In truth I love it; I had once been an English teacher in Spain over thirty years ago and I am enjoying the chance to repeat the experience. I had forgotten what a delight it is to teach young Spanish people in a typical state school. They are polite and listen as I explain my journey and put forward some of my views as to the current state of Spanish society. I am slightly cautious, as I know Antonio is a man of conservative views and I do not want to upset him or abuse my status as a guest in his house and his classroom.

However, the students start to probe some of Antonio's views as to the reasons behind the current Spanish crisis. Antonio has been quite clear on the subject of future employment for his students: they need to be prepared to travel and perhaps leave their families and country behind in search of employment. With Antonio everything is black and white, it is "*sí o no*", while the youngsters want a bit more colour. I have no doubt that Antonio's advice is sincere and probably accurate but the class want to know why the economic crash has hit Spain so much harder than other EU countries, who is to blame and why should they just accept the need to emigrate and become exiles? Antonio is reluctant to go there and the students, emboldened by my presence, look at me and want my view. I feel the need to respond. My frustration at seeing a country that I love fall apart before my eyes overcomes my sense of responsibility as an invited guest. I speak of how I still see a country with huge divisions between the affluent and the poor, a country that has not dared to confront its past, a transition to democracy that was flawed and introduced with the old guard looking on and still firmly in place, the weakness of the monarchy, the strength of the EU. How much has really changed in the last forty years in terms of democracy and justice and how robust is the new world in Spain?

I hesitate to go further, sensing a certain discomfort on Antonio's part as the lesson draws to a close. The students all thank me individually and shake my hand. Antonio is fine. I haven't stepped too far across the line. I feel pleased afterwards and hope that the students have found it a positive experience to ask questions and not just receive a black or white answer. One young pretty girl, no more than sixteen, passes me a note surreptitiously. She whispers to me that it is the name of a TV journalist who speaks frankly on austerity and has not signed up to any "*pacto de olvido*". Antonio asks me about it afterwards and I show him the note. "OK," he says, "but you have to watch that one – she is the daughter of a socialist councillor and wise beyond her years in all sorts of areas." Another member of the class comes up and says she has enjoyed the class and the broader than usual discussion. She lowers her voice and I think, *oh no not again*. She says, "*Nuestro professor puede ser un poco cabezón, ya sabes.*" (Our teacher can be a bit pig-headed at times). It is said with humour and a smile and I feel the respect that exists between pupil and teacher. Antonio shrugs his shoulders when I tell him this. "You have to be firm with them," he says.

As a teacher with only two hours' experience in the last thirty years I am happy to bow to his wisdom.

In Córdoba I find that traditional values of Spain and Andalusia still live on. I see evidence that the art of *La Corrida*, or bullfighting as the English inaccurately insist on calling it, and the passion for flamenco and *Cante Jondo* still thrive well away from the tourists who relentlessly seek out the make-believe Spanish fairy tale world that is sold to them at lower and lower rates as the real Spain crumbles all around them.

Lee got closer than most English observers to understanding the role of Spanish totems in their complex society, the dichotomy of religious fervour and pagan traditions, the life and death ritual of the bullfight, the paroxysms and contortions of the flamenco dance or the deep song recital. In "Song in August", Lee wrote of love in a pastoral setting flourishing while war raged all around him:

> Wheat bleeds upon a wind of steel and ivy splits the poisoned sky... Your lips are turreted with guns and bullets crack across your kiss, and death slides down upon a string to rape the heart of our horizon.

Almost certainly it was about Lorna and Kent but it could just as easily have been death sliding down a Spanish Lorca-esque string in the darkness and heat of a Spanish summer.

*   *   *

Antonio takes me deep into the heart of the old city to Santa Marina. He points out the intersection of two narrow streets and tells me that Spain's finest bullfighters were bred here, including the best of them all, Manolete.

We go into a small bar full of bullfighting posters and photographs of Spain's finest. We have a drink of coarse local red wine and he tells me of the reality of the bullfighters' lot. The power, the glory and the limelight goes to the matador, he tells me, but the reality of their lives is somewhat different. They rely much more than the public realise on a back-up team that stays in the shadows. Every successful fighter has a right hand man who researches the bulls, devises tactics and strategy and stands in the wings at the fight, dispassionately analysing the progress of the contest. Occasionally a bullfighter would freeze in the unremitting and murderous heat and light of the afternoon and the bull would sense an opportunity. This is the moment for the man in the corner to act, as a shout or a gesture at the critical moment could turn the contest around and often did. These men shun the spotlight, perhaps lacking the nerve to enter the ring themselves, or perhaps they are just men who prefer to live rather than die a glorious death. I ponder the thought that throughout life there are observers and there are activists, I have always been an onlooker on the sidelines.

It is the breeder of bulls that really makes the money, Antonio tells me, and yet it is a fraught business to identify the right breeding programme that will produce a prize bull. Identifying a sire is the easy bit; it is selecting the mother that is more difficult. She has to show high levels of aggressiveness herself to produce a fighting bull with the right balance of aggression, cunning and patience to outwit the most skilled of human adversaries.

*   *   *

Antonio secures me entry into a large room above the bar in the Taberna de Beatillas in the *barrio* San Agustín, a faded newspaper cutting tells of a visit to the bar in 1935 by Federico García Lorca on Good Friday. I would love to discover that Lorca had met Lee but I am certain it never happened. Back in Stroud in England, when Lee was in his late teens, he had had come across a group of anarchists, the Whiteway Colony, just two miles from Slad. The colony's founders had been inspired by Leo Tolstoy. Lee went there to recitals; he met the mysterious Cleo there who he would follow to London in due course. During the Spanish Civil War the colony took in a small number of Republican refugees. There had always been rumours that Lorca had visited the colony in the 1920s, but I have never been able to substantiate that.

The long room is a Spanish version of an English middle class club-room. It is filled mainly with men but with a smattering of women. The walls are covered in photos of male and female singers and dancers. One proud man stands out on the wall, *Fosforito*, emblazoned along the bottom of the photo. It is Antonio Fernández Díaz known as *Fosforito*, born in 1932 in Córdoba. He was a singer and winner of the fifth Golden Key for flamenco singing. Only five of these have been awarded since the award's inception in 1862. Other winners included Camarón de la Isla (posthumous) who died young and tragically just a few years ago. *Fosforito* translates literally as "little matchstick" – his nickname referring to his tallness and thinness. He would take advantage of his height and light his cigarettes from the gas lamps above the stages in the 1950s.

On the stage are two men, a younger man with a guitar and a middle-aged man, seated on a simple chair on the bare stage. Silence falls as the guitarist begins to strum the opening chords. The singer, dressed in black trousers, a creased white shirt hanging over a paunch, begins to sing, his hands resting on his knees. He sings of the allure of the south, of love and pain and death. His voice scratches the air and tears the sounds out of a rasping throat. The guitarist leans over his instrument and caresses the strings. The singer, eyes closed, ringed fingers stretched out taut, reaches a crescendo and begins to clap in a mesmeric rhythm until there is just silence. He takes a bow as the room erupts. Only the fan, the hat, and the black shawl decorated with red and white flowers and frills hanging down almost to the floor, all secured to the wall behind the stage, stay still. The singer mops his brow with a handkerchief passed on by the guitarist. *Fosforito*, looking on from the wall, smiles approvingly. I have seen flamenco in Valladolid that was intense in its charged atmosphere and sensuality, this is more measured and cerebral but no less raw.

Lee visited Córdoba in the 1950s with his new bride Kathy. She had spent part of her childhood in Provence where she had watched

Spanish dancers and gypsies. She would endear the young English couple to their new Spanish friends by dancing *Sevillanas* and *Malagueñas* while Laurie strummed the guitar.

Pilar, by chance, that summer had reread Lee's account of his walk through Spain and had been surprised at the unsparing view of her country it painted. For her the Spain it conjured up seemed a brutal place and was and not somewhere she wished to revisit. She could not see the wonder evoked by the book in an outsider, she was too close to her own country or that is what I told myself. She loves the plays of Lorca, and suggested I read *Rosita, la Soltera*, the only one of his plays I have not read. It is the tale of Rosita, a woman left on the shelf. Pilar tells me that in the 1960s, when she was young, she used to visit two aunts who lived together. Both claimed to be widows but Pilar knew one of the aunts had been jilted by her *novio*, (fiancé). It was a public disgrace, a humiliation for the family and never spoken of in public.

In discussion with Antonio and Pilar's erudite set of friends, mostly teachers and academics, we touch on the city and how it has featured in the arts, over and above Góngora. I mention Lee's poem, Falla's tribute is put forward and Lorca and the Generation of 27 are cited. Jesús intrigues the group by stating that perhaps one of the most iconic war action works of art was made in a village just outside the city. Antonio and the others look quizzical. Jesús refuses to say more but promises to take me there the next day.

True to his word, he arrives the following morning and takes me to Espejo, a village near the city. On the way he tells me a true story. A young Jewish/Hungarian photographer, Endre Friedmann, fled from Berlin, via Vienna, to Paris. He was an atheist, an anti-fascist and a Jew and knew there was no future for him in Hitler's new Germany. He carried in his memory the sound of Nazi boots marching on the Berlin streets and in his hand he had the only possession he valued, a basic Leica 1 camera. He struggled to get well-paid work in Paris, pushed out by more popular western European and American photographers who could command premium rates for inferior photographs. To get around this, Endre decided to invent a persona who could be the vehicle for his work. Enter newly-arrived American photographer Robert Capa.

Capa was an instant success and Endre was soon securing him lucrative commissions. Before long, Endre decided to fade away into the background and he became Robert. Capa's career took off and he was sent to Spain to cover the civil war, along with his lover and equally proficient photographer, Gerda Taro.

Jesús brings me to the top of a hill overlooking a valley of olive trees, three whitewashed olive presses dotting the landscape, a Sierra ridge undulating away in the distance. "This is my *pueblo*," he says, his home village. He pretends to take a photograph and then takes out a black and white print of a photograph that I recognise instantly – a Republican soldier, dressed in a white shirt, head jerked backwards, a dark face, so dark it looks like a dark nylon stocking is stretched taut across it and tied up with a neat knot at the top. He is falling backwards and has just been shot in the head. No blood is visible: it is a very clean kill. I never knew the name of the photographer, nor the date, nor the location but the photo, but for me and thousands of others, is the iconic symbol of the civil war. It was taken on 5 September 1936, and made Capa into a superstar.

However, as I discover later, the site that Jesús took me to saw no military action in September 1936 and there is no evidence that Capa had ever been there.

There is nothing about this photo that is clear-cut.

The man in the picture was, for many years, believed to have been Federico Borrell García. However, in 1996, his death was shown to have taken place elsewhere and not in similar circumstances.

I discover that a village called Cerro Muriano, also near Córdoba, had originally been cited as the location of the shot. A battle had taken place there on 5 September 1936 and Capa and Taro had been identified in a photo which showed a stream of refugees heading away from the village while they strode purposefully in the opposite direction, towards the raging battle. There is also controversy about the veracity of the photo itself. Was it staged, simple propaganda, a cheap shot? Taro died in 1937 on the Spanish front at the Battle of Brunete and, as far as I knew Capa had been silent on the subject up to his death in 1954. There was no negative of the print ever discovered, not even in a famous cache of Capa photographs discovered in 2007, known intriguingly as "The Mexican Suitcase Lot".

And there no doubt the mystery would have remained, had I not confronted Jesús after that day nor mentioned it to Antonio. Jesús would not admit he was wrong; Spanish men rarely do. Antonio had his doubts though. Afterwards when I investigated these discrepancies I was to come across an interesting recording. Capa had been born on 22 October 1913. A hundred years later, as part of the celebrations in the USA surrounding his centenary, The International Centre of Photography (ICP) released a recently discovered recording of Capa talking on a 1947 NBC prime time radio show *Hi, Jinx*. He was promoting his new book *Slightly Out of Focus*, and was interviewed by the husband and wife talk show pioneers, Jinx Falkenburg and Tex McCrary.

The radio programme recording is crackly but clear. Bob Capa is introduced before Jinx cuts away to an emerging news story about the delights of saffron coffee, which I realise it is an advert. Bob is talking about a recent trip to Russia with John Steinbeck to photograph places like Stalingrad. There is much banter about the Russian censors and the Iron Curtain. It is an interesting insight into American Cold War thinking, in perhaps more innocent times, before the McCarthy-led witch hunts of the 1950s when photographers, writers, journalists, actors who had a hint of pro-Russian feelings were hounded out of public life in the democratic, free and open West.

Capa's book had been panned by Time Magazine, "Terrific pictures but frivolous writing", while others described him as a "miniature Goya".

Capa tells the tale of another war photo that took on an iconic status. In Leipzig, on the last day of the Second World War, Capa takes a portrait picture, on an open overlooked balcony, of a "clean cut earnest" young American soldier. As he clicks the shutter, a shot rings out and the boy falls dead. The photo becomes famous as the last American soldier to die in the war. Is the story true? Capa seems to have a charmed life and a charming tongue. Don't I know someone else like that?

Finally Capa is asked about the famous Spanish Civil War photo. He has never before (and would not be heard again for another 65 years) spoken on tape about the picture. He sketches a scene of himself in the trenches with twenty Spanish Republican militia. Their position is overlooked by a nationalist machine gun position dug in to their right. Periodically small groups of the men slip over the top with cries of "*Vámonos*" (Let's go) and are mown down by the lethal fire. The men continue to be sent over and Capa risks standing up and fires off the camera, held high above his head and then sits down again. He never develops the film and sends it off back through the lines to his editor. The frame of the dying soldier, caught in free-fall, was published and went, as we would say now, viral. Capa pauses and says, "My most famous photo and I never saw it in the frame."

The tape finishes and I sit back at my desk.

I never had been sure of Jesús's story and now having heard the great man speak himself I am even more unconvinced. I think back to that day in Espejo and remember thinking how hard it was to really find the truth in a story.

Here I am, following in the footsteps of a man I had once so admired, and still do. Doubts are still harboured in my mind though about whether the tracks in the dirt are really his, whether his traces have been kicked over and away or whether they were ever there in the first place. The camera does sometimes lie, history gets airbrushed and writers tell fibs.

Lee was a secretive man, like all of us he accumulated and hoarded setbacks, short fallings, guilt, shame and bitterness. Abandoned by his father, he would flee from a civil war, he would be rejected by a lover, he would fail, twice over, as a father, once due to neglect and once due to a smothering tendency. Suffering already from epilepsy and recurring fevers, he would become a depressive and an alcoholic, he would be allocated a reserve occupation over fighting in World War II, hide the stain of an illegitimate child, not quite make it as a poet. He would choose a safe marriage. His writing would soar to heights but gradually disintegrate; he would choose one last hurrah and meet his nemesis.

That exposed nerve, hidden deep inside him, would twitch and throb, kept quiet by pills and spirits. Insecurity never lies dormant for long. Lee could take an ordinary truth and infuse it with wonder, brush the dried up dirt off an everyday object and flood it with new life, breathe in the rarefied oxygen-starved colourless air of a desolate spot in nowhere and exhale rich ozone-layered violet-hue prose passages of transformation.

He could do all of this but he could not correct the congenital fault, the curvature of his emotional spine. There would come a time

142

when the words would not form, the sentences would not fuse, the poetry would not mask the one essential truth that he was *not* all that he claimed to be. He would be found out, the narrow stretch of brick road on which he was carefully picking his way would open up and start to crumble, chasms appearing on both sides as he stares ahead. His storyline now disassembling, individual black letters, some bold, some italicized, some underlined but all now falling and clattering onto stony ground.

Back on that day as I looked at the scene of either an extraordinary moment of war action or the studio set of a master photographer or illusionist, I wondered not for the first time what sort of man I was chasing after.

I cannot leave Córdoba without visiting the Mezquita, built originally by the Moorish occupiers of Al-Andalus, as the lands of Iberian Spain conquered by the Moors were known. The Mosque is an Arabic masterpiece with a Catholic cathedral inserted and secreted within its heart. I weave in and out the brick-red and white striped arches, a sort of Dalí surreal painting of striped English barber poles, a May Day fair with maypoles, high church organ music filling the air already sweetened by incense. A lonely Christ on the crucifix hangs below a Moorish arch. The Latin inscription INRI, standing for *Iesus Nazarenus, Rex Iudaeorumis, Jesus the Nazarene, King of the Jews*, is etched into the wood. At the time of the crucifixion it would also have been translated into Hebrew and Greek.

Elsewhere Arabic calligraphy is overlaid into the ornate stonework. There is an interpretation panel on the wall, a guide to the individual stonemasons' signatures, both Muslim and Catholic that have been carved into the stone. Each signature has a plaque, a simple white stone square with an array of lines, loops and circles. These master craftsmen worked under the rule of Al-Hakim 11, the Caliph of Cordoba in the 10th century, who oversaw the extension of the Mezquita. The lines etched into the white stone resemble spermatozoon, solidified and preserved in time as if coated by a wash of Pompeian lava, flattened egg-shaped heads, elongated necks and thrashing tails all striving to achieve mortality by impregnating the ovum. They had done more, like the words of poets; they had found immortality in this ancient space. I have a picture in my head of Thomas Hardy's tragic hero *Jude the Obscure* carving his stonework in Christminster. Did he leave his mark too?

I had once attended a talk by Edmund de Waal, an English ceramist who had trained with Japanese master potters in Tokyo. He spoke of the work of potters "breathing in and breathing out and in between the making" and showed me a plain white shard. It was a piece of Tang Dynasty porcelain, a reject, discarded by its makers one hot humid afternoon long ago in China. He said, "You cannot recall what you make, me keeping this is a synapse, from me to them, passed across a thousand years." I thought of these words as I looked at these signatures frozen in time.

Lee must have come here to this meeting place of two great civilizations, of east and west, a living cradle of *duende*.

A war memorial with the names of forty-four priests of the diocese stands within the cathedral. "They gave their lives", the inscription reads, "during the period of religious persecution between 1936 and 1939." It is an interesting description of the Spanish Civil War that saw the Catholic Church siding with the ruthless dictator Franco in its successful attempt to overthrow a democratically elected government: another reminder to me of Franco's narrative living on in this great monument. Franco may have gone but the Church has still its grip on Spanish society, its lands, its gold, its power.

King Juan Carlos proclaims from another plaque, "the light from the cathedral shines brightly for us, it fades not nor flickers, it lights up our path." The path to where and from where, I wonder, as I leave the hallowed ground?

Outside, I meet another congregation gathered in the street, partaking not of the blood of Christ but glasses of *vino tinto*. I look around for the bar and see a sign *Bar Correo*, Post Office bar. It is at best a small district sub-post office with a single bar counter the size of a postage stamp or small chapel altar, dispensing communion of spirits and delicious tapas of honey-smothered aubergine tempura fritter parcels and a more secular example of the fusion of great civilizations, one perhaps more to mine and Lee's taste.

I am serenaded by an immaculately dressed elderly gentleman, sporting a dark blue suit, white pressed shirt, red and yellow knotted tie and a black Cordoban hat worn at a rakish angle. The ensemble is set off by a swirling black cloak, with a red and yellow silk lining. He raises his long stemmed slim glass of *vino fino* and toasts the stranger, the guest in his land.

It is time to leave and follow the wide Guadalquivir down to Seville.

Seville

Orange Groves Lining White Dusty Roads

15 September 2012, Palma del Rio

I have tracked the river out of Córdoba down to Palma del Rio, passing orange groves containing trees over 200 years old.

Small villages alongside the river cling onto vertical hilltops as I walk directly into a setting sun, seeking shelter for the night.

I lie on a bed in the early hours in a monastery cell, the early morning sun is streaming in through the window, the oak shutters are flung open and the spreading pattern of light filters through a low black latticed shade positioned in front of the floor-to-ceiling window. A small naked fairy is swinging from a fern as part of a ceiling fresco. If I were to open the window, I would be able to reach out and pick an orange. The monks here were famed for their orange cultivation right up until the end of the 19th century when the monastery passed into private ownership.

The smell of the herb garden in the courtyard drifts up into the bedroom, past the inner cochineal-crimson coloured arches. The crimson dye originated in South America, was extracted from small insects that lived on the cacti and was exported to Europe in colonial times.

The exotic feel continues with the bright yellow exterior walls. The pigment used for the vibrant colour was prized in the 16th century. It was achieved by feeding cows in Bengal an exclusive diet of mango leaves and then collecting up the urine-sodden sand for processing. It was popularised in Europe by the Dutch traders of the time.

It is Sunday morning and the bells are summoning the faithful and not so faithful to early Mass. For a moment the ringing reminds me of Góngora and his beauty and the beast and Notre Dame and hunchbacks. The drumming sound of leather shoes on the stone flagged cloister corridors intrude into my 16th century musings, the early morning serenity of soft shoe shuffling of the padded feet of brown-robed monks fractured for ever long ago.

In the evening I dine alone in the splendid restaurant attended by a retinue of elaborately dressed staff.

The following day I ramble around the outskirts of the town. I find, by the railway line, a huge shell of a deserted building. It recalls the misty cliff top church ruins in Whitby, the setting for Bram Stoker's Dracula and for a moment I am expecting a big black dog to leap out from the shadows and take me by the throat.

The sign above the building declares that it is a flour mill and jute factory. Jute is more commonly grown in India in the Ganges delta and its presence here is another reminder of the immensity and fertility of the Guadalquivir basin as it launches the great river on its downward sweep to the Golden Tower of Seville, the Atlantic Ocean and the treasures of the New World beyond. Like Spain itself, the factory is broken and defeated, left behind by the inexorable march of progress and the capitalist system.

I am walking along the Río Bembezar up into the Sierra de Hornachuelos, past oak and cork-shaded meadows. All is quiet. A black eagle leaves his nest built into the overflowing crowns of the treetops and swoops along the valley surveying his domain.

My feet scrunch over cork and acorns, the bees are humming and the honey dripping, free range pigs are snuffling in the meadows. Wild boars roam the pastures and I see a stag flit through the woods.

I am alone in this wilderness, thrown down towards the river and snug-tight in a holloway, when from seemingly nowhere, come snatches of sound, of conversation, stray syllables floating on the breeze. I stop, listening intently, anxious not to succumb to thoughts of voices from the past or even the future, calling me back or urging me forward. I think briefly of desert nomads experiencing a *sarba*, a spiritual revelation. I realise finally it is the gently flowing water that is speaking to me, or rather it is the water that is carrying the faint strains of fellow walkers down to me from behind the hill and around the arc of the river.

I wander through the groves, apparently frost-bitten trees greet

147

me everywhere, the lower trunk, stripped of bark, stands exposed with its pink flesh shivering in the cool breeze. The upper trunk and branches are dressed roughly, limbs covered with mottled and snagged greeny-black stockings, branches encased in long Edwardian gloves drawn tightly up to the elbow, sticky green buds peering out from black mottled mittens. Delicate light green star-shaped clusters of flowers are growing, almost in sympathy, around the tree roots.

Some of these oak trees lining the track are hundreds of years old and have been welcoming home the workers on the outlying farms for centuries as they neared their village.

I look down now upon the river as I have ascended into a hanging wood on the side of the slopes. A pale sun is picking out the riverside trees and bathing them in a luminous yellow glow, interspersed with shards of white brilliance as the rays reflect off a rock. Hardy green and blue bushes cover the stony ground in front of me and fall away down to the riverside. I climb up higher and look back towards Córdoba.

A tall thin gelid spire of rock looks down on me from the heights of the Sierra; it looks cold and menacing up there. I recall that walkers would call such a rock formation a *hoodoo*, and a shiver runs through me. The early heat of the day is coming to the end and a slight chill is in the air. Autumn is coming and I need to get to the sea.

18 September 2013, Ecija

I pause briefly in the small town of Ecija on the banks of the Genil. I approach it in the cool of an early autumn afternoon. In the hot Andalusian summers it is known as *El Sartén*, (The Frying Pan), and renowned as being one of the hottest places in Spain. As I look down on the town in the distance, I recall Laurie Lee's words when he arrived in the town in the winter of 1952 on a return visit to Spain on his honeymoon with his new bride Kathy, "Ecija at noon was a city of black and gold – gold of the roofs and towers in the sun, and black of the shadowed alleys and of the widows passing through them. This was post civil war Spain, a land peopled by widows and ghosts of men and soldiers in starched and pressed tunics, soldiers who didn't fight but ruled with an iron fist and no glove."

It is, as Lee described it, a town of towers and palaces with great oak doors studded with hundreds of black circular nipple-shaped discs and two door knockers in the shape of giant hands caressing what could be a breast each or possibly a brass apple. Large pale frescoes line the elaborate walls of the Peñaflor Palace, an elaborate baroque terracotta red and white tower ascending gracefully beside it.

A large blue and white poster on a church wall announces the forthcoming October pilgrimage to an outlying rural parish church. A plaque featuring two hooded penitents holding a sword and bible stands above the poster.

I pass a foot clinic as I walk towards the edge of town; I decide not to make an appointment. I move on down a street named, not after a Spanish saint or sinner, but after a musician from Liverpool, John Lennon.

I am fairly sure that Lee would not have found a business offering balm for his aching feet other than in a wayside inn with a grandmother offering up a pumice stone, a sprig of heather and a clove of garlic, and I am confident that he could not have envisaged a street would be named after an English pop idol of the future. What I did know for sure was that Lee had visited the bullring that stands in front of me.

It does not look so very different from his description of it at the time, of an old barely used building. At best it is functional, hemmed in as it is by bars, a garage, flats and social housing. It is not a building that is venerated and has pride of place in the town. Its mustard yellow exterior with its corrugated iron gates denies access to its inner arena. Rusty signs continue to announce the class divisions within: the *Sombra* section for the town squire and the well-to-do *Señoras* who needed the shade to protect their complexion; the *Sol* section for everyone else, condemned to swelter in the heat and glare of the sun at its highest. Statues of past bullfighters line the square alongside and a forlorn Toreador School sign suggests hope of a new golden generation. It is an *Escuela Municipal,* a council-owned school. Even bullfighting, it would seem, has now been nationalised.

In the lee of the Plaza de Toros is a house with an open inner courtyard accessing the ring, perhaps the place where the bloodstained carcasses of the bull are left out to hang.

Lee seemed fascinated with the bullfight as a symbol of Spain's spirit, its *duende*. Secretly perhaps he longed to show his valour as a man and lay his life on the line, not for his art, but for his beliefs. If indeed he had such strong convictions about anything that could be called by such a name.

Perhaps Lee was spoiling for a fight. In Seville he would pick up the scent not just of the zest of oranges but of an impending conflagration.

25 September 2013, Seville

I am in a cool shaded room in the Museo de Bellas Artes. I am sitting gazing at a painting of San Bruno by Zurburán. He was a 17th century painter much praised by Lee's Spanish poet mentor, Federico García Lorca, who talked of his *"moon-frozen heads"* as an example of the real *duende* of Spain. I am looking at such a head, at least, I think I am. I am not sure exactly what Lorca meant by the phrase, wonderful as it is. I do not know whether Lee ever sat here looking for Spain's soul. It is clear to me though that this is what Lee was set on, trying to unlock Spain's secrets, for himself and his reader. Probably not as a drifting twenty-year-old but certainly as the poetic writer that he became later in life when he looked back and wrote about the Spain of his youth. Lorca talked often of the holy trinity of muse, angel and *duende*: inspiration, flow and the devil perhaps to the modern reader? Lee did not lack the former: he often found a rich flow of words and always had the shadow of the *duende* hovering over him. He loved the irresistible verve of the Spanish character but he was often drawn to its melancholy streak, the cold damp air of a Granada winter morning visiting the cemetery on the *día de los difuntos* (The Day of the Dead).

I had walked earlier through the museum's green cloister. The flowers were still blooming in the late summer, early autumn warm weather. Brightly coloured murals with climbing vines lined my way. I was observed by what appeared to be a semi-naked bearded middle-aged man, hands clasped together but not praying, a cord tightened around his biceps, his groin covered by a tasselled velvet blue strip of material and a frayed green cloth hanging at his hips. He was positioned at the heart of the mural and I hoped didn't represent a vision of myself in an earlier life.

A solitary ripe green apple sat on the path directly ahead. In the distance a red rose was just flowering, its buds opening up in the sun, giving off a sweet perfume. I looked more closely at the flower, its blood-red petals slowly unfurling. There was a small tear on one of the petals and this imperfection seemed to serve just to make the whole creation more perfect.

I am back upstairs in front of San Bruno's moon-frozen head. He adopts a humble pose with his gaze fixed firmly on the floor in front of him as he sits in a chair in the papal presence. He is a Carthusian monk and has taken a vow of silence and lives frugally and fasts as a rule. His sunken spare figure is enveloped in a white robe and is covered by a black cloak. His shaven head is bathed in a warm golden glow that places his austere figure into sharp relief. The Pope sits alongside him, dressed resplendently and looking confidently at the artist and onlookers down the ages. It is a still life but is it a moon-frozen head?

Lorca was well known for his plays as well as his poetry. In *Bodas de Sangre* he tells a local Granadino folk tale of a gypsy wedding that ends with the groom and the bride's lover dead in a dark forest lit up by a full moon. The moon, in Lorca's surrealist way, appears as a character in the play, symbolic of impending death and a presence full of bitterness at being excluded from the inner lives of the village folk. He sings a lament and promises bloodshed; he is cold and calculating as his voice cuts through the darkness, "Let me enter! I come frozen, over windows, over walls! Open roofs, take me to your breast and let me warm myself! I am cold... I'll have no shadows. And my beams must get in everywhere."

As I look at San Bruno the golden glow cannot hide the dullness in the eyes and the stoop of the shoulders, perhaps the golden glow in which his head is bathed is nothing but the sorrowful pitch contours of the moon's song freezing as they meet the closed mind. Or perhaps the light is of his own making and just noted by Zurburán.

When Lee and Kathy were on their honeymoon in Seville in the early 1950s, they had a song dedicated to them by Spanish friends and it became their party piece. It was called Lorenzo and Catalina and went like this: *"El Sol se llama Lorenzo y la luna, Catalina. Cuando se acuesta Lorenzo. La luna se levanta Catalin."* (The sun is called Lorenzo and the moon, Catalina. When Lorenzo goes to bed the moon Catalina rises.)

I wonder if Lee was aware of Tarot cards. He was born under the sign of Cancer, on the 26 June 1914 (though actually Lee freely admitted that his mother was not absolutely certain of that, only that it was a Thursday as she recalled that it was laundry day). Cancer is symbolised by the crab. Card number eighteen is The Moon. It represents the 18th stage of the hero's rite of passage quest. A crab, symbolic of the primitive unconscious, is immersed in a deep pool and is attempting to extricate itself and crawl onto dry land. In the distance, a wolf and a dog, guides to the land of the dead, guard their position. Behind them are the stone pillars of Hades, gateway to the darkness of the underworld. Overseeing all before her is the Moon, the Queen of the Night. The hero is at the turning point of his journey, if he succumbs to the draw of the moon along with the tides and the fertility cycle, he is lost. If however he keeps to the straight and narrow he will emerge into the dawn of a new day.

Lee's mind was often a place of darkness and torment, cold chills breaking out into sweating fevers, shaking from fits, then still with unconsciousness.

I suspect that Lee fought battles with the Queen of the Night on a daily basis. I feel I have only recently fought a similar battle, one from which I had emerged, scathed but renewed in spirit.

Lee, like Lorca, was fascinated by the moon. Whenever he saw a new moon he would stop in his stride, turn round three times and make a bow.

Late in life, safely ensconced in his Slad cottage, he would slip into the garden and stare up in wonder at the stars and the moon. He once said, as a frail and elderly man, in conversation with a pretty young journalist: "The moon will rise over **there** tonight, behind that tree or hillock, at the appointed time a kind of primeval reverence surrounds the orbit of the moon. Before a full moon rises, there is a quietness in the valley, almost an anticipation."

I walk along the corridors of the museum and find a painting of Triana from 1890 by Emilio Perrier, just 45 years before Lee first came to Seville. Triana is not a person but a place, a place on the wrong side of the river. It's where Lee stayed in 1935 and visited in 1952 with his new bride. The picture has the bridge in the background. Lee had stood on this bridge with his wife Kathy "in the midst of the muddy river, the sun burnt down slow into the rigging of orange ships, waiting the winter harvest." Paintings, like photographs, suspend time and give you the illusion of a timeless world, in the same way the imprint of a footprint can remain long after the walker has moved on, so a sheet of contact prints, exposed to light, can reproduce the past long into the future.

It was on that same bridge back in 1935 when Lee first got wind of an impending war. Lee was leaning over the rails looking at the dark river waters at midnight. A young sailor approached him asking for a cigarette. As Lee struck a match for him, his face loomed into view from the dark. He was young like Lee but had seen much more of life. In broken English, learnt on the coal quays of Cardiff Docks, the rating spat out, "I don't know who you are, but if you want to see blood stick around – you're going to see plenty."

Lee had written of Seville, "The slow time dripped musically from fountains, wine-barrels and the guitarist's fingers." The pace of his journey had just quickened and the stakes had been raised.

In the foreground of the painting, Dickensian slums stand along the north bank of the river. Rotting stakes are just visible above the waterline. Trees with bare branches wilt in the thin soil of the bank. Lee talked of lunchtimes spent drinking cheap wine with a companion called Queipo and then sleeping off the afternoon in semi-sunken boats just like the ones painted by Perrier. Queipo was a one-handed gypsy beggar who lived in a cave with his wife and fourteen children. His left hand had been bitten off by a mad dog in Madrid.

Gypsies are not so common in Triana nowadays. In the 1970s whole gypsy communities were moved away down to the south of the city in a social experiment that smacks now of Francoist ethnic cleansing. Franco tolerated the gypsies to a degree, as he felt that they gave the impression to the outside world of a country steeped in the romance of flamenco, and word has it that he enjoyed private evenings of the dance form himself. Gypsies however, have always been outsiders in Spain and still are. Very rarely these days do you see someone like Queipo. In the 1970s, when I first knew Spain, it was a common sight to see one-armed street vendors or beggars with no legs getting about on wooden trays using their arms to propel themselves along the ground. However, if you venture into some of the no-go areas on the outskirts of the city, home now to gypsies, the homeless and those exiled from mainstream life, you will still find communities ravaged by drugs, drink and disease. Evidence of the narcotics war fought in these parts can be seen daily, with junkies haunting the streets, heads bowed down, looking for the next fix.

Gang warfare is rife in the notorious shanty town accorded the Orwellian name of *Tres Mil Viviendas,* or Three Thousand Households. Here in this lawless suburb of the city, the rival gangs of Los Perla and Los Marianos are fighting a street war for control.

The modern city of Seville seems to be flourishing despite the damning unemployment statistics and regular evictions of families by banks foreclosing on mortgage and rent arrears.

Lee, whose social awareness antennae were beginning to function at this stage in the journey, had noted the stark class divides within Seville.

He wrote, "Seville lived for itself, split into two halves, one riding on the back of the other."

Lee cantered around the city on his honeymoon in the 1950s on a horse-drawn open-air carriage, "Seville of sweet wines and bitter oranges, of dandy horsemen bearing their girls to the parks, of fantastic villas and radiant whores, of finery, filth and interminable fiesta centred around the huge deadweight of the cathedral."

The whores are still there, I note, when dusk falls in the Alameda de Hércules but appear to taking a laid-back approach to their trade, lounging drowsily in the cool of the avenue of trees.

The essence of a place is made up of the people who live there and their stories. I feel I know Seville partly because I have lived here before in a previous life, as a student in the 1970s, and partly because I have experienced the city through stories and music. I love the opera *Carmen*. Opera is not real of course, it is drama, coincidence, farce and tragedy. And yet life is an opera, human drama played out over and over again down through generations. The seasons and annual reference points play their part. Seville is a different place at Christmas or Easter. I can remember the magic of spending Christmas in Seville, attending *Misa de Gallos* (Midnight Mass) in the cathedral. A young man living abroad, in love for the first time – an unrequited love that sharpens the senses. I shared my life and a flat at the time with three girls. All three of them living out dramas that would shape their lives. As usual my role seemed to be that of an observer, a narrator. We lived in a quarter of Seville called *La Macarena*.

Two of the girls were Americans, Caroline and Ann, who were students on a study year like myself. Caroline had left a boyfriend behind in the States and missed him terribly. I would watch sometimes as the two blonde, fair-skinned girls would walk in the street and be harassed by men, well-educated men, family men, at every turn. The Spanish called it *"piropear"*, the art of flirting by making approving comments of a girl's figure. In fact it was more crude than that. The girls learnt to give as good as they got which was not part of the game for the men. They would get in first the moment they smelt a lecherous pheromone in the air and saw a gaze lock on to their erogenous zones. *"¿Quires sacar una foto?"* (Would you like a photo?) or *"que se lo metas en el culo"* (go stick it up your arse), they would say, the use of the familiar form of address almost as shocking as the words themselves.

The third girl was Mariá Carmen Angeles, a local girl, in her late teens. She had been excommunicated by her family, for dating a married, older man. To make it worse he was an anarchist/communist. To be a communist even in 1975 was dangerous in Franco's Spain. Mariá Carmen Angeles was, like many of her time, ignorant of many of the facts of life. She sought help from her more experienced flatmates, excluding myself, on issues such as her monthly periods and needed, gently, to be given some advice on hygiene and cleanliness. She knew nothing of contraception, not that it was available for single Spanish girls, and Carlos, her boyfriend, did not believe in it anyway – it was against both his anarchistic beliefs and his right, as a man, to heightened sexual pleasure. Inevitably, despite the best efforts of her new English friends, she got pregnant and went back to her family to be secreted away until the birth. Carlos was faithful to his sense of responsibility and disappeared, leaving not only a bastard baby in an unforgiving society but his pet dog, Trotsky.

Pedro appeared on the scene, a young handsome bearded student, he had the look of an apostle but not his sense of morality. He had a Spanish *novia*, Teresa, who tolerated, for a while anyway, his nomadic eye for the ladies, especially American ones. I watched as he first snared the young Caroline and then drew Ann into his clutches. Teresa also watched from the shadows. Pedro, however, was himself being played cleverly by Teresa who, just as the two girls were preparing to fight it out for his affections, played her trump card. She announced she was pregnant, a terrible mistake, a failure of approved Catholic methods of control. He had not withdrawn quickly enough then, but he extricated himself rapidly from the ménage-a-trois. Hats were bought by mothers-in-law, sacraments pronounced and all was well. And life in the flat went back to a state of normality.

Now as I walk the streets of old Seville, I pass by the gates of Seville University, the Faculty of Arts, housed in the old tobacco factory. When built in the 18th century, the factory was the second largest building in Spain. Philip II's Escorial Palace was the largest. It was build on a site known as *De las Calaveras* (Skull Place), an ancient Roman burial ground.

I wander around the interior courtyard, students coming and going from classes. The factory provided the setting for Bizet's opera *Carmen* that opened in Paris in 1875, a hundred years before the death of Franco. In Bizet's time the factory was more or less run by an all female workforce with more than 6,000 *Cigarreras* (Cigarette girls). Carmen was a *Cigarrera*, a *femme fatale* who seduces a young naïve soldier, Don José, and then deserts him for a more glamorous Toreador, Escamillo. The work climaxes with Escarmillo delivering the *coup de grace*, despatching the bull cleanly and supremely in the bullring while outside at the exact moment of Escamillo's kill, Don José is stabbing Carmen through the heart. He then enters the bullring and confesses all to the adoring masses.

I can hear the opera's final notes playing in my head as I consider whether the fictional fantastic life of Carmen matches up to that of Lee and his two loves of Lorna and Kathy in terms of dramatic tension and soap opera content. I work my way through the life stories of Bizet, Carmen, Lee and the loves and rivalries of his life.

Consider: Bizet, as a young man, fathered a bastard child, as they were called in those times, with his father's housekeeper. He was 24. The child was brought up by the housekeeper with Bizet taking no responsibility for the child, choosing to focus on his flowering career instead. Lee, as a young man, fathered a bastard child, as they were still called in those times. The child was brought up by the mother Lorna and her husband Wish. Lee had little contact with the child, Yasmin, until she was twenty years old.

Lee had walked through Spain on the brink of civil war, been repatriated at the start of the war and met and fell in love with Lorna

Garman on a deserted Cornish cove. Lorna was the sister of Mary, who Lee had met on his walk in Toledo, and with whom he had been entranced, by whilst receiving the hospitality of her husband to whom he looked up to as a father figure. He had defied Lorna and returned to Spain to fight against Franco for the International Brigade, having made an epic climb over the Pyrenees in midwinter. He was invalided out of the war but wrote a classic book extolling his feats on the battlefield. He was accused of plagiarism, just as Bizet had been when the highlight of his career, *Carmen* was premiered. Lee had no strong socialist beliefs unlike the cuckolded Wish, the husband of his lover and the man who raised Yasmin as one of his own. Lorna, possibly the most beautiful and perhaps the most amoral of a long line of ravishing sisters, in time left Lee broken-hearted and took up with a young, almost feral, artist Lucian Freud, the grandson of a world-famous psychoanalyst.

Lee considered first killing Freud and Lorna and then his thoughts turned to suicide. Lucian himself was then rejected for a younger model and threatened to kill Lorna with a gun. Both suitors recovered and some years later each marry one of Lorna's nieces – Kathy for Lee, Kitty for Freud. Not before, by the way, Lee had bedded Kitty and moved on quickly. Yasmin became a talented artist, like her mother and is infused with Lee's creative juices. She did not work professionally, and choose a quiet life. Lee had a second child with Kathy, named Jessy. He did not like to see her growing up and wanted to keep her innocent. He failed, he grew older, succumbed to drink and demons and depression and epilepsy. He died and like Carmen, he became a legend, a myth, whose stories are read over and over again. You couldn't make it up, I concluded. Well, Bizet did, but for the most part Lee didn't.

Oh, all these bastard babies, Mariá Carmen Angeles's, Teresa's (though legitimised just in time by the magic of the church), Bizet's, Yasmin...

Lee wrote a beautiful prose poem in honour of his "Firstborn." The opening lines recall his feelings when the new born child arrived:

She was born in the autumn and was a late fall in my life, and lay, purple and dented like a little bruised plum, as though she'd been lightly trodden in the grass and forgotten.

I loved this piece from the moment I first read it and treasured it, a feeling, an emotion that I felt I would never experience for myself. I had a fear of being a father. There came a time though when I realised that the poem, written for Jessy, should have been entitled "The Secondborn", for the firstborn was Yasmin and she was born in the spring of his life, a windfall, unexpected and inconvenient. If Lee had named his two plums, then Yasmin would have been an Early Prolific perhaps with Jessy being an Old Greengage. I read the closing lines now of Lee's piece and fight off a sense of anger and allow the poignancy to seep out, "Having a child alters the rights of every man, and I don't expect to live as I did without her. I am hers to be with, and hope to be what she needs, and know of no reason why I should ever desert her." It was late 1964 when Lee wrote these words. On the same day as Jessy was born, Esther Wishart, Lee's granddaughter, Yasmin's first child was born. Yasmin was 24, Lee's age when Yasmin was born. Perhaps "The Firstborn" was written not just for Jessy but for Esther and for Yasmin too. I would like to think so.

It is certainly true, I think, that Lee did not wilfully give Yasmin away. She was born out of wedlock to a mother, happily married but needy of affairs and stray poets and artists and a penniless and perhaps, at the time, feckless father, just back from the war. It was for the best perhaps that Yasmin was brought up lovingly by Wish, a steady and reliable father. While Lee succumbed easily to the conventions of a society that disapproved of children being born out of and raised out of wedlock, at the same time, he quite happily flouted other conventions of loyalty and honesty in relationships, earning an honest living, and later on in life, the observance of marriage vows.

Yasmin was unaware of her real father's identity until she was twenty-one and even then she had to work it out for herself. Within a year of reconnecting with her real father, Yasmin did the one thing that fathers dread: she married and committed herself to another man. Julian David, her husband, was a psychologist fascinated by Jung. Yasmin had found a soul mate: they were both concerned with "the long-despised unconscious of Man", the creed of Jung. David explored the means of connecting the conscious to the subconscious using his conscious logic and intellect. Yasmin sought it through her paintings.

Julian and Yasmin had an adventurous life that in some ways seemed to mirror that of Lee's. They went to work in Sicily in the

1960s and found themselves often in conflict with the might of the Church and the Mafia that, yoked together, ruled life on the island in a fascist dictatorship. They went to South Africa in the 1980s to carry on the work of Jungian analysis in a country where Jung himself loved to sit out in the open to watch the dawn break over the African veldt and watch the coming of the light and the world turn to flaming crystal with the only sound being the cry of the bell-bird. In 1989, they witnessed the last gasp of the modern fascist state, apartheid. It was the same year that the Berlin Wall came down. It must have been euphoric for Yasmin and perhaps for her, the completion of her father's and stepfather's struggle against fascism and the control of the state and an opportunity for her to please both.

It would seem that Yasmin lived her life in Lee's shadow. She could love him from a distance and meet with him occasionally. Kathy knew of her. Things got complicated though when Jessy came along. She knew nothing of her sister until she herself was a young woman. Perhaps she was content with that. She was adored by her grandmother Annie, Lee's mother. Annie had lost a four-year-old daughter, Frances, when Lee was two. Lee had described her as slipping away from life, almost unnoticed as Lee himself battled with a life-threatening fever. Yasmin, perhaps, was always Frances in Annie's mind. Annie died in 1950, long before Jessy came along. She was buried in the Slad Church graveyard alongside Frances. Lee, buried there now himself, placed a poem and a photo of Yasmin in her coffin.

To the last, Yasmin understood her place in the Lee family. At her father's funeral she is reported to have slipped into the service quietly, at the back.

Back in Seville, I stand looking up at the statue of Carmen, another mythical figure with supernatural appeal, just by the Plaza de Toros, La Maestranza. She towers above me, her Spanish skirts swirling, her enigmatic gaze going right over my head. It is a statue of freedom we are told.

Carmen died at a tragically young age having defied the conventions of her age. Lee lived to the ripe old age of eighty-three, a great writer, but one whose artistic inspiration was his own young life and his adventures in the heat and passion of Spain. His young first life ended too early, like Carmen's. Lorna lived a long life too, towards the end becoming a converted Christian and burning all her love letters, a mistress to the last. Her tales of passion and revenge snuffed out by a struck match. Perhaps a match used to light a cigarette, perhaps a match made in Spain, perhaps a match made in a tobacco factory in Seville.

Yasmin outlived them both.

Much as I love the Andalusian city jewels, in the heat of the summer they can become suffocating. I need to feel the wind in my face again. It is time to leave the city and head for the hills.

Aracena

Dark Angels Ascending

I sung of Chaos and Eternal Night,
Taught by the heav'nly Muse to venture down
The dark descent, and up to reascend...

– John Milton in Paradise Lost

28 September 2012, Aracena

I am on the final leg of my journey, heading down towards the Atlantic Ocean but first I need to make a slight diversion from Lee's route. Pepe, who I had met in Castile earlier on in my journey, had told me of how his grandfather risked his life in post-war Spain by illegally smuggling food back to Madrid from the south-west of Spain. I want to see where he foraged for food in those desperate years of the 1940s when the defeated of Madrid were being starved into total and utter submission. I am now heading towards this region, the fertile groves of Aracena, west of Seville and high up into the hills.

The cafes are packed in Pajanosas, a small village on the edge of the Sierra Morena. I am steadily climbing. The temperatures are mild as autumn approaches. The food on offer is getting more robust. *Jabalí, Cola de Toro, lagrimitas de pollo,* wild boar, oxtail, and chicken teardrops – a new take on chicken strips. The posters on the wall are not promoting football or bullfighting but the annual *Romería* of years past, the recent past. It is still a major event in the community calendar where the ladies and the men both get dressed up in their finery, put on hats and set off on foot, horseback and horse-drawn cart to the local shrine. There are houses and inns in the village, built in a bygone age when each family kept a working horse stabled in a space underneath the living quarters. The animal's body heat and steam rose up and provided under-floor heating in the cold winters. It is a typical leftover ribbon village, hugging the old roads up into one of the wildest parts of Andalusia. The area is well known throughout Spain for its succulent ham including the famous *Pata Negra marque* (black foot ham).

I opt to lunch on two small oranges and a bread roll for 35 cents from the greengrocer's that frames the entrance to the bar. I wash these down with a bottle of mandarin juice I'd bought from *El Corte Inglés*, the Spanish equivalent to Marks and Spencer's in Seville for five euros. The old and the new in Spain coming together in a simple meal.

Once more I am flirting with the Portuguese border and straying from Lee's probable route. I had been introduced by a friend to an intriguing couple Alfonso and Marie, pig farmers in the Sierra foothills. Alfonso is in his 70s and has led an interesting life including spells in America where he met, or in his words acquired, his American wife. He comes from a family rooted in Andalusia, landowners down through many generations and very well connected to the local establishment. In this area that is code for being fully signed up supporters of the Franco dictatorship and its post transition right-wing cousin. Pig farmers in this part of Spain are a different breed to those, say, in the valleys of Wales. Here, they are aristocracy. Alfonso is too young to have fought in the civil war but his father and several uncles all fought for Franco, except one. He has forthright right-wing views, Marie does not. I am looking forward to the encounter.

As I sit in the shade of a cork tree, I eat my bread and oranges. All around me are free range pigs snuffling their way through their own picnic of acorns. Here, *La Bellota,* the humble acorn is king. Ahead of me the Sierra looms, a browny-green backdrop with occasional splashes of white, like chalk markings. Spirals of smoke rise above the scattered white dwellings. There is no shortage of wood here to burn in the *Dehesas* of Aracena, the acorn-rich golden meadows.

All around me are large private *Fincas,* landed estates, which have been under the same ownership for hundreds of years. The proliferation of the *Latifundios,* the large landowners who employed local peasants in a feudal system that had not changed for centuries, was one of the triggers for the civil war. How much has really changed today? With unemployment in Andalusia running at 30% and 50% of young people with no job and no prospects, it seems surprisingly little.

*   *   *

High up in the Sierra I feel like a US Cavalry officer in the Wild West looking down on an Indian Reservation. A solitary funnel of white smoke curls up into the blue hills perhaps sending out a message to other indigenous tribes. A large boulder juts out from the escarpment and a Spaniard with long straggly greying hair tied back with a braided string of many colours, sits on his haunches and chants. It is a wail, a strident call to the rain gods. It tears into the blue sky and shatters the silence, echoing back from distant rocks. The purity of the sound is akin to the choristers in Gloucester Cathedral that Lee would have listened to many a time. A black eagle circles overhead, unsure as to whether the shrill notes are to be welcomed or feared. Alfonso completes this ritual every morning and evening at sunset and sunrise. It is the sound of a man released from exile, a man with a strong connection to his native land.

Alfonso welcomes me warmly and invites me to sit on the terrace overlooking his land. Marie appears bearing glasses of chilled *fino* wine and some *tapas* of bread and oil and *Pata Negra* ham.

Alfonso asks about my journey and I tell him the background to it. He has not heard of Laurie Lee, although he knows of Gerald Brenan. Everyone has heard of Brenan in Andalusia.

He also asks after John, our mutual acquaintance, and we share thoughts on his latest book, *The Angel of the Stories*. It is set in Aracena and has been well received. I tell Alfonso that I will be seeing John in a few days, at one of his writing retreats across the valley.

Alfonso says, "So you are going to be a writer then?"

I am taken aback. "Why do you say that?"

"You are following in the footsteps of an adventurer, like me, across a nation. This man later writes about his journey and becomes a great writer. You are visiting John who mentors writers. I am not a wise man with great powers, I just observe."

It is true perhaps the ultimate tribute to Lee would be to become a writer myself and commit my story, like his, to print. It is something to think about.

Alfonso goes on to tell me about his life. Born just after the civil war had ended, he was very much a child of the Franco era. His family were on the winning side in the war so his childhood was a comfortable one and life was good. As a young man he had then gone to America to seek his fortune. A trained actor, he lived a picaresque existence, travelling around the continent, odd jobbing here and there. He tells me a story about how he almost got poisoned when he was apple picking in Washington state, and another about getting caught up in smuggling in South America. He met his wife, Marie in the USA, a left-wing firebrand, and brought her back to Spain. He has talked little of his politics but I get a distinct impression of him as a young man rebelling against his conservative upbringing, a young man, who like Lee, had gone on a quest to find himself and become a man. He had met his guru out there, in the deserts of New Mexico, who taught him how to chant and find peace in spirituality. He talks of the freezing cold nights in the Arizona desert, the full moon casting long shadows over the shifting sands and of other warmer nights gazing at the shooting stars.

Marie joins us and we sit and while away the morning. A light breeze wafts down from the mountains bringing with it a hint of eucalyptus. The *cortijo* or estate house stands proud, surrounded by acres of farmland and shady groves where pigs roam freely. Alfonso describes how the farm works. They are not his pigs. They were delivered a few weeks before from neighbouring farms to be fattened up before slaughter. His land has been cultivated over decades to provide ideal grazing for pigs. When the animals are delivered, they are weighed on a large set of scales and the weights independently audited. On departure, weeks later, they are reweighed and Alfonso is paid according to the *Arroba*, the amount of fat put on by the pigs during their stay.

The scene looks idyllic but Alfonso explains that this is deceptive. The land is baked hard during the long hot summers and often in the autumn there are long rainy seasons. The land has a granite surface but underneath there are five natural springs. Every few years or so there comes a reckoning and nature runs wild. He talks of the floods of 2006 when the farm was under water and in great peril, the rushing waters destroying a 2000-year-old bridge in the process. A neighbour was killed trying to rescue the pigs. There was talk of human bones floating in the debris, rumours that an old mass civil war grave had been disturbed.

"Even now," Alfonso continues, "we are suffering an infestation of a parasitic worm that is attacking the oak trees and affecting the supply of acorns, the lifeblood of the farm. It attacks trees close to water, the worm thriving on the humidity."

Alfonso has, in passing, now uttered the forbidden words, civil war. I seize the moment and ask him if he has any memories of the war. Alfonso says nothing. Marie is silent too. Alfonso stares into the distance, then begins to speak.

"I was a young boy, it was late and I was sitting on the stairs inside. My parents were talking to my uncles. It was probably a fiesta night. They were talking quietly but I could hear every word on that still night. They were talking of the war. My family were, are, very conservative and they all fought for Franco against the Reds. All, that is, except for Uncle Rafael. He had got caught up in the hysteria of the Second Republic, the revolution, a new start. He was a friend of Martínez Y Barrio, the President of the Second Republic for a short while. Martínez came from Seville and he was well known to Franco himself. My uncle was in a very dangerous position. I had never before heard my father speak of him. I realised I was listening to a family secret. It was like picking the forbidden fruit from the tree: exhilarating and dangerous at the same time. It was a cold night but the sweat was running down me."

"Was he still alive then, your uncle?"

"I think so, but I never met him. That night my father and my uncles were talking of the day that they took a decision that could have led to their deaths. The civil war had been over for a year or so but recriminations against known Republicans were rife. My family, even though they were all proud nationalists and angry at what they saw as Rafael's treachery, were close. Blood in Spain is very much thicker than water. I realised that my uncle had been hidden away in the *cortijo*, in a secret room, since the end of the war. If he had been found, the entire family would have been in danger. However, Franco then issued a new decree saying that if Republicans gave themselves up they would receive a fair trial. My father was sceptical but saw a possible way out. He decided to attempt to smuggle Rafael into Seville and let him give himself up. He hoped their own good connections with the regime would secure him a good hearing."

"That was a dangerous course of action. What did the women of the house think? Did they have any say in the matter?"

"Of course. My grandmother was a strong woman, she was not one to be argued with. In fact, she devised the plan. Rafael would travel in the car masquerading as my father. He would have a scarf wrapped around his lower face, protecting a toothache, the reason for the trip being a visit to a dentist. My father, you see, had a prominent scar on his face and he was well known. They were stopped by a patrol of civil guards and the tension in the car was high. Luckily my grandmother knew one of the policemen. She had helped him before the war, supplying him with fresh milk from the farm, when it was scarce, for his daughter who had tuberculosis. She miraculously recovered and her father put it down to the milk. My grandmother chatted with him, distracting his attention. Rafael was so scared he was pinching her bottom to stop her talking."

"Was he shot after he gave himself up?" I asked.

"He would have been, but my father bribed the prosecutor with a new Buick car and Rafael was given a life sentence instead. He went to prison in Burgos for five years and was then released and exiled to Granada. He was never allowed back to Seville. For the rest of her life my grandmother said a Mass each day for his soul."

Alfonso carries on talking about how money has always ruled in Spain. He talks of his uncle who secured a divorce, illegal in Spain, by bribing the papal officials of the Santa Rota to annul the marriage on the grounds of non-consummation.

I see a smile starting to form on Marie's face, just a trace, a slight movement of the lips.

"Honey, there's nothing new under the sun, you know. Take this thorny issue of divorce – Franco wanted to keep Spain in the Dark Ages. They taught me back in the States about Spanish history and divorce and men. My favourite was Catherine of Aragón, Henry the Eighth's first wife. She was married first to Henry's brother, Arthur. Henry, as you know, tried to annul his own marriage to Catherine on the basis that Arthur's marriage had been consummated and therefore his subsequent marriage had been a sham. Catherine claimed that the marriage had never been consummated with the fifteen-year-old Arthur being overcome on the night and unable to rise to the occasion. He had kept a clean sheet, you could say. Honey, don't pull a face, I'm making a point. I remember the date clearly – my history teacher was hot on dates. It was 11 June 1531, 500 years before your uncle took his case to the Santa Rota. In Zaragoza Cathedral, on a very hot summer's day on the banks of the river Ebro, the elite of the Church's hierarchy were in attendance. At the command of the Pope himself, a tribunal of the Santa Rota had been called to investigate Henry's claims about the "Great Matter" as it was called. Salvador Felipe, the herald of the tribunal announced in Latin that the King of England had been summoned to Zaragoza to explain himself. Did he come? The hell he did, that's not the point. Five hundred years, darling, and Spain has not changed. Franco's only aim was to keep it that way."

Alfonso says, "Well my dear, I know how Henry felt. I have my very own feisty queen who doesn't do what she's told."

We sit in silence for a while. It is a great story of a country at war with itself and a family in crisis, caught in the middle. I have no doubt that it's true, and I wonder if Alfonso secretly admires his uncle Rafael or whether he is truly the son of his father.

There have been a lot of stories in the press recently about the new law of historical memory introduced by the previous socialist government that had allowed, under certain circumstances, mass civil war graves to be exhumed and bodies, if identified, to be reburied in consecrated ground. What, I wonder aloud, do Alfonso and Marie think about this? Alfonso, having relaxed a little during Marie's journey into the Golden Age, looks up abruptly and for the first time I see anger in his eyes.

"Young man, I am not in favour of this. The war is long over. We live in peace and in democracy – we do not need to disturb the dead. Let things lie and do not meddle."

Marie says, "These poor men and their families have never had justice though. Is it not right to give them the respect accorded to their victors, a burial with decency and honour?"

Alfonso looks at Marie, perhaps remembering why he had fallen in love with her so passionately as a young man and not wanting to admit, even to himself, how much he had changed since that time.

"No, *hijo de puta*, these men, they wanted to destroy my life, my farm… they burnt the churches, killed nuns and priests and for what? An ideology that could never work."

"Darling, please do not talk to me like that. We have a guest."

Alfonso looks at me. "What do you think then? What did your precious writer think? It is so easy now to condemn Franco. He saved Spain and gave us a good life for 40 years."

I look at Marie who offers me no guidance, then and back to Alfonso.

"I believe that Franco did what he did to protect the status quo, to protect the establishment, the Church and the ruling classes, to protect a feudal society from new modern ideas of equality and to give him the power that his ambition craved and that he consolidated for over thirty-six years. I believe he felt threatened by socialism and communism but that did not justify his actions. I believe that if a similar threat to the establishment were to occur, even now, in Britain, we do not know what the army, the Church, the monarchy and the establishment would do. I remember a time in the 1980s in my country. The miners were on strike suspecting that the British government was intent on closing down the mines and destroying communities across the country, in effect a class war on the working class by the right. The government insisted there was no policy in place to close down the mines. Thirty years later the government records were released, and they show that there was such a policy and Mrs Thatcher was prepared to enlist the police and the army in delivering it."

I pause briefly, before continuing, "I was in Madrid in the summer and saw the striking Asturian miners arrive in Madrid. Our countries are not so different. However, I am your guest and I respect your views but I do not necessarily agree with them."

Alfonso looks at me, and Marie says quietly, "My, honey, this young man reminds me a bit of you way back."

Alfonso laughs, smacks Marie playfully on her arm and says, "Woman, go and get some more wine, I need to tell our guest a few home truths and you are not helping my cause."

"I know honey, I know."

The tension is broken and we drink some more. Alfonso asks about my links with Spain over the years. He is not interested in Laurie Lee. He wants to know about me.

I tell him of some of my memories of visiting Spain and share recollections that I was only vaguely aware of and had not linked together ever.

"I remember lying on my back in the Mediterranean, off the coast of Valencia. I am seventeen and on a study visit to Spain. I am thinking not of *Horchata*, the milky ground almond drink, a speciality of the region, nor of the Tribunal de los Aguas, the ancient Water Tribunal that had been meeting for decades on a Thursday outside the cathedral, to solve water disputes in the rice fields of the region – we had been studying *La Barraca*, a novel by Blasco Ibañez on the issue. No, I am thinking of my educational forays into the wiles and bodies of the opposite sex. For three weeks we had been segregated into male and female dormitories and then, on our last night, we had foolishly been granted a joint unsupervised leaving party.

I remember meeting an old school friend, who had been on that same study visit many years later at a function in an expensive hotel in Stratford-upon-Thames. He was then working for the company that printed banknotes for South American countries. When he was seventeen he had been a Monday Club Youth Wing member, a 1970s right-wing organisation, a follow on to Mosley's 1930s black-shirted fascists. He would have fought for Franco, I thought. That night in Stratford we couldn't work out how we knew each other and then he walked out of the room. He had a peculiar gait and a distinctive way of swaying his bottom. I remembered instantly who and what he was. I told him when he came back into the room and he smiled and said that his last memory of me was that night in Valencia when he and other students had to carry me half-naked from my room where I had collapsed onto the body of a half-naked female student and had promptly passed out."

All this comes back to me as I think of that perfect day lying in the Mediterranean.

"I remember sitting in the Plaza de San Nicolás in Granada watching the blood-red sun sinking down over the Alhambra Palace and the Sierra Nevada. I am thinking about how my life is going to work out, I am twenty.

I remember sitting on a long balcony overlooking the sea in Nerja, near Málaga. I am twenty-one and my mother is visiting me fleetingly during a year spent, in theory, studying abroad. She has come to tell me that she is divorcing my father. She leaves me for a bit on my own and I cry for myself, and for her and for my father. Twenty-one is a very young age.

I remember lying in bed with my first girlfriend in a flat in Santander, Calle Santa Lucía, next to La Bodeguca where we would go for tortilla and rough red wine. She looks at me and informs me that I will not, after all, be the father of her babies.

I remember waking up in Seville in 1975 and being told Franco had died and looking out of the window in my flat in Santander, that long night in 1981, when the army coup against the new democratic government, led in part by my own landlord, was in the balance.

And now, as I am sitting talking to you and Marie, I am thinking of my wife and daughter. My wife who is divorcing me and my daughter who does not know what to do. She is twenty-three, not much older than me that day back in Nerja."

It is a long speech and Alfonso and Marie have listened quietly. They offer me a coffee and I receive a hug from Marie and firm handshake from Alfonso, no words of homespun wisdom or well-meant advice for which I am grateful.

*   *   *

I take my leave of Alfonso and Marie, a couple still very much in love but with very different views on life.

I walk on towards Aracena and then up and away from the town back into the hills. I am off to visit a small community of writers, led by my friend John Simmons. The writers are called Dark Angels. I have little idea what to expect. I once asked John where the name Dark Angels came from. He said,

"It's a nod to Milton's *Paradise Lost* and the idea that our creativity comes from our flawed human nature; that as Dark Angels we are neither those who have ascended nor those who have fallen, but that we occupy the fertile, if broken, territory somewhere in between."

I briefly ponder that Laurie Lee, as I am increasingly realising and coming to accept, could have very much been a Dark Angel and that I very much seem to fit the bill at the moment too.

It is early in the morning as I climb towards the *Finca El Tornero* where the group meets. All is silent and still save for a cock that unnervingly crows just three times.

170

I wonder about these Dark Angels I am going to meet, a group of angels grounded by earthly toils seeking new inspiration and renewal at the top of a mountain. As it turns out they are a friendly and eclectic group. They have flown in from all parts of the world, from Seattle to Prague and Edinburgh.

I have a good sleep and awake refreshed. The next morning, the warmth of the early morning sun burns off the mist hugging the contours of the lake below and the mountains stretching away to the horizon. I gaze, in awe, at the hazy impression unfolding before from me. It is as if the shifting sands of North Africa have settled in the folds of the hills, creating great seas of desert sands, shimmering and gently rippling in the cool breeze. Gradually the full majesty of the Sierra emerges, its serrated edges cutting its way through the wispy cotton wool clouds that offer little resistance to the steadily increasing burning intensity of the early morning sun.

I had been awoken by the harsh cry of a cockerel followed by the sweet flute like tones of a bird drifting through the still air. The gathered writers of the Dark Angels go about their work in the cloister like surroundings of the *finca*. Short spasmodic episodes of writing punctuate the air at regular intervals sending the collective creative juices cascading down into the parched gardens below.

This, despite the heat of an early autumn day, its soporific humidity sapping the very life from the marrow of the bone.

In the middle of the courtyard there is a tree with exotic-looking fruit hanging from its branches, tantalisingly just out of reach, just as those ripe apples always seemed to be in childhood. The fruit is luscious and the juice of one, a victim no doubt of predators, is dripping down onto the ground. Rachel, one of my fellow students, wanders over and takes pity on me. "Lift me up," she says, and I do, enabling her to reach up with a nut-brown slender arm and pluck a fruit off the branch. She shines the fruit against her denim-clad legs and hands it over. It is a quince. Its perfume fills the air now, picking it from the tree seems to have released its sweet and sickly smell, cloying like honey.

I love the quince's shape, with its generous curves and bulges. It is a voluptuous, even magnificent fruit to look at, like a Rubens' bottom. Rachel warns me not to try and eat it raw as she takes out a handkerchief, moistens it with her lips and wipes off the white pubescent fluff covering the yellow bulbous skin. She tells me that it can have a bitter taste and the best way to remove this is to wash the fruit in salt water or the sea, a process of alchemy that produces a thing of sweet beauty. Spaniards make it into a paste, *membrillo*, and eat it with slices of hard *Manchego* cheese. It is at its best if the Spanish year enjoys an Indian summer, a late autumn of higher than normal temperatures. Indeed it has led to the saying in Andalusia, "*El veranillo del membrillo*", which translates literally as "the little summer of the quince" – a term used to describe a Spanish Indian summer.

Rachel and I have been working together as a pair on a writing exercise. We have to tell each other something of our lives and then, in the main group, describe the other person using an appropriate metaphor. Rachel is a slim, pretty and vivacious young lady with a love of the sun that has given her a dark oriental look. I toy with metaphors, ranging from silk off-the-shoulder kimonos, scented exotic orchards, dark rum and coconut cocktails, soft paws padding across a dark mahogany floor. In the end I settle for a siesta snooze, languorously, lazily, stretching out in the shade of a eucalyptus tree. She seems content with that and responds with a portrayal of me as a quilted pullover keeping someone warm on a cold winter's night. I am happy with her description and slip the quince into a pocket to join my shell and locket.

Rachel whispers to me later on that evening that Indian summers or little summers of the quince happen in life too, a second chance in life that shouldn't be foresworn.

One night John reads from his recently published book, *Angel of the Stories*, which is set in Aracena. It is a novella written in a magical realism style that seems to capture the rather strange set of experiences that I have had in these hills to the west of Seville.

John had been inspired by a Dutch artist, Anita Klein and her work of illustrations entitled *Italian Angels*. I particularly like her *Angelo delle arance*, The Angel of the Oranges. This shows a voluptuous angel with emerald green wings, sitting cross-legged under an orange tree and holding an orange in her hand. Simple clean Dutch stroke lines conveying a hint of the orient.

The main character in the novella is a young lady, Julia Buendia Allone, living in Aracena, an aspiring writer but one stuck and grounded, devoid of inspiration. The choice of name suggests some inspiration from another of my favourite books, *One Hundred Years of Solitude* by Gabriel García Marquez, the Colombian writer. In John's book, Aracena is bathed in a special aura that washes over Julia and endows on her the gift of wings and bids her fly. John reads a short piece from the beginning of his story, our story:

"Julia felt drawn to look upwards at the pure whiteness of the moon. There was no cloud in the sky and the sheer emptiness looked like an invitation. She looked back briefly and she smiled when she saw the wings on her shoulders. She stood on the railings of the roof and she plunged off the side like a diver into the depths. But she didn't fall, she soared, higher and higher, enjoying the sensation of the slow-beating wings, up and up towards the moon."

A tingle goes through me as I listen to these words, late in the evening, the light of the candles flickering, I am taken back to that summer afternoon on the top of that Oxfordshire hill, plunging through the gap in the clouds, the sun going down, entering into a new Spanish world of heat and colour, a glorious Indian summer awakening, my very own little summer of the quince.

The days I have spent with John and his Dark Angels have been precious ones. We have talked about Lee and his writing as a group. A group of strangers, we have shared our personal journeys in the intimate way that only writers seem able to do. They seem to understand, at times more than I do, why I am on this particular quest to find Lee and myself.

2 October 2013

Surrounding the *finca* are acorn strewn *Dehesa* groves, dominated by the *Bellota* tree, under which black pigs roam freely, playing out their role in the natural cycle of the region's eco system.

Truly paradise on earth and yet...

High above the Sierra circles a *buitre negro*, a black vulture indigenous to the region. He hovers on the warm thermals waiting his moment for a kill. He is alone as his flight plan bisects the azure blue sky.

I manage to get hold of a local newspaper. The headlines make grim readings: they talk of Black Saturday, the day when the latest economic figures were released; 25% of the population across Spain is unemployed; in Andalusia the figure rises to 30%; in Andalusia

50% of people under twenty-five are unemployed.

There comes a reckoning in the affairs of a nation and with the strains of the Arab Spring playing hauntingly in the background, Spain, once a colony of Africa, and one that is prone at times to take its cue from there rather than Europe, is teetering on the edge as its economy implodes and unresolved tensions rise to the surface.

I recall a conference that I had recently attended at the London School of Economics on "The Role of the Monarchy in the Transition to Democracy in Spain". The session was chaired by Professor Paul Preston, biographer of King Juan Carlos and a self-confessed close friend of the chief guest of the conference, Alberto Aza Arias. Arias is a former Spanish ambassador to London and was present in the Cortes parliament building in Madrid that day in 1981 when an attempted coup by the army failed. He was Adolfo Suárez's right hand man in steering through the legislation to create a new democracy in Spain in 1978, albeit a government packed with former Franco regime ministers. He also went on to head up the Spanish Royal Household. It was an interesting session without too much of interest being revealed. I was struck however, by Arias' reply to a man from the audience, who had dared to defy Professor Preston's declaration that there should be no questions about present or future events. The man talked of the unspoken but inviolate agreement to adopt the *Pacto de Amnesia* (the Pact of Amnesia) in 1978. It invoked the entire population of Spain and future generations, to wipe from its collective mind, all memory of the civil war and its war crimes and the long slow strangulation of the country by the fascist reign of a dictator and to carry on as if that bloody interlude had just been a "spell of magical realism." Now, nearly forty years on from Franco's death, the perception that the pact if broken would have the direst of consequences remains ingrained on the national consciousness. He finally came to the point and in the now silent chamber came the question, delivered with all the economy of a stiletto to the heart. "Is it not time now for Spain to awake from this state of denial and truly become a modern state?"

Arias paused for a long time, looked at Professor Preston for support and slowly said that the question had taken him by surprise and that he could not give an opinion "off the hoof", but in these desperate economic times it was possibly not the best time to raise such issues. The questioner stood up and simply replied, "With respect, sir, you have had over thirty years to reflect on the impact. I interpret your answer to mean that it will never be a good time to revisit this terrible period in our history. A very convenient state of affairs for some one might think." He sat down to a crescendo of silence and Professor Preston hurried us on.

I wonder if Spain has missed its second chance by burying its bodies and memories on unconsecrated ground all those years ago and then denying their existence for more than seventy years. I sense an opportunity, however, to revisit the ghosts of the past, free the skeletons from their incarceration, afford them the respect of a burial in hallowed ground and learn the lessons from their sacrifice. That would be a true act of remembrance and enable the nation and its citizens to collectively and individually confront their demons and spread their wings and fly away, just like the Dark Angels as they return to England, Scotland, Wales, the Czech Republic and Oregon.

I am not at all sure it is going to happen though.

Utopia, though, will always be searched for by each generation. Lee wrote of paradise and described it as "a holding on to the familiar contained within some ideal scale of the past." In my research into the current state of Spain and its forward direction, and during the course of my journey down through Spain, I have talked to many commentators, activists and ordinary people. I met Giles Tremlett, the writer and Spain correspondent for *The Guardian* in a Madrid bar near his house. He has a Spanish wife and has two children. He was late for our meeting, as he had been covering the story of the Asturian miners arriving in the capital. We talked of the current Euro crisis and the implosion of the Greek economy and their descent into social chaos. "Could it happen in Spain," I asked him. "Are we at a dangerous point in the country's history?"

He paused, took a long draught of his beer and said, "The people of Spain are being pounded economically by the government's austerity programme and it is going to get much worse before it gets better. Brussels is in charge and dictating the narrowness of the prime minister's room for manoeuvre. Spain, in fact, is being humiliated by the EU and yet they are taking it on the chin. Yes there are demonstrations and strikes and anger, real anger, but at the end of the day the Spanish middle classes are in love with the European Union and I see no sign of a divorce."

Back in London I had met Olga Abasolo, a publisher and translator of Tremlett's books into Spanish. She is also a passionate supporter of the *Los Indignados,* the grass roots Occupy-linked movement. She was there at the Puerta del Sol in Madrid on the 15 May demonstration that has become a byword for Spanish protest against the neo-liberal capitalist agenda. I told her what Giles had said and she had smiled.

"I am not quite with Giles on that point, I think there is a point at which the Spanish could say enough, no more, but I understand his perspective. The trouble is the opposition to the capitalist agenda from Brussels is disparate, as ever, and we are easy to ignore. It would be great if the southern European countries under threat from the northern European elite could unite in opposition but it is not going to happen."

My friends had told me of an alternative approach, a sort of Andalusian Shangri-La, a utopia in the heart of the region, a town called Marinaleda. I had been unable to get there but had heard all about it. Run by a Robin Hood style mayor for over thirty years and elected just after the transition to democracy, Juan Manuel Sanchez Gordillo dared to fight for the ideals that so many had fought and died for over the years since 1936, He vowed to uphold these ideals of equality, shared land ownership, co-operative workplaces. He declared a Third Republic, forty years on from the demise of the second. Did it represent the future for Spain that Laurie Lee had dared to dream of and risked his life for? What would he have made of it?

The tales I hear of this small republic are of harmony and fairness, a community working together for common goals. No unemployment, no shareholders benefitting from dividends at the expense of workers. I also hear of a charismatic leader who brooks no challenge to his authority, a local democracy that works well so long as you do not challenge the leader. It has faint echoes of Orwell's *Animal Farm.* There is no local police force. Gordillo creates his own laws but breaks the rules of the parent nation. He has been imprisoned several times. There are whispers that if you do not back the mayor's plans and protests with direct action, then you are excluded. It sounds too good to be true and with Lee's longing for "a holding on to the familiar" in his paradise perhaps he would have found it uncomfortable. The picture emerging of the town has echoes of Lee's Slad at the turn of the century where there were few laws; disputes and scores were settled in secret; neighbours looked after neighbours. The squire was the Gordillo figure – the figure of authority but one of less obvious occasional benevolence. Lee, as we know, loved life in London and though a man of the soil, he loved the good life of the city and by no means was a socialist figure.

I am glad in a way to have avoided Marinaleda on my journey. It is a good story and even if the reality lived up to its billing, it is one tiny community in a huge country of inequality. Its model has not been replicated anywhere else in the country. I am not seeking paradise on earth just some hope to cling on to and perhaps some space to create some clarity in my thinking.

My mood is that bit lighter, my step a touch quicker. The tang of the sea cannot be far away.

Walking in the hills all is total stillness and calm. There is a fresh feel to the air as the weak sun occasionally breaks through the cloud. Nevertheless, my skin glistens with beads of sweat that trickle down with more moisture than the dried up river bed beside me. I pass a church where a funeral is taking place. I gather the deceased is a ripe old age. I read somewhere recently that a good death creates a welling up of love from those left behind on earth. I have never found death a particularly depressing concept; I often wonder what life would feel like without that aura of melancholy that lingers, the ever-present knowledge that life begins and ends. As we move into autumn and then into winter one's mood often dips. Not for me, not at the moment: I am beginning to really enjoy my Indian summer.

Can life be measured in terms of goodness accumulated over a lifetime? And on death is its equivalent weight distributed as grams of pure love to those kneeling at the graveside living out their grief?

The image of the weighing machine still used to calculate the added value of fat and muscle achieved in the *Dehesa* comes to mind. Your worth is assessed as you enter the promised land and reappraised as you depart; if you are in credit, you live on in the goodness of others.

I am following an ancient track that runs between dry-stone walls, swathes of bountiful *dehesas* are all around. The track gradually becomes cobbled and harder underfoot, it is the ancient drovers' path of *Las Dehasillas*, once a principal livestock route across south-western Spain.

I walk through the small village of Linares de la Sierra. Its main street is Calle del General Franco. Other streets are called Virgen de la Salud, Calle Limón. Mass times for dead souls are listed on the church door. A poster looking to recruit parishioners for the annual Twelfth Night Wise Men procession stipulates that you must provide your own mule. Yoga classes are twice weekly. The Plaza de Toros doubles up as the main square. It is a very up-market village to find so high in the hills.

I come across an outpost of England, marooned and becalmed like a Rock of Gibraltar in the hills. Sam and Jeannie have been running a very smart country-house establishment, Finca Buen Vino high above the town of Aracena for many years. I arrive at teatime and am immediately required to relate the tale of my journey. The guests comprise Stavros and Catrina, Greek and Austrian respectively. They are both high-flying EU officials and married to each other. Virginia and Harriet, two friends from England make up the group.

It is a slightly surreal experience for me. The hospitality is wonderful but I am unused to the kitchen supper home counties feel of the place. I think of Lee in Toledo, staying with the Campbells and the servants and wonder if he felt as out of place. The food is English cordon bleu at its best. Jeannie had been trained in London at a finishing school for soon-to-be-brides in the 1970s. I am astonished to hear that such places still existed as I grew up in my middle class suburb south of the river. Jeannie had learned much and could trap a rabbit and kill it with one blow from her formidable fist. She did not demonstrate. Sam and Jeannie are excellent hosts and do their best to help me to fit in.

We all eat together at one large dining room table. Fish and quail is followed by a Queen's Pudding, seemingly a distant cousin of Eton Mess. I do not dare to proclaim my deeply Republican sympathies.

The experience overall is superb, the food lovingly prepared – in fact they now have their own published cookery book – and the welcome is sincere and thoughtful.

It gets me thinking about England, my home, but a place in which I am not at ease.

I cannot help but think though of the similarities between England and Spain, both still divided societies, held together by a compliant middle class. Much of each country is still based on a rural economy, dominated by landowners and tied tenants in a not too distant past and controlled by right-wing governments and an establishment still very much in charge in Madrid and London.

Stavros and Catrina and their two young children live in Brussels. They had been based in Egypt where often the ministers would break off meetings for prayer. Catrina is worried about the rise of the right wing across Europe, in Austria, Hungary and Greece. Stavros is concerned about Spain. His main concern is the prospect of Spain as a nation breaking up with Catalonia and the Basque country seeing the Euro crisis as a once in a lifetime opportunity to become independent. I am reminded of Antonio in Cordoba, telling me that where these two regions go, Andalusia will follow. I cannot imagine the poor and rural Andalusia having the slightest chance of making it alone though.

I need to leave this part of Andalusia that will be forever English and head south again to rejoin the Guadalquivir River and follow it down to where it drains into the Atlantic, a historic departure point for so many other navigators, explorers and conquerors setting off for new worlds. Many of these journeys, like Lee's but hopefully not mine, were to end in warfare.

Sam stands in the doorway of the finca and waves me off. His parting words sent a shiver down my back on this warm autumnal day, "Watch out for Cádiz," he says, "it always reminds me of Havana on a bad day."

Cádiz

To the Sea

Every valley shall be exalted, and every mountain and hill made low; the crooked straight and the rough places plain.
– Handel in *Messiah*, 1742

10 October 2012, Sanlúcar de Barrameda

I am standing on a wild, exposed spit of land. The wind is whistling around me, I am finally reunited with the sea, the Atlantic Ocean. The River Guadalquivir is emptying itself into its vastness. It seems a very long time since I sat on that overhanging rock high above Vigo harbour watching Lee step ashore.

The waves wash over my feet, soothing them and refreshing them for the final leg of the journey, east to Málaga. I have not yet reached my final destination, but the re-acquaintance with the ocean seems like a significant milestone.

Las Piletas bay stretches away in front of me. A breakwater of jagged rocks, visible only now at low tide, is spread out before me. It teems with crustaceans and other marine life. Away beyond this is the wild expanse of the Doñana National Park.

The park is once again under threat from the proposed reopening of a tin mine that caused Spain's worst ever ecological crisis back in 1998 when a dam burst and carried poisonous residue from the tin mines into the water system. Plans have been outlined to build an oil pipeline through Doñana, while other developers have announced proposals to expand local tourist resorts whose new hotels and golf courses would demand water supplies that would further erode the local table. Silt washed from nearby farms is also choking the channels that crisscross Doñana. The wetlands of Doñana are under threat of a death by drought. Yet more fallout from the economic crisis that threatens to engulf Spain.

The park is the refuge of one of Europe's rarest mammals, the Spanish lynx. Its yellow-brown fur with dark brown spots blends into the natural habitat and the shy creature is very rarely glimpsed by human eyes. I am gradually getting more and more insight into its human equivalent, the young English poet walking towards a war not of his own making but one that would shape his life.

Javi, my friend from Madrid besotted with all things Irish, had told me to visit a small church in the town, the parish church of Our Lady of the "O." I ask the way to the church from a very well dressed gentleman. He is on his way there himself and shows me the way but makes me go on ahead as he is walking very slowly and the wind off the Atlantic is fierce. I never find out exactly what the "O" stands for but the church certainly has a presence. As I enter a performance of Handel's Messiah is being enacted by a touring English choir. I slip in just before the interval to hear the soprano and the counter tenor duetting and reaching a glorious climax as the Son of God is born: "Learn of him, for he is meek and lowly of heart and ye shall find rest unto your souls." It is a poignant moment: I have heard Elizabeth sing this so many times.

I have come to this small church, as I get closer to completing my own odyssey, to experience the place that Columbus and Pizarro sought out. They wanted the blessing of Santa Maria before setting sail for the New World. They sailed down from Seville along the silvery waters of the Guadalquivir, the river reeking of spilt blood, mixed races, of greed and ambition, of hope and fear. I wonder if Magellan came here before he set sail for the Spice Islands?

Laurie Lee, inspired by his visit to Seville in 1935, chose the subject of Magellan's voyage for his first radio play broadcast in 1946 by the BBC on its experimental Third Programme. This is a Spain at the height of its glorious empire, a Spain, that in truth, Lee never saw. The Spain he saw was a European power brought to its knees after a 400 year decline ending in a civil war.

The play is narrated by a survivor of the epic voyage. Only eighteen returned to Seville out of the 262 that had set off three years earlier on the five ship convoy: "five ships, five creaking worlds in a green universe of ocean."

The sailor tells his story to a blind beggar and recounts the sight of his master on the eve of the voyage, checking the seaworthiness of his vessels "Each thread of sail he tested for his shroud." These great men knew the perils of their voyages and they were seeking succour from the gods of the time.

I sit in front of the statue of Santa María in the church, looking into those piercing blue eyes. What had she said to those explorers and warlords in response to their exhortations? Had Columbus asked her to protect him from the unknown? Had Pizarro turned his even, unforgiving gaze on her and demanded that Mexico and its treasures be delivered unto him in the name of the queen? The very same queen, it is said, who looked out of the window from the imposing castle along the street and gazed upon the ocean for the first time.

My eyes search hers for compassion or pity and find none.

My fine gentleman hails me on my way out from the church like an old friend, shaking my hand.

The strains of the choir accompany me out, "How beautiful are the feet of them that preach the gospel of peace and bring glad tidings of new things."

12 October, Cádiz

I am sitting in a bar sipping my drink, a cloudy *anís* from Huelva, when I hear the sound of music coming from the far recesses of the bar. The melody is enticing but difficult to place. It has the rhythm of flamenco and the soft drumbeat of Africa. I make my way round the corner of the bar and find a small stage. There are two performers, a beautiful dark skinned young lady, dressed in the vibrant colours of Africa, gold, oranges and bright yellows, a slash of colour around her head in a scarlet bandana. She is playing the strangest guitar I have ever seen, the same width across as a typical flamenco guitar but only half the depth. It is enfolded tightly into her frame and her fingers dance across the strings. She sings in snatches of Andaluz but the chorus is African. Her companion, a young boy of no more than ten years, is softly playing a single drum, its surface no bigger than a dinner plate.

When they take a break, I approach her and introduce myself.

"Great music, I love it! Where did you get that extraordinary guitar from?"

"*Hola, encantada*, I am Rosa from Cádiz. My mother is from San Fernando, not far from here and my father is from somewhere in Africa. The guitar is my grandmother's. The style is called a *Petenera*, it was made especially for women to play – its shallowness is easier for us. My grandmother was a great performer and an even better prostitute." She smiles at me, enjoying my discomfort. "And this is my little boy, Gonzalito."

I offer to buy them a drink. The boy has a Coke and we have a cold glass of the local Manzanilla – it is bone dry and has the salty tang of the Atlantic.

She goes back on the stage to complete her set but not before she has agreed to meet the next day for a coffee. I want to hear more of her story. The further south I have journeyed towards the narrow straits separating Spain from Africa, the more I have seen of African immigrants trying to eke a life out of a region that is itself impoverished but still attractive to the African world.

The next day I find Rosa on her own as Gonzalito is at school. She tells me more of her story. Rosa is *una gitana* – she comes from gypsy stock. Her grandparents were both flamenco artists and made a living from performing for rich benefactors in specially performed concerts, *juergas*, in grand houses in the Plaza de San Antonio. Often her grandmother would perform in her other occupation at the behest of the same benefactors when they wanted to commission more than just a tune.

They were well connected, "*enchufado*" she says, literally, "well plugged in" to the *crème de la crème* of the city.

"They performed with some of the greats of Cante Jondo of the time, the Cádiz slums were perfect breeding grounds for *el duende*. My grandfather sang with Enrique "*El mellizo*" (the twin) – though he didn't have one – and with "*Hermosilla*" (the little beauty) who was tall and ugly. They could sing though, my father would tell me of listening to them and feeling the moment when "*los tercios fueron coronados*", true perfection, was reached. My grandmother, she had another phrase for this, used frequently in her second trade, "*Estoy por acabar*." Or as you English would say, "I am about to come."

She pauses and looks up at me, just the faintest of smiles showing and the tiniest lift of an eyebrow revealing her coquettish glee at my English reserve. She continues, "Of course for my grandmother, for her it was all a pretence, a sham. For my grandfather it was deadly serious and for real. When his song reached a climax, the room would be quiet for an age before the clapping began, the devil of darkness was doing its work, eating away at the soul."

"And your own parents, were they performers too?"

For the first time her mask slips. "My father, he was a performer with my grandfather, but he was also my uncle, well, probably my half-uncle."

I am just trying to work this out as she continues, "He married my mother, his niece. It was quite common in those days but often caused problems in the family, worse for them because of his African roots. My parents, they had to leave in the end, go to Seville to Triana, to live in exile. My mother though would bring me back to Cádiz, she was a *Canastera* (a basketmaker). She claimed she was the cousin of Camerón de la Isla. Have you heard of him? He was the greatest flamenco artist of the last century. In English, his name means, "the Shrimp of the Island" and my mother worked with his mother for a while. Was she really his cousin? I don't know, with gypsies it's often difficult to know. Cameron died young from drugs and tobacco poisoning. He is buried in San Fernando over the bay. His grave is a shrine to his followers. My mother would take me there and we would sleep by the grave sometimes at night. They are both dead now. I came here with Gonzalito when his father abandoned me. I get along okay. I lived in England for a while, in Liverpool... great city, great music."

"Your parents grew up under Franco. Did they tell you much about that?"

"Not much, but they didn't starve like many. Franco closed down much of the music industry; there were curfews in city centres after 9pm, but he left flamenco alone. More to the point though, was that the people in power, the people with money, they carried on the patronage of flamenco. They liked the music of the underclass. My parents and my grandparents knew them all, despised them I think, but they were a good meal ticket. And then after the war, the Second World War, I mean, we had new customers – German naval officers. In the civil war you know, the area around here and down to Gibraltar, you know where *los llanitos*, the lowest of the low, lived."

At this point she spits on the floor of the café, the tiled floor, no sawdust here, and whispers, "The Maltese and the like, you know. Anyway, in this area in the civil war, it was full of spies. The control of the straits of Gibraltar was vital for the nationalists. Your precious government did nothing to help the Republicans and they let the Germans roam free. Hitler sent his elite U-Boat commanders here to train and learn to kill my people. The British, all they wanted was their Rock. These U-Boat captains, they grew to love the coastline and after defeat in the next war, they slipped back into Spain and set up home. They loved the flamenco, they loved to listen to the children of the parents whom they had sent to an early grave, probably a mass unmarked grave at that. The Deutschmark was a good currency, while the peseta could buy you nothing."

Time is getting on and Rosa needs to leave. She has been an interesting companion and given me what I wanted, a good story. It feels wrong but I give her what she wants, a bunch of euros and she goes back to her life, not quite on the streets but certainly not anything like mine. Is this what Lee had felt on those occasions when he took advantage of what was on offer when he stayed in the roadside brothels? His transaction was more physical in nature but both have an element of sordidness about them. Have I taken advantage of Rosa or has she fleeced me with a pack of lies that I wanted to hear?

Lee wrote of Cádiz, "I'd been travelling through Spain in a romantic haze, but as I came south the taste grew more bitter."

While Lee was preparing himself for trouble, I was beginning to find peace.

I wander about for a bit on what is turning into a filthy day with the rain teeming down on the old port. I find the Barrio de Santa María where Rosa had told me her grandparents had lived. It is on the other side of town along with La Viña, which was pretty much an Arab ghetto a hundred years ago. It was where her father was bien enchufado. I can't find any of the old haunts in the centre that she had described to me, the flamenco hotspots of the good times in Cádiz before the civil war.

Rosa had told me a tale of sycophantic dependency running across three generations, a tale that, as far as I could see in many parts of the country, is still being told today.

I had, prior to reaching Cádiz, dropped into yet another slice of England, the sherry town of Jerez de La Frontera. Seemingly full of *bodegas* on every corner, the town has a damp musty smell. It's as if white yeasty flower spores have dropped from the trees lining the avenue, fermenting away, mingling with the heavy spray dragged into the town from the Atlantic waves pounding the beaches. I imagine the locals going home at night in the hot summers, itching to change their day clothes, wiping away the sugary veneer of fungi cells. I can't help but be transported back to Valdepeñas and that brothel with the air infused with, not the angel's share of escaping evaporating alcohol, but a more devilish concoction.

I realise though that it is a bad memory but that is all. I have moved on, literally from the dry plains of the *meseta* to the flow of the sea but spiritually to a better place.

I hadn't stayed long in the town. Just long enough to be shown around a *bodega*. Sam, from Aracena, had introduced me to a senior director, Gonzalo, an *enchufe,* of his. He spoke perfect English and had been educated at Oxford. Though a pure bred Andaluz gentlemen, he seemed more English than me. The old sherry barrels had been signed by visiting dignitaries from over the years: US presidents, British prime ministers, film stars. Red *Claveles* (carnations) grow in the courtyard. He suggested I try a sherry from Sanlucar, a dry sherry cooled by the salt tang coastal breezes. He must be careful, he said, not to break the thin film of yeast lining the top of the barrel, the *flor* that protects the liquid below from oxygen. The wine, like Spanish brides, in older days, had to be virgin, the *flor* intact and untouched by man. The Spanish though, down the centuries, had perfected the art of sampling the product without breaking the seal!

An immaculately turned out man appeared and served me a glass of sherry. Pinstripe trousers, white shirt, beige jacket, a red cummerbund wrapped around his slender waist, he dipped his curved silver ladle into the barrel from a small opening in the side, having removed a bung, and poured the chilled honey-coloured liquid into a cut glass flute. It was undeniably liquid but its wetness seemed to have disappeared on contact with the warm air in the vast cellar. It tasted as dry and sharp as the desert sand of the Atlas mountains carried over from Africa on the Levante wind.

I was, after all, a long way from the warm viscous liquid that passes for sherry back in England.

On my last day in Cádiz I walk by a large poster promoting an Ibero-American trade fair. At the top of the poster is Jesus Christ, sitting cross-legged on a cloud. He is a puppet-master controlling a diverse group of marionettes positioned below him: a Che Guevara figure saluting a gentleman in top hat, tails and white gloves; Don Quixote; a satanic skeleton with horns; an admiral; a princess; a Spanish Inquisitor dressed in purple velvet; a young bearded man playing the guitar. I have no idea what it all means but it is the sort of scene that, after months on the road, I could easily have conjured up in a dream.

I have had enough of my glimpses of England in Spain. I set my compass east for Málaga, fully aware that I have yet to negotiate the ultimate bastion of England on the Iberian Peninsula, the Rock of Gibraltar. Lee had spent a few days there, bound by a curfew imposed by the immigration officials. He had arrived as a tramp dressed in rags and shoes worn to the bone. The Gibraltar police were suspicious and glad to see the back of him as he stepped back across the border.

I have no real desire to cross the border and may indeed not.

East to Málaga

White Elephant Hills

Far away, beyond the river, were mountains.
— Ernest Hemingway in *Men Without Women*, 1928

15 October 2012, Algeciras

Quite by chance I stumble across a piece of English history. I am in Algeciras in southern Spain, a smuggling town at the tip of Europe, looking across to Africa. The Rock of Gibraltar casts its long shadow over the town.

Lee had been unable to resist slipping into Gibraltar as he neared the end of his long walk. The novelty of English sights, customs and tastes soon palled and threatened to suffocate his hard-won freedom and he left after a couple of days. I cannot bring myself to follow in his tracks there. I feel no need for English calm and order.

I have little appetite either to follow Lee's trail along the Costa to Málaga, now a series of concrete strips and urbanisations linked by fast flowing freeways. I am tempted to go inland in search of the quieter corners of Andalusia that Lee so loved.

Algeciras was one of those places. It was a frontier town in the 1930s, a place that winked at you with its one good eye, possessing all the charm of a *Pícaro* (a Spanish Oliver Twist). He stayed here for a while and slipped under its skin – busking, chancing his arm and learning the craft of the streetwise. He came back as a married man on his honeymoon in the 1950s and fell in love with the town all over again. The second time around he discovered the town's glorious hinterland, the Alcornocales Nature Park.

On this occasion, I find myself on a Mr Henderson's trail, rather than Laurie Lee's. To be more precise I find Mr Henderson's legacy, his snaking railway line buttressed by two classic railway hotels. Henderson was a Scottish railway pioneer whose vision and entrepreneurship was recognised by the Spanish government. He would go on to become a leading figure in the British Railway success story of the 20th century.

Railways and Spain had always seemed to go together for me. My first experience of entering Spain was not by sea as it was for Lee, but by train, back in that magical summer of 1974.

1 July 1974, The Spanish Border

The night is still as the train slips through the countryside. Occasionally we stop at a station but nobody gets on and nobody gets off.

We are nearing the border where we will stop to change tracks. The French track is not compatible with the Spanish. Opposite me is a young man, a reluctant soldier, doing his mili, his compulsory national service.

"Cigarette?" I venture.

"*Gracias.*"

The harsh black tobacco bites at the back of the throat and reappears coated in a phlegm-flecked bullet.

"You got long to go?"

"Three bloody months."

"Must be hard."

The soldier pauses and takes a long look into my eyes, weighing me up, calculating the risk.

"Tell me about it – it's ball-breaking hard. The parades, the pointless discipline... but it's the boredom that kills you. We drink to forget, play cards, fight, go with the whores down by the river. We pay with our shoes, but then back in the barracks, no shoes, you're up on a charge, then solitary confinement."

We lapse into silence.

I enter the station cafe through misted-up doors, the cold early morning air meeting the steaming warm front loitering inside. The coffee still smells of Paris and the bottles above the bar, silhouetted in a large mirror, boast dancing girls from the Moulin Rouge. I sniff the air though and I smell Spain. The barman slams the metal coffee holder against the side of the bar, the used coffee grounds spill onto the floor and lie amongst the paper screws and shells and cigarette butts. Fresh coffee is pounded into the container and attached to the machine with a wrench of the barman's wrist. The machine explodes into life. Hissing and spitting and smoking like the trains that used to pull into the station of old. Black liquid gold drips out into a fresh cup. The barman passes me the cup and nods.

I have the coffee with a strong slug of cognac and anís, one of each, a *Sol y Sombra*, they call it, light and shade. In this I am following the example of my fellow customers. There's not a man under sixty and barely a tooth in sight. They watch as I take a sip and their faces remain blank as I choke and splutter as the cocktail hits my already raw and nicotine-stained throat.

I am about to enter the shade of a fascist state for the first time.

Thirty-four years before, in 1940, General Franco, fresh from victory in the Spanish holocaust, and Hitler had met here in Hendaye in a railway carriage in a siding. The talk was of war.

16 October 2012

I am staying at cheap hotels on my journey, like Lee did when he wasn't sleeping rough, or earning his supper at a local brothel, playing his fiddle well into the night. I have to sneak a look inside the stylish Reina Cristina hotel overlooking the British Rock. It was Mr Henderson's first hotel, an iconic local landmark when it was built at the end of the 19th century. A twin hotel, Reina Victoria, was later built in Ronda. The Reina Cristina's glory is now rather faded, but its story still resonates with the events of the tumultuous first half of the 20th century. On entering the hotel I am met by a wall of black and white photos of eminent visitors, including Federico García Lorca and a young Winston Churchill.

Mr Henderson, later to be Baron Faringdon, built the railway and the hotels partly to enable the British occupying forces in Gibraltar to escape the heat of the coast by transferring to the cooler air of the hills, and partly to open up the coastal hinterland by connecting it to the coast, thus increasing trade and denying the hill-based *bandoleros* the isolation in which they thrived.

I am reminded of a great, great uncle of mine, Cedric Vinson Thomas, a railway engineer who discovered his own new world, working on the emerging railways at the turn of the 19th century that were opening up Brazil's tropical forests. He was not much older than Lee was when he walked through Spain. It was the eve of his first period of home leave back in Wales, after three long years away, when he succumbed to yellow fever. Two days later he was dead.

I decide to take the train and travel the route created by this pioneer, not just to save time and another long steady upward climb into the hills but because I have remembered a time and a place, a turning point in my recent life, the reason why I am here in the first place.

Laurie Lee had crossed to Morocco from Algeciras in 1936. It just so happened that this was the very same time that Spanish Army plotters were engaged in secret meetings on the African coast to plan the 1936 coup that triggered the Spanish Civil War later that year. Lee knew nothing of this, but the dated stamp in his passport almost led to his execution as a spy two years later after he had joined up with the International Brigade to fight Franco's troops. His interrogators were unhappy at the coincidence of dates. He survived, however, and returned to Algeciras years later on his honeymoon and spent a day lazing in the Alcornocales. He wrote about it in his book *A Rose for Winter*: "It was a different country there from the dusty coast; a wooded valley, green and fresh, with grass and flowers among rocks and a mountain stream running cool...birds flashed through the cork trees like motes before the eye...Then at last, in a blue dusk, we left the valley and walked back to the town. A curved moon, like a quartered orange, hung low over Morocco, and the wide sky filled with big bright stars."

We pull out of the station and the Rock of Gibraltar slides by.

The first stop is San Roque-La Línea, a small quiet station. In the languid heat of the October afternoon, it feels like an English summer's day.

We steadily climb up into the hills where white villages cling to the hillsides. From the bare urban surroundings of the port we are swallowed up and enveloped in a green cooling canopy. I have been here before, staying in one of those white villages and then taking this train to Granada. That was only a decade ago, but it seems more distant. I was with my wife, Elizabeth, and even though she did not leave me for seven more years, the first signs of the marriage's derailment surfaced here, alongside the single-track railway line, that is now carrying me high up into the hills.

Lee visited these hills and wrote about them, looking down from here on Europe and Africa and the Straits of Gibraltar.

We stop at Jimena de la Frontera. Green wooded hills surround the station platform – the same platform from which my wife Elizabeth and I had boarded the train that time. The shimmering hills in the distance bring to mind a classic Hemingway short story – *Hills like White Elephants* – that is set in rural Spain. It is the story of a man and a woman waiting for a train at a small rail station request stop halfway between Barcelona and Madrid, deep in the Ebro valley. Nothing much happens as the two of them talk around an unnamed subject. It becomes clear that the issue is one of life or death, whether or not the woman should abort the baby that they have conceived. She looks at the hills in the distance, compares them to white elephants and wonders if anything will ever be the same again. He just wants to catch his train and move on.

Elizabeth, like Lee, is out there somewhere, walking across the railway line and away into the distance – both forever just out of reach. The lemons on the trees are within my grasp, just by the station platform. They look ready for picking, but I don't need to try them to feel the sad taste of bitterness already on my tongue.

San Pablo, the next stop, is announced; it's a request stop only. We pass slowly through the station that has a neat shaded restaurant terrace and red carnations growing up the sides of the black iron railings. There is a wood fire alight in the station, the smoke curling up and drifting on the air, bringing woody hints of *encina, chaparro y naranjo* – young oak, older oak and orange zest. It is a fine clear day, no hint of the fiery *Levante* wind from the east, or the cooler *Poniente* wind from the west. The *Barba de Levante*, the Levante Beard, the sea haar that clings close to the hills, has stayed away today. Orange trees, almond groves and fields, flecked with white cotton buds, line our route as the railway follows the river valley. There used to be bandits in the hills; in 1952 Lee had an armed escort as his horse-drawn stagecoach took him and his new bride to Seville.

Many people walk the railway route now and lots of the small station buildings have a second life as restaurants and small hotels. I alight at Gaucín. I will complete the journey to Ronda later today, but I want to spend an afternoon in this quiet corner of tranquillity. I sip a cold draught beer in the small bar next to the station. The local men are in for their pre-lunch drink. The woman behind the bar swats away the men's coarse but humorous comments, as if they were flies hovering over the *tapas* of squid, kidneys and pork marinated in sweet Málaga Virgen wine. Occasionally and without warning she breaks into song.

I climb up into the wooded hills seeking shade from the hot October sun, there is just enough of a covering from the turning leaves to provide some relief. Much as Lee did, that winter afternoon back on his honeymoon, I doze away the afternoon. My rest is interrupted only by the trees above spitting out occasional acorns into the undergrowth beside me.

Lee ended his walk in Almuñecar, a town along the coast from here and holed up there for the winter and spring and sleep-walked into the start of the civil war. As the acorns thud onto the ground around me I am conscious that this valley would not have been so peaceful back in 1936 when Franco's national rebel troops were seeking to overthrow the supporters of the elected Republican democratic government in this part of Andalusia.

I rejoin the train and am waved off by the station-master. He has his own office and looks after eight trains (four travelling up the line, four down) a day, and a level crossing. He has the look of Mr Perks, from Edith Nesbit's classic book, *The Railway Children*, about him. No children waving red petticoats though, as we plunge through the dark. Tunnels come thick and fast with deep gorges in between with fast flowing emerald green waters. Toy houses, dropped into a ravine far below, flash past, hugging close Irish green postage stamp gardens.

The countryside is opening up now into wide plains – bandit country. The hills are farther away now, solitary hunched trees hanging on as slopes soar skywards. I want to come back and walk this route sometime. The ever-changing landscape is unable to keep pace with the train and I cannot take it all in.

It is mid-October, five o'clock in the afternoon and it is still 30 degrees outside. Enticing green pools of ice-cold mountain stream water trickle into view.

I have to end my journey at Ronda, a town that clings to the top of a steep gorge. I make a last call at the Reina Victoria hotel, where I sit on the terrace and look back along the valley as the sun sets over the Sierra ridge. I walk across the bridge over the gorge and look over to the valley below; it is a sheer drop to the river. Over the centuries, heretics, adulterers, traitors, and people in the wrong place at the wrong time, have been thrown to their death from here – or worse, invited at gunpoint to jump off.

Neither of these things happen as I make it to the other end of the bridge.

I have been offered the chance to hole up in a small farm belonging to a friend high up in the *Sierra de las Nieves* above the village of El Burgo. It offers a rare chance to pause awhile in the wonderful Indian summer that Andalusia is enjoying. I am nearing the end of my journey and though tired I am more at ease with myself than I have been for a long time. I do not want the journey to finish. I want to linger and reflect.

The dusk comes quickly as if eager to assert its hold over the day.

The village of El Burgo is laid out below me, the burnt-out hills that fall away to the chalk houses are all dark greens and browns dotted about with black trees, it looks like a Neolithic theatre backdrop, a scene etched onto a cave wall by primitive man.

I go to Pepe's bar as I have been directed. Juan, my friend, is not there but Pepe who has known Juan, *El Escocés* (Scottish John) for many years greets me with warmth.

He takes me to Juan's house, a couple of kilometres outside the village, my home for the next three weeks, where I will slowly recover from the rigours of my journey.

Approaching the house we ford a shallow stream as we walk up the short incline to the house.

The flies buzz all around me as the hens peck at the scraps on offer.

I can see a man in the distance, a neighbour of Juan's who has a smallholding under the lip of one of the many scrubby hills dotted with olive trees. Manuel is a grizzled, kindly man, with toothpick jutting out from under the white bristly moustache. He welcomes me and carries on working as we chat. Working the land here is hard work. He collects up earth mixed with olives and sifts out the small sharp pebbles with a metal tray punctuated with holes. There is a twang that echoes uneasily as he picks out the olives and dumps the stones onto a cairn of previously collected stones. His children and grandchildren all live away in the city now he tells me. He collects up some of the ingredients for the local staple diet, *La Sopa de Siete Ramales* (Seven Ingredients Soup), dropping wild asparagus and tomatoes into his basket.

He is retired now, like Lola, who scurries around my legs. She is one of his dogs, a slim elegant *potrenco,* a whippet-like breed. She is a hunting dog, her instincts honed over generations to hunt and kill rabbits. Manuel points out another dog, Diana, who is Lola's puppy. She is dragging a bone retrieved from some poor animal's carcass. Like her mother, she is redundant as there is scarcely a rabbit left in this arid landscape. "The land has been poisoned by man," says Manuel. "Too many pesticides."

Manuel is stooping low again, this time picking the onions that he says taste so sweet. He reminds me of an elderly Don Quixote.

The olives are harvested in December but Manuel shows me another smaller variety, his gnarled fist opening up to reveal a cluster of green olives that have been growing on this land for centuries. He presses one onto my hand.

I caress the olive between my finger and thumb as Manuel points out that these olives are different. They can be picked now, not December, bathed in water with a handful of salt for a month and then eaten.

I don't have a month to wait. I leave Manuel being tracked by Lola, Diana and Moon, another of his dogs. The posse pick their way through the allotment. They pass giant, white, round *Calabazas* (pumpkins). The pumpkins appear to be fussing over the smaller vegetables like earth mothers.

I have no routine for these weeks other than in the mornings and in the evenings I have a gaggle of hens to care for. There are eleven in all, of different shades and varieties. I have never before had so many girls to look after. They seem to trust me implicitly, and present me with eggs. They ask only for a daily feed, perhaps some scraps as a treat and to be locked up safe at night when Mr Fox comes calling. They escape their run only once. I try everything to get them back in, clashing saucepans, swearing at them in English, Scottish and Spanish. I plead with them to no avail. They have the run of the grounds and as darkness falls, I am contemplating an all night vigil with no shotgun. I feel helpless. Then, just like that, nature kicks in. Whether it is a survival instinct or an instinctual fear of the night, I am not sure, but as light levels fall I hear rather than see a sudden move en masse back into the run and the shed.

It is fiesta time in El Burgo, they are celebrating the frontier period when the hills around the village were full of *bandoleros*. The outlaws would prey on stagecoaches carrying the better off townsfolk and visitors. I go into the local bar and find Pepe dressed in a white shirt, a scarlet cummerbund across his waist, half-mast black trousers. On his head he has a red beret and he wears a brightly embroidered woven sash over his shirt. Oh, and he is carrying a shotgun. Luckily he is also wearing a broad smile. Outside the bar people are arriving on horseback and attaching the reins to a bar.

I overhear a conversation between two elderly men. They are recalling the times when one of the major industries of the village was ice-cutting. In the winter when food and money was scarce and snow covered the hills, the villagers would create ice wells. They would shovel the snow into piles and compact it. When it was frozen solid, they would cut it into blocks and descend to the coast at night, when the temperature was below freezing and the ice would not melt, and sell it to the bars and restaurants.

I am invited into the kitchen to see Concha at work creating a giant bowl of soup for all the customers to share. It is *La Sopa de Siete Ramales* that Manuel had been collecting vegetables for. The Seven Ingredients Soup comprises onions, asparagus, potatoes, red peppers, tomatoes, mushrooms and bread. Concha shows me a bowl of wild asparagus grown locally. It looks to me just like a bunch of marsh samphire picked off a Blakeney mud bank in the Norfolk Broads. Those who sought it had to be quick in picking it, as it only grew for a very short summer season in wild, desolate areas. Its presence was marked by a wash of emerald green on the black mud. The delicacy would be snipped off with scissors by foragers intent on their task, but also listening out for the return of the flooding Norfolk tide.

El Burgo is far from the sea, but here too the asparagus is elusive and the amount gathered has taken three days to collect.

There is a crowd of helpers in the kitchen, all women, all chopping, frying and tasting. Five eggs at a time are frying in a vat of olive oil.

The final touch is the addition of the bread, roughly divided up into small pieces. The bread is not added to all the assembled communal bowls, some prefer it without.

The bowls are put out in the dining room and friends. It is a truly communal dish: neighbours and strangers all eat from the same bowl. The soup is delicious and I learn I prefer the bready version. I am told that on 28 February every year, a huge fiesta is held to celebrate *El Día de Andalucia*, the newly constituted National Day of Andalusia. Enough soup is prepared to feed 5000 residents, relatives and tourists. There is no mention of fish.

I am having a siesta when I am woken by an urgent squawking from outside. I rush out and through a haze of dust and feathers, I see a large Alsatian dog with a hen in its mouth, the bird's snapped neck hanging limply to one side. There is a stand-off between the dog and me. Its hot mustard yellow eyes are locked on to my own pale green frozen ones. It is calculating its chances but not wanting to loosen its grip on the still warm but lifeless body in its mouth. It blinks first and departs, leaving behind seven more corpses. Miraculously, three of the most petite of the hens, one jet-black and two milk-white, are still alive and cowering behind the dead bodies of their companions. I feel sick and close to tears. I had been charged with the welfare of these hens and I had failed them.

It was almost dusk, the time when the hens would retreat, en masse, from the run into the coop. The dog had beaten me to them, somehow digging a tunnel under the wire fencing and pouncing on his prey. I can only think that because I had been away for three days the dog had grown bold. It had timed its attack for when dusk came. Darkness arrives suddenly at this time of year. The fresh scent of the hens would have been hanging in the air as the dog circled.

Chicón came to clean up, remove the dead and consign them to the large ditch at the back of the house, rich pickings for the predators always waiting near the farm. I asked about the survivors, expecting to be told that they too had been put down and recycled too, but they were to be re-housed, or their value re-couped perhaps, by a switch to the mother-in-law's farm. He wouldn't let me see the dead, he could see I was upset and though, hardened himself to the savage ways of the animal kingdom, he had the empathy to spare the feelings of this English urban sentimental creature who was mourning the loss of the hens.

I look up and the kites are already circling.

Every day as I walk down into the village for bread and milk, I pass a plaque by the side of a road. It commemorates the reprisal execution of a Republican family back in 1936. Nobody, other than me, seems to walk along this road that is reserved for cars, so I guess that the plaque is not really seen by anyone much these days. The locals know and don't really need reminding.

This morning, my last morning here, I sit on the terrace and listen to the Sunday morning church bells tolling down in the valley. The Iglesia de la Encarnacion was built in the 16th century on the site of a mosque, at the highest point of the town below. I had met a bell-ringer, Cristiano, outside the church earlier in my stay. As we stared down on the fast flowing River Turón and across to the Cabrilla mountains, Cristiano described the range of sound of his bells. "Think warm dark molasses, a black-cherried Rioja wine, the seductive sweetness of a Málaga Virgen wine." He speaks softly but clearly, like a muffled clapper resonating against the sound of a bell. Orwell, I recalled, had likened the tolling of a bell to the last cries of the condemned man on the gallows, reaching out to his god.

I am a Londoner and allegedly was ushered into life by the sound of Bow Bells ringing in the morning in East London. Peter Ackroyd in his biography of London had talked of its bells, "Beyond the time measured by human memory there exists sacred time evoked by the sound of these bells... they provided that sonority where sacred and secular time meet."

Sonority, such a lovely word. Not much of it was about, I am guessing, for Lee as he approached the end of his journey, looking for a well-deserved period of rest and peace.

The next morning I have an early start. The sky is a black sea of stars, the road unmarked and unlit. All is still, not a breath of air. Nothing stirs; even the birds are not yet awake; the shadows are tinged with light as I turn a corner and a scene, as old as time, unfolds before me. A small village is awaking below in the valley. It is like a Christmas grotto from my childhood, shadowy dwellings lit up from inside casting a reddish glow outwards.

In the distance, a bruised sky is emerging. A cock crows over to the west and is answered by one in the east.

I am on my way down to the coast on the last leg of my journey.

Almuñecar

Don't Open without Reason or
Close without Honour

25 October 2012, Almuñecar

I have come down to the coast to Málaga and am within striking distance of the end of my journey, Almuñecar, a small town just along from here. Málaga is the home of Picasso, the painter of *Guernica*. It is the place where Lee's trusty fiddle broke and fell into pieces. Lee had survived the journey but his fiddle gave in at the last.

I want to make one last pilgrimage to a small part of England in Spain. I am standing in front of a Victorian Gothic-style entrance-lodge. Unlike Gibraltar, the place I have come to is not full of Barbary apes, duty free shops, English teashops and thousands of British tourists. The tourists are not far away though, lying on the beaches and drinking in the bars in Marbella, and other hot spots.

I am outside the English Cemetery. It is home to some British long-term residents and I have come looking for one in particular. Writer Gerald Brenan is a legend in these parts, even though he has been dead for 27 years. He didn't put his life on the line in the civil war, like other British writers and artists, better known back in the UK. He is held in great affection by Spanish people of a certain age because he wrote sympathetically about Spain in a post Second World War period when Spain lacked many friends abroad. Brenan has always fascinated me as I saw in him what might have become of Lee if he had settled in Spain.

Brenan was living in Spain in Churriana near Málaga at the outbreak of the civil war. He was, reputedly the last Britain to leave Málaga in 1937 with Lee having been one of the first. Brenan had first lived in Spain in the 1920s high above Granada in the Alpujarras region. He had moved there after a distinguished period of army service during the Great War, in which he won both the *Croix de Guerre* and the Military Cross. He served in Lee's local regiment, the 5th Gloucesters. Like Lee, as a young man, he had undertaken a romantic walk across Europe. In his case he set out to walk to China, but he didn't get much further than Italy. Brenan has been likened to Roy Campbell so, if their paths had crossed, Lee might well have fallen under his spell. As it is Lee, and Brenan were only really acquainted in the 1960s when Brenan would play host to visiting writers to Spain.

Brenan, like Lee, had cultivated a reputation as a humble man of letters and a lover of all things Spanish. He is known mainly for his book *South From Granada*. He was in reality a somewhat unpleasant man who preyed on young women and was a controlling husband. He fathered an illegitimate child with his housekeeper in Yegen in the Alpujarras. Later, after he was married, he adopted the child. An insight into the spiteful and bitchy nature of the expat colony in Spain in the 1960s is given in an extract from a letter to Lee, about showing visitors the *Romería de Rocío* – an annual pilgrimage to a small shrine – from the Stewarts. John Stewart was a British engineer in Gibraltar and a friend of Lee's: "We're tired of taking deadbeats there, ineffectual gapers. We even took Gerald Brenan who was chasing after a piece of Torremolinos tail and must have seen quite a unique view of Rocío through her languid thighs."

Given that Lee was not averse to "chasing tail" himself, a fact that Stewart would have been very well aware of, suggests there is perhaps more than a hint of snobbery here.

Of more interest perhaps was a diary entry that Lee made about Brenan's wife, Gamel Woolsey, an American from the Deep South. Lee observed "wife charming slow-spoken Southern American bit like Aunty K (Kathleen Epstein)" And here we have the extraordinary link again to the Garman sisters and Lee. Kathleen was the aunt of Lee's wife Kathy and sister to Lorna. Gamel Woolsey, before marrying Brenan, was the mistress of Llewelyn Powys, a hedonistic writer in the 1920s. After Brenan had succeeded in capturing Woolsey's affections, Powys turned to Lorna and they embarked on a long affair. Powys and Lorna were both free spirits and professed to believe in sharing lovers rather than possessing them. As it turned out, Powys could carry this off, Lorna could not. When Lee came onto the scene, a few years later, it would seem that he was sharing Lorna with Powys. How much Lee knew of this is not clear.

The English Cemetery stands on the road from Málaga to Velez. I walk in past a pair of lions guarding the entrance, each with a paw resting upon, or perhaps pinning to the ground, a globe.

Lee talked of the English debs chaperoned closely by their parents who were abroad in Malaga. Some of them are, no doubt, buried alongside Brenan. Lee had escaped from the English suffocation of Gibraltar to get to Málaga. If he had visited the English Cemetery he might have felt that he was still there. The elderly English volunteer in charge in the Cemetery Gatehouse has a sun-blistered face and deals with me in an efficient and brusque manner. She could have been parachuted in from any Surrey parish fête committee. Pink glossed lips and blue-coated eyelids, she gives me the rundown on the cemetery. Later I hear her lambasting another helper on the phone who is ringing to apologise for being late.

Weeping willows give shade to the graves from the still strong winter sunlight. Many of the graves are shell covered and reminiscent of the grottoes once fashionable in English gardens.

Brenan's gravestone is understated and modest, like the public image of the man. He lies there with his wife. Gamel Woolsey died from cancer on the 18th January 1968. Brenan had asked for these words to be inscribed on her gravestone: "No longer need you dread the heat of the sun or the furious rage of winter."

His last years were unusual. He had been taken back to England, gravely ill and in need of nursing care. His Spanish admirers took this as a slight and he was spirited back to Spain and provided with the best care. He died in 1987 and left his body to medical science; some say to save the funeral expenses. Untouched for fifteen years because nobody wished to dissect such an eminent body, it was left floating in formaldehyde in Málaga University until 2001 when he was interred alongside his wife, in the warmth of the cemetery. His ashes were mixed with earth from the two Andalusian towns, Yegen and Alhaurín el Grande, where he had been resident. His epitaph reads simply: "*Escritor Inglés, Amigo de España.*" (An English writer and friend of Spain).

Ian Gibson, Irish writer and Hispanist, made a short speech in which he described the English Cemetery as the most beautiful in the Mediterranean region. I am not sure about the claim but it is certainly a lovely piece of living English history in this corner of Spain.

The Anglican Church of St George sits at the heart of the cemetery. Normally the church is locked but I creep in while a tradesman is distracted and keep an eye out for the Chair of the Surrey Fête Committee.

I had been told that before the creation of the English Cemetery in the 1830s, if an English Protestant were to die in Málaga, the ensuing burial was harrowing: they were not permitted to be interred on consecrated ground; nor were they allowed to be buried in daylight. They were taken in secret down to the seashore by the light of a flaming torch and buried in an upright position. They would later, depending on the state of the tide, be torn apart by dogs or washed out to sea.

In echoes of what happened to Lorca and could have happened to Lee, the first person to be buried in the cemetery was an Englishman called Robert Boyd. He had helped to orchestrate an uprising by Spanish Liberals in Málaga against the absolutist government of Ferdinand VII.

The plot had failed and the Spanish authorities executed all involved, including Boyd, by firing squad on St Andrew's Beach. William Mark, the British Consul who set up the cemetery, ensured that Boyd was buried in the cemetery in daylight.

Marjorie Grice-Hutchinson, one of the few English people buried in the cemetery after the 1990s, and the author of the lovely guide the English Cemetery at Málaga wrote: "Melancholy, to be sure, dwells in this place, but it is a melancholy tempered by a certain comfortable, and very English, propriety."

I often sit in churches to think. I have no faith left but it is hard to shake off a Catholic upbringing.

I leave the church and cemetery and go back to Spain, leaving Brenan behind in his final resting place high above the sea in the heart of their beloved Spain, fussed over daily by an English society that he had long forsaken before his death.

*   *   *

It's a damp autumnal day on the Costa del Sol and my walk down to the south coast of Spain in search of Lee is at an end, I have arrived at Almuñecar.

I feel a peculiar lack of elation at having reached my final destination.

I do feel a sense of satisfaction though. In the end I have carried through my desire to make the journey. I feel a bit like Lee felt though when he first came back to Almuñecar (or Castillo as it was called in the first editions of the book published in 1969. This was done to protect identities, Even this late in Franco's dictatorship, the threat of reprisals was still ever-present) in 1952. Nearly all of his friends and comrades-in-arms that he came to know during the nine months that he spent here as the civil war fermented and then exploded into life, had disappeared, were dead or in exile. Those that he did recognise would not talk of them. Like me, Lee was chasing ghosts.

I find the obelisk and plaque dedicated to Lee by the town. It is hidden away near the seafront. I go into the local church *La Iglesia de Encarnación* in the square where Lee lived with Wilma, a middle-aged English writer who had befriended him. They are celebrating a Mass with the three-strong congregation scattered to all four corners of the church. In the porch there is a leaflet celebrating the saint's day, a few days earlier, of my saint, San Judas Tadeo, he who looks after lost causes. A coincidence, serendipity or fate? Whatever it was, he had brought me safely to the end of my journey.

✳   ✳   ✳

In the morning I walk along the warm sands lining the small cove below me, still following in the tracks of Laurie Lee to the end. As I progress along the water's edge, the imprints left behind are washed away. The calm blueness of the sea contrasts with the spray-drenching green-crested Atlantic waves that had sent me on my way all those weeks ago. Out of habit I bathe my scallop shell in the sea.

Later that day I sit on the outside terrace of the hotel overlooking the cove.

Warm raindrops fall softly onto the clear roof above me, and run like tears, down the glass window that faces the sea. A pale shaft of sunlight plays on the window and the figures beyond become a blur.

I look through this pane of glass to a scene played out below me 76 years ago.

31 July 1936, Almuñécar, East of Málaga

> *Now I am still and spent*
> *And lie in a whited sepulchre*
> *Breathing dead*
> *But there will be*
> *No lifting of the damp swathes*
> *No return of blood*
> *No rolling away the stone.*
>
> – Laurie Lee in "Words Asleep", 1936

Laurie awakes, it is night and the shells are still exploding away down the coast, the flashes of light and muffled roars help clear his head. An innocent in war no more, the many-coated man has slipped on a new alias: gunrunner for the Republicans fighting Franco's rebel nationalist troops. The rebels had poured into Spain from the Spanish enclaves of Africa, Ceuta and Melilla across the strait of Gibraltar just two weeks earlier. Laurie was no more just a poet, a lover, a musician: he had taken on the mantle of freedom fighter. His state of unconsciousness had been induced not by sleep, though he is weary from the nerve-shredding weeks of the war build-up, followed by the grim reality of the real thing. The catatonic state stemmed from his latest episode of epilepsy, from which he has suffered since the age of ten. He had known that an attack was imminent. The outbreak of open warfare had indeed stirred his blood, tightened his stomach muscles and constricted his throat with spasms of pure terror. However, only the onset of a fit could generate the "state of startling illumination and euphoria." Even as he had witnessed his first dead body – a young boy from a nationalist family, lying in a ditch – the nausea that it induced was mixed with a primitive exultation that both thrilled and repulsed him. He had danced around the burning pyre of a grand piano torched in the Plaza Mayor. On the beach, he had warmed his hands on the flames licking around the charred remains of the holy relics and images looted from the local church. Then the icy grip of epilepsy took hold and he had keeled over, as if shot by a sniper. The attacks over – both his own personal assault of the senses and the bombardment of the coastline – he wonders whether his "falling sickness" was observed by his new comrades. He could deal with the illness, but not the public knowledge of the affliction. He knows he should go to reassure Wilma, the bohemian middle-aged English lady who had adopted him early on during his stay in Almuñécar, of his well-being. He stares across at the sea and notices a new boat on the horizon as he goes home to a mild scolding from Wilma and to sleep the sleep no more of an innocent.

16 November 2012, Almuñécar

I wonder about that boat on the horizon that Lee had seen. It would have been the Royal Naval boat sent to evacuate English expats from the coastal areas. I knew from my research in the British Library that it was HMS Blanche, captained by a Captain Edward Richards and it picked up Lee and Wilma the day after his epileptic fit. Lee had written, "A ship's cutter was drawn up on the sand, guarded by pink-cheeked British sailors. The King of England had sent a ship for the hotel fiddler and his friend, and our departure was a dramatic necessity."

As I drink another glass of cold beer on the terrace, I wonder what Captain Edward Richards made of the situation.

1 August 1936, Off the Coast of Southern Spain

Captain Edward Richards of HMS Blanche is on the bridge as they steer through the strait of Gibraltar. He and his crew have been on alert for many months now as the signs of civil war in Spain have become evident. The night before, he had monitored the shelling of a position east of Almuñécar. It had come from a small gunboat. He had instructed his crew not to intervene. Although only two weeks into the rebel insurrection, the British government, led by Prime Minister Stanley Baldwin, had adopted a firm stance of non-intervention and Gibraltar had already been sealed off to prevent arms importation into neighbouring Spain.

Captain Richards takes the view – which he suspects is shared by his government – that the nationalist rising is much needed to restore law and order to a nation afflicted by five years of mob rule by the elected Republican government of Spain. The conservative British press reports that the wide-ranging social and economic reforms threatened the settled order. In Britain, as much as in Spain, this sends a chill wind across the massed ranks of the establishment. He is then the representative of a neutral state and the painted red, white and blue stripes on his front gun-shield will hopefully afford him protection from both sides of the escalating conflict.

To starboard is the African coastline of Ceuta and Melilla, the Spanish enclaves that had harboured the initial assault force of the rebel nationalist army. To port is the Republican-held area of Malaga and eastern Andalusia. His remit is to repatriate any British citizens caught up in the conflict. He has no authority to force a return to England, but reasons that no Englishmen or women would have cause to take sides in the conflict. This is surely an internal affair for the Spaniards.

Cabins have been prepared below for any evacuees and makeshift arrangements for deck shelters hastily set up in case of larger than expected numbers.

He sends a cutter ashore and awaits developments.

The boat returns with just two evacuees. A middle-aged woman of about fifty with cropped hair wearing a brightly coloured lemon shawl and black baggy corduroy trousers, smoking a roll-up cigarette of dark tobacco. She could be a handsome lady, Captain Richards reasons, but he has no way of telling and feels it unwise to pass any comment to that effect anyhow. She has in tow a bronzed, fair-haired young man of delicate appearance and nature. An odd couple indeed. He salutes them, an action ignored by the lady and acknowledged only with a polite nod by the young man. They are escorted down to their quarters and the ship sets course for the short journey to Gibraltar.

Lee exults in his reception on board HMS Blanche as he is piped on board along with Wilma. Before he slips below he waves farewell to the few villagers gathered on the beach to see their very own Englishman rescued as a hero and returned to the green fields of England. His sadness at leaving his friends and his comrades to the fate of the civil war is somewhat diluted at the prospect of returning home with a story to tell. He does not know if he will ever return to the green waters of the Mediterranean, by whose side he has spent almost a year. He looks into the Spanish waters and glimpses in them his past, present and future.

In truth, the fate of his comrades has already been decided by a rapid series of events and meetings across the rest of Western Europe. France, with its popular left-leaning government, had been expected to ally itself immediately with the Spanish Republican government, but has been talked out of this action by the "neutral" British Conservative government, led by Stanley Baldwin and Anthony Eden. In the meantime, General Franco has been instrumental in securing the support and involvement of the fascist states of Germany and Italy. Britain's Conservative government, which has never trusted or respected the Spanish Republic, elected in 1931, has allowed its establishment instincts to cloud its strategic judgement. It has effectively and tacitly supported the nationalist rebels, allowing the German/Italian axis to steal an advance on Britain in terms of the lead in to the Second World War. Franco's messengers have met with Hitler's envoy, Rudolph Hess. Hitler, on holiday in Bayreuth, attending the annual Wagner Festival, has set in motion "Operation Magic Fire" and the German vessel, the aircraft carrier Usaramo, has already set sail for Spain, laden with modern fighter aircraft, bombs and ammunition. The die has been cast.

Of course, neither Laurie Lee nor Captain Edward Richards appreciate these significant events of the latter half of July as the odd couple are introduced into the world of Gibraltar of tea in china cups and cucumber sandwiches. Slipping into the English port feels like going through the looking glass; from the hell of warfare to an oasis of calm, tumbling down a rabbit hole into a wonderland of Alice and the Queen of Hearts. Lee is ensconced in a comfortable hotel, a far cry from his quarters on his previous visit the winter before: the cells of the Irish jail which had been made available to him due to his penniless state. In the meantime, Britain continues to position itself as a neutral power and drafts a Non-Intervention Agreement, which twenty-seven major nations sign up to, including all the major powers. The agreement is overseen by Britain's Lord Plymouth who proceeds, in the spirit of Nelson, to turn a blind eye to the axis of Germany and Italy, who flout the agreement's existence with impunity. In truth, the British government is in hock to the country's financial establishment, which has significant investment in Spain. The money men set up shadowy meetings in discrete country houses, as the nation sleeps through the fug of an English summer, ensuring that a stable benign Spanish dictatorship is allowed to form. This is only a sideshow to the main action, in which the British financial establishment brings their influence to bear over policy towards the rising fascist states of Germany and Italy. "Appease, appease," they whisper into the ears of the grey government officials. "Reds under the beds," they warn as Mosley's black-shirted fascists begin to prowl the streets of London and other European cities.

The reality is that Franco will rule with a fist of iron for 36 years and leave behind a legacy of a country whose individual and collective will has been so crushed that when democracy does came along it is sometimes hard to distinguish it from the previous regime.

9 August 1936, Dover, England

Laurie Lee and Wilma Gregory arrive back in England in Dover on 9 August 1936. As Lee says, "Back in England it was August, bank holiday time, with the country deep in the grip of a characteristic mid-Thirties withdrawal, snoozing under old newspapers and knotted handkerchiefs."

He is glad to be back though:

So do I breathe the hayblown airs of home,
And watch the sea-green elms drip birds and shadows,
And as the twilight nets the plunging sun
My heart's keel slides to rest among the meadows.
*   – Laurie Lee in "Home From Abroad"*

2 November 2012, Almuñecar

There is no doubt that Lee returned over a year later to fight for the International Brigade. He did walk over the Pyrenees French border into Spain in the harsh winter of December 1937, and he did join up with the International Brigade. He was almost shot as a spy, twice, by the Republican movement. But he also suffered epileptic fits during his training and as a result he was not deemed fit to fight and was sent home.

There is no doubt that his account of his return to Spain to fight, as chronicled in his final memoir published in 1991, *A Moment of War*, is deeply flawed and carelessly written. Dates of critical battles are confused. He puts himself in places at times that could not have happened. After his death in 1997 he was heavily criticized by historians and civil war veterans. The case for his defence? He was well into his 70s when he finished the book, he could not rely on diaries as they had been stolen back in the 1960s, he was a writer and writers make things up.

I think what really infuriated his critics, is that he insists in the book that he saw action and was involved in killing. I have my doubts about this too.

Even now I do not really know what happened then and how much of Laurie Lee's war was fought in his head and through his pen.

One small conversation in *A Moment of War* has always stuck with me. Lee had been released from a cell in the International Brigade quarters in Albacete. He had been under suspicion of spying for the enemy. Nobody believed his tale of walking over the Pyrenees with a fiddle slung over his shoulder rather than a rifle. He was talking with an American volunteer fresh from defeat in a battle. He had witnessed horrors: the ill-equipped Brigade volunteers had been no match for the elite Moroccan troops, once commanded by Franco himself. He described how the Moors had taken no prisoners and had cut the throats, in cold blood, of prisoners.

The American had then taken a deep-bladed clasp knife from his pocket. As Sheffield is famous around the world for its steel, Albacete is famous for its murderous clasp-knives. He had handed it over to Lee. Lee opened up the clasp and exposed the long sharp blade. Inscribed along the blade were the words. *"No me saques sin razón, no me entres sin honor."* (Don't open without reason or close without honour). I have a feeling that these words stuck in Lee's brain and haunted him down the years.

I am weary but I have one more place to go before I return to England to pick up my life again. I have to go to Granada for it is only in Granada that I can really end this journey. I opt to take the bus just as I used to do when I was a student.

3 November 2012, Granada

I lived here for a year in 1975.

On a Sunday evening I would walk up the slick black winding cobbled streets of the Albaizín, the Moorish quarter. I would not go up as far as Sacromonte, where gypsy families still lived in caves and underground dwellings.

I would take a right turn from the main street and climb steeply up a narrow whitewashed alley, past the house with the broken guitar affixed to its creased outside wall, and enter the Plaza de San Nicolas, my plaza.

On those autumn evenings, I would sit on the low wall, feet dangling in the cool dusk air circling upwards from the valley far below. I would drink in the silhouette of the Moorish Alhambra palace, the green watered gardens of the Generalife still woozy from the drugged warmth of the early autumn Spanish sun, as darkness fell. The snow-coated outline of the Sierra Nevada sitting above the palace in a blood-red sky. A nightingale's song would occasionally break the stillness. I would trace its journey down from that sky, through a rainbow of colours, to the gardens of the palace.

I am drawn to this place when in need of solace. A place where African princes conversed with the birds from their homeland, mourned their melancholy songs, rejoiced in their love refrains and whose lovers in the harem were rocked to sleep by the lullabies of the homesick birds.

I met an old man once who kept birds and sold them in cages on Las Ramblas in Barcelona. I was sheltering once under the trees just as a storm broke. The birds were unusually silent. I said to the old man that I had heard that birds normally sung when a storm was imminent. "They are usually the birds in the countryside," he said. He hesitated and then took out a needle from under his coat, "but my birds sing sweeter when I spike their eyes out."

Spain is a beautiful country but like nature it can be cruel too and I should never forget that.

I am here again now, 37 years on from when I first came. Then, like now, it was both a beginning and an end. It is my first visit since that time and a whole lifetime has passed.

I had risen early to see the sun rise over the Alhambra. After 37 years my internal compass was not set correctly and I had walked up too high and to the west of the square. Glimpses of the church steeple finally led me back down through the years.

It is a cold, damp November morning, like many in Granada – a magical but melancholy city. At 21 minutes past seven, the time of sunrise, the Sierra behind the palace is covered in a grey sheet.

Granada is the home of Federico García Lorca, a soulmate of Lee, and someone who influenced greatly his poetic and lyrical style of writing, though they never met. It was also the home of Manuel de Falla who captured the soul of the city and its people with his music.

The wind ruffles the leaves on the square of the plaza and spreads them out over the indented images of the *Granadino*. The *Granadino* is the symbol of the city, the pomegranate, whose black shells and seeds carpet the cobbled floor.

Down below me the city of Granada is spread out. I can pick out Alhóndiga street where Lee stayed when he returned to Andalusia in the winter of 1955. Granada is a beautiful and melancholy city but often damp and cold. Lee succumbed to one of his regular fevers but this one worsened quickly and things looked serious. He pulled through and wrote of looking out at the street below as he convalesced. I had walked down the street earlier, trying to identify which window he had gazed down from. This time I had been unable to catch his eye.

Blue sky is breaking out all around me now. Smoke from a factory way down to my east snakes across the valley, like the coal smoke trailing from a steam engine. Lorca lived in the countryside as a child. Falla's house, with its blue front door is below on the hill.

There is no snow on the Sierra, just cloud. The clouds hiding the Sierra Nevada peaks seem to have taken on their cordillera outline, darker clouds perch on lighter cloud tissue covering the towers and turrets and spires of the Alhambra. The light and green gardens of the Generalife lie hidden behind the castle.

The highest man-made point on the horizon is a large cross. From my vantage point it is just the size of a little silver cross that a child might wear around his neck. I wore such a cross once.

On the wall beside me I lay out one Saint Christopher medal, one scallop shell, one locket. The sun appears from behind the clouds and glints off the metal of the locket.

The sun has risen on a new day and there is forgiveness in the air. I have wanted to feel a reaction ever since I arrived in Almuñécar. It had all just felt a bit flat.

The pilgrims, who walk *El Camino* to Santiago de Compostela celebrate the end of their pilgrimage, by making their way to Cape Finisterre on the north-west Atlantic Coast. They burn their walking clothes and their boots on the beach. They attend a special Mass in their honour in the cathedral.

Here on my own, I do not feel like celebrating.

I have, though, gradually become aware of a change in me that has caught me by surprise. As a child I was told to forgive, it was a tenet of the Catholic doctrine that one should seek forgiveness for one's own sins and in turn forgive others. I would pray every night, "Our father who art in heaven, hallowed be thy name, forgive us our sins as we forgive those who have trespassed against us." I have not prayed for a very long time and I have not been very forgiving of myself or of others. During this journey I have, I think, been learning how to forgive. I have realised that forgiveness is not a passive feeling. It is an active choice. It is a choice that has to be made not once but over and over again. My journey down through Spain has been all about constantly "moving on" from one place to another. It is only at its end that I understood that in order to find hope – and after all it is hope that keeps you alive – you have to find a way of forgiving.

I think the past is a place that many of us want to escape from. The literal translation of "to forgive" in Aramaic is "to untie".

The Spanish people, I think, have not yet grasped this concept, they may well have disengaged emotionally from the conflict of the past, they have put it out of their minds but they have not faced up to it. They have not chosen to forgive the sins of the past. They have compounded this omission by choosing to forget these past sins. True forgiveness, I think, is to choose to forgive but always to remember, forgive but never forget.

I have started a longer journey, that of asking forgiveness of myself, to stop listening to all those silent screams echoing soundlessly down all those empty years. Fathers and heroes often call out for forgiveness and I have finally been able to listen.

Many a time I have come back here to Granada in my mind, usually at dark times, now I am here and feel at ease. My journey is done.

I turn away from the plaza to a nearby bar for a well-deserved warming breakfast. I think of Lee's final thoughts as he left Almuñécar, for what he certainly thought would be the last time in his life, as he set sail for England:

"Spain drifted away from me, thunder-bright on the horizon, and I left it there beneath its copper clouds."

Slad

A Sprinkling of White Tea Rose Petals

But Laurie did not rest in peace...
      – Valerie Grove in *Laurie Lee: The Well-Loved Stranger*

Friday 9 November 2012, Victoria Station, London

I am back in London, stepping off the train, the final leg of my return from Granada. There is no-one to greet me here.

I have decided to go straight to Slad, back to where my journey, in truth, really began.

I want to be there for the eleventh minute of the eleventh hour of the eleventh day of the eleventh month.

Forgiveness is about remembrance too.

Sunday 11 November 2012, Slad

Remembrance Day must have been an annual day of torment for Lee.

He was nineteen when one midsummer morning he left his home in Slad, walked out to London and then on and down through Spain on the eve of the Spanish Civil War. He returned to London in 1938 a war hero, an International Brigade soldier who had risked his life to fight fascism. He had no valiant part to play in World War II; he was not fit for active service due to epilepsy and worked in reserve occupations instead.

If it is true, as I have reluctantly come to believe, that he had greatly exaggerated his active service in Spain then this day must have troubled him every year. I doubt that Lee ever forgave himself for his

214

perceived failure to make a difference on the front line in Spain. If he had done, then the 11th November each year could have been a positive experience. As it is, I think that this day, every year for more than fifty years, was probably an ordeal.

Before he finished *A Moment of War*, Lee had had over fifty years to get his story straight on the civil war. Perhaps like J P Ismay, the owner of the Titanic, he just couldn't think that way. Ismay had an episodic mind – he couldn't see his life unfolding as a narrative story. In a split second Ismay chose to step down into a lifeboat, leaving behind women and children to perish. One small step that blighted his life. He was forever vilified and never really recovered. With Lee, it was the step that he didn't take that cost him dear. He never did step on to that battlefield and engage arms. He could never explain or own up to that omission thereafter, he could not construct a narrative that worked for him and for others. He wrote one lie too many.

Lee died on Tuesday 13 May 1997. One of his last Remembrance Sundays would have been in 1995, also the 50th anniversary of the end of World War II.

I wasn't there in Slad that day in 1995 but just as his amiable spirit seems to live on still in this homely, sparse pub, paying little heed to the generally held principles and dimensions of time and space, I feel that I could have been there. If I had been, I would have sat quietly in a corner and observed.

Lee was four when the Armistice was signed and World War I came to an end. He had described the scenes in The Woolpack. He looked in through the window from the outside, "the bar seemed on fire with its many lamps. Rose-coloured men, through the rain-wet windows, seemed to bulge and break into flame."

Now in 2012, at the end of my journey into Lee's past, I sit inside that pub and look back out of a rain-wet window and imagine the scene that November day in 1995 when Lee must have known he did not have many years left.

Remembrance Sunday 1995, The Woolpack, Slad

The old writer is frail and practically blind now. He does not have long to live but he has his Spanish Civil War medals. The following year he would be granted honorary citizenship of Spain as an International Brigade Veteran.

I would have looked at him, sitting in his old coat, his British Warm, accepting tankards of ale on the house with a look from those rheumy old eyes that along with a silver tongue and assured pen had charmed the world all his life.

Earlier that day Lee would have taken part in the Remembrance Sunday service at the village Cenotaph just up the road from the pub. Albert and Cecil, Frank and Lionel would have been remembered, fathers and uncles of Lee's classmates, who had also walked out to war but hadn't come back.

I stand at his shoulder at the Cenotaph, look on and listen in to his private thoughts.

There is a bright blue November sky overseeing the scene, a single white stream of cloud piercing the blue expanse, tracer from a resurrected Spitfire perhaps. Dry browning leaves drop from overhanging branches and settle on the ground like poppy petals. Lee joins in with the hymn:

A thousand ages in thy sight
are like an evening gone
short as the watch that ends the night
before the rising sun.

Lee's medals, pinned to his chest, tinkle in the breeze like spinnakers in a crowded marina. His thoughts race through his fevered mind…

…quiet, stop thinking, they might hear, the thoughts that stir in the early black hours, that stab me like hot needles steeped in shame, keep the chattering teeth still, purse these lips that long to speak the truth. Am I in that machine that sees right through me, exposing my dark heart, laying bare those ageing bones with marrow rotten to the core, oh my God, can they see me now as I am?

The bearer of the Legion's standard stands tall, the flag held high, his red beret worn proudly, his white gloves gripping the flagstaff tight. He lowers the flag until its velvet drapes rest on the leaves. The reveille is sounded and the flag is slowly raised again.

Lee's head jerks up, to attention, alert, the scrambled thoughts still persistent, he is back in Madrid in 1938.

The crowd around are screaming "*no pasarán*," they shall not pass, and yet those bearers of fascist arms keep coming through and I wave them on and look the other way...

The man with the red beret is talking now. "When you go home, tell them of us and say – for your tomorrow, we gave our today."

I leave Lee and this scene at the war memorial just up from The Wool-pack to think back to a distant day when it was quiet on the western front. I was not there either that day but my mother had told me this story of her father, my grandfather. It is 1917 and close to Ypres.

The early morning light picks its way through the fragile bones of the blue-grey skeletal cloud tissue. As the day brightens the church spire of the nearby Belgian town appears into view. From the top of the spire the undulating land sloping away to the horizon, once a rolling sea of green, is but now a bed of mud stuck in time, belonging to nobody.

The April-pale sun alights on a sliver of metal, glistens momentarily and is gone.

Second Lieutenant George Vinson Thomas sits on a rough wooden slat at the bottom of a deeply-dug trench, his back resting against a wall of white china clay luminous mud. He opens his top left breast pocket and takes out a silver cigarette case.

It is quiet, as is common at this time of the day, both sides still drawing breath and waiting for their blood temperatures to rise. There is no dawn chorus, no birdsong, no wood warbler spinning his coin and allowing it to settle, drop and rattle onto a wooden board. Life is still a game of chance though.

Nicotine-stained fingers release the catch and the case springs open. They extract a cigarette from those held in place by the fraying but taut yellow elastic band.

He closes the case and the rough tobacco-stained fingers caress the dent in the metal, a small crater on a lunar-smooth surface. He taps the ends of the cigarette lightly against the metal cover, taking care to select the smooth side of the case. He cups his hands around the cigarette, strikes up a match and lights the tip of the cigarette. The smoke curls up, over his neat trimmed moustache, his rheumy blue eyes and over the top of the trench, disappearing into the early morning haze.

The red glow of the cigarette can be picked out from the top of the church spire.

A scene had played itself out in the sea of mud stretching away from the spire some days back, though for George it seems a lifetime ago. Second Lieutenant Thomas is going over the top in slow-motion movements into the deathly quiet of No-Man's-Land. It is deserted, save for the fallen stricken body of his fellow soldier. He hears nothing and does not register the puff of smoke from the rifle recoil. The thud of the 370 grain bullet into his chest knocks him backwards. Somehow they make it back, the two of them, to the safety of the trench.

Recommendations are made in despatches and a Military Cross is commissioned, cleaned until it is shining and pinned on to Captain Thomas's breast.

The cross sits in a dusty drawer. Only the metal of the cigarette case that absorbed the impact retains an imprint of that moment for ever, a memory that is barely, if ever, spoken of by George, a memory nevertheless, whose groove is worn smooth by the rubbing of a yellow finger over the course of the 20th century, right up to 1965 when the case could protect him no more.

The rescued soldier lies still in a cemetery in Belgium, a white cross marking the spot. He did not survive, unlike my grandfather. He lies undisturbed, but he is remembered.

The cigarette case sits proudly in the French glass-fronted cabinet in the front room of a thatched cottage in a village in Oxfordshire. It is taken out, as new generations appear, and is passed from daughter to grandson to great-grandchildren and even now to great-great-grandchildren. And so it will continue.

We are back in The Woolpack now, Lee drinks his ale and tries not to remember on this day of remembrance.

I am thinking that I, like those bitter International Brigade veterans, should be denouncing this man for a fraudster, a fantasist, a scoundrel who has tainted my grandfather's memory. I should but I don't; he had every intention of fighting and killing if he had to. He crossed the line of courage and put his life on the line. That can never be forgotten and needs to be respected.

From my window seat in the bar I can see out across Lee's valley, to Swift's hill and the woods beyond and I can see a lonely man sitting in his seat, lost in his thoughts and all his yesterdays.

Although I am not there, I leave him to his memories.

13 May 1997, Rose Cottage, Slad

I try and picture Lee in his last hours.

A pale imitation of the early morning May sun penetrates the gloom of the room. He lies amidst damp sheets, not yet changed from the night before. Soft tears on his cheeks sting from the chill wind from the open window. His sleep has been disturbed by the sounds of the night; he is infected by the stars. He considers that boy weeping, covered by green, green grass towering over him. The cool green valley, the hot flushes of black fever, gentle loving sisters, one taken early by grey death. He is the promised one, the golden boy. His father is long gone.

Now consider the man who was that child. A poet, a writer. All his life he has been running away and if not running, then walking down the open road. Searching or escaping. What does he see lying there in artificial darkness, gasping for breath? His eyes have stopped functioning. What, if anything does he hear? The drums in his ears were silenced long ago.

Does he see Capa's falling man, captured in his moment of death in Córdoba? Can he hear the soft click of the black Bakerlite telephone receiver being returned to the cradle as the Captain ends his son's life?

Is that Roy, Roy Campbell, stroking his hair? Roy, who gave shelter to the nuns and priests in Toledo, Mary's sisters in Christ. Mary, Lorna's sister. Maybe she was the one – not Lorna, not Kathy.

Cocks crowing thrice, his firstborn Yasmin in a basket, flowing away down the river, betrayed, forsaken.

Does he see the newsreels, flickering black and white shadows dancing on the screen? December 1938, the men from the International Brigade arriving home at Victoria Station, defeated but proud. He's not there at the station to greet his comrades, he's in Cyprus. Sent away while Lorna has his child, his Yasmin. Brothels, Spanish ones, Cypriot ones, wandering cunning precocious fingers. Fred Copeman, on the front line, brown men moving over the field of battle, Rosie, marrying a soldier, Fred the strike leader from Putney. Lee's first taste of revolution, swoony Chanel No 5-soaked one pound notes, Cornish beaches strewn with wet seaweed ribbon, shipwrecks, lives wrecked. Fred rousing the men to engage with the enemy and fight, daring him, Lee, to fight. Only he hadn't, had he, he hadn't taken up arms and engaged, he had slunk back into the country, under the radar, no Royal Navy six-gun salute this time. Just Lorna is there to greet him, that smell, her smell, Fleurs de Rocaille.

He's just six now, recovering from yet another fever, a rare outing to the cinema in Stroud, great excitement on the screen, Victoria Station again, the Unknown Soldier arriving, the coffin appearing through clouds of steam. The roaring masses, bereaved wives, orphaned children, lost mothers, all wanting to touch the coffin, to feel something at last, to forgive, to say goodbye to their husbands, lovers, sons, fathers, all abandoned, nameless, numberless on French fields.

And Lorna is there, at the station, waiting for him, she has come. And he tells her a lie, a small lie and she tells Wish and she will tell Yasmin and he tells the world of tales of heroism, of courage in the face of the enemy and the taking of a life. But there has been no life taken. He may write a poem about killing Lorna, he may kill Lucian Freud in verse in years to come. In future dreams he may kill, but in the killing fields of Spain, no.

There is always a reckoning.

The wake from the boat as it steams into Vigo, Lee stepping ashore, his new life in Spain. Wakes are aftermath too, consequence. Wakes apply balm to the soul, set grief in train.

Lee would not wake again.

Laurie Lee died at home in Rose Cottage. The day before his death, he suddenly called out to Kathy to come.

"Yes, Lol," she said.

"I've got a secret," said he, and not a word more.

He died at 9.25am just as a brilliant rainbow swept across

his valley and all the colours of the rainbow danced across his face. Kathy and Jessy went out into the garden and picked white tea roses, Laurie's favourites, and let the stream of petals fall silently on his still body.

Epilogue

We shall not cease from exploration, and the end of all our exploring will be to arrive where we started and know the place for the first time.

– T.S. Eliot in Four Quartets

16 March 2014, Oxford

I have been back from Spain now for over a year. I have indeed become a writer, perhaps a natural consequence of tracking a writer to the end.

I have written a book of my journey, the Indian summer of my life journey or as the Spanish say in the south, my "little summer of the quince" journey.

I still sometimes go to the top of the Wittenham Clumps. It is so quiet up there and I can dream of Slad Valley and Moorish castles and white dusty roads lined with orange groves.

I have come to Tewkesbury, nor far from the Slad Valley, on a typical wet Gloucestershire winter evening. It is the opening event of Laurie Lee's Centenary Year celebrations.

There are seventy of us squeezed into a pub. Laurie would have liked that. We are all fans of Lee, the man and his writing. I think we have all journeyed through our lives, accompanied by Lee.

Lee's surviving family are there – his daughter, Jessy, and his wife, Kathy. Yasmin is not there; she passed away a few years ago.

I never did get to meet Laurie, though I felt close to him at times during my walk.

The evening begins with a scratchy taped recording of Lee reading one of his favourite poems "Apples". Jessy reads "Fields of Autumn", which is Kathy's favourite.

Frank Mansell, a local poet and a great friend of Lee is remembered. Lee championed his poems. Poems are read of Cotswold lads lying sleeping, ships of many sails, the roads going down to Gloucester town and the Severn seeking the sea.

Johnny Coppin, a locally based folk singer, sings songs of Lee poems set to music; he once recorded an album with Lee himself. Jessy talks of Lee and his fondness of talking about death.

This is all very surreal. After two years tracking Lee and following in his footsteps and asking him questions that received no reply, finally I can communicate with him through his two women.

I introduce myself to Jessy and Kathy, not without trepidation. I have no idea if they know of me or of my book. I explain about the book and my journey. Jessy is already quite emotional about the commemoration of her father and has been holding back tears all evening. My story seems to touch her as I explain that I had meant to write a straightforward biography of her father and of how Spain had shaped his life. I tell her of how during the journey I realised that what I was really searching for was a better sense of myself, and forgiveness for my own father.

Lee seemed to have become a surrogate of the father I always wanted. I do not feel self conscious in telling her all this. I tell her of my discovery that you have to ask for forgiveness yourself before you can forgive others. To succeed in finding a sense of Lee, I had first to make peace with myself and my own father. I tell her that the book is by way of a thank you to Lee.

We, I, have been talking for twenty minutes and the concert is about to start again.

Jessy swallows hard, touches my arm and says fiercely that if her father were standing now at her shoulder, listening to me, he would be nodding his head, saying how he quite understood and what a lovely chap I am.

I feel I have at last made my connection with Laurie. I can now go and find a place to call home and live my life.

Tribute to Laurie Lee

In a way, this book is my tribute to a great writer and a flawed hero. I wanted, however, to make a practical difference to Lee's legacy through the book. I am donating a percentage of all proceeds from the book to the Gloucestershire Wildlife Trust, who manage Laurie Lee Wood.

I first went to Laurie Lee Wood in the autumn of 2013 and this is what I wrote.

Knitting Socks, Wet-Eyed Squirrels and Drinking *Cider with Rosie*

It is the beginning of a magical sunny day as I drive across the Cotswold Way, high up overlooking the Gloucestershire countryside, lovely views once the early morning mist burns off under the gentle intensity of a warming-up autumnal day.

It is a real *Veranillo del Membrillo* day, as the Spanish in Andalusia say, "a little summer of the quince" – an Indian summer day – and the English are out en masse to enjoy it.

It feels like a moment snatched away from the inexorable march towards the darker days of winter and I am looking to enjoy it to the full.

I am on my way to the inaugural Walking with Words event, inspired and led by Kevan Manwaring, a quiet, gentle Gloucestershire poet. The collection of guided walks and tours stretch from late summer, through the winter and into spring 2014. They celebrate Gloucestershire's links with classic English writers who took their inspiration from the natural beauty of the county, including WH Davies, Edward Thomas and Robert Frost, Ivor Gurney and John Drinkwater. Today though it is all about Laurie Lee, who would have been 100 next year. He is a hero of mine and I am writing a book about his Spanish Civil Wars years, that time shaped him as a writer and a man, and a walk that started, well it started from here in Slad, a tiny village in a sumptuous English green valley on the edge of the Cotswolds.

We assemble in front of Rose Bank cottage where Lee grew up. We gaze down the steep bank to the cottage and imagine the scene of little Laurie Lee, only three, being set down from the carrier's cart. It is 1917 and the Great War is still raging on the once-green fields of France. Laurie recollects his arrival in the village in his first memoir *Cider With Rosie*: "The June grass, amongst which I stood was taller than I was and I wept."

There are no tears from our slightly surreal group, but I think it is close. Chantelle, a professional archaeologist – IT boffin in the public sector by day, a backing vocalist for a progressive band at night – is distracting herself by knitting socks as she watches on. She is not digging up bones today, just gently sifting the earth and the air for traces of the spirit of a dead poet. Sylvie, a retired classical violinist who toured the world and once played with the Grateful Dead and taught Joni Mitchell's daughter, is imagining a stained glass commemorative centenary piece of Lee flailing against the grass much like a young Don Quixote confronting the whirling blades of the windmills on La Mancha. Sylvia, as vivacious as the uplifting vowel at the end of her name implies is another singer and a poet to boot, whose muse was Joni Mitchell herself. She would be in grave danger, I think, if an older Laurie were to appear, armed with his charm, silver tipped tongue and come-to-bed eyes. In the words of the great American singer, that could have been written for Lee, he was all about "*Court and Spark.*"

We are an eclectic group, many, like me, looking for something, a second chance in life perhaps, after divorce, the ending of first careers. Some first lives move into a second phase seamlessly, others end abruptly. Perhaps we are all looking for some of Lee's alchemy to inspire and transform our lives. Anything is possible, I think, on a day like today, with grasshoppers chirping and apples, both red and green, ripe for the picking. The opening words of Lee's second memoir *As I Walked Out One Midsummer Morning* also have Lee standing where we are now. It is 1934, he is 19 years old and he is leaving home. He has no plans other than to walk to London, he doesn't know that after a year in the capital, his feet will feel restless again and he will walk out again, this time down from the Atlantic coast of the north-west of Spain to the Mediterranean...

We walk for about five miles and circle the valley, like the red kites above us, stopping from time to time to admire views. We relive scenes from *Cider With Rosie* and read extracts from the book. Sylvie reads a piece about Peace Day and the annual blessing from the squire, a man always close to tears on these occasions apparently. Somehow Sylvie creates a more evocative scene than intended when she speaks of the party being welcomed by a "wet-eyed squirrel" on the steps of the manor house. I feel this is in keeping with the spirit of our pilgrimage and that Laurie would have loved the slip of the tongue.

The highlight of the day is visiting the newly christened Laurie Lee Wood, acquired recently by the Gloucestershire Wildlife Trust and now protected from the threat of redevelopment. I had heard recently a BBC Radio 4 programme on the wood and how an appeal from the Trust to its members had resulted in £36,000 being raised in just six weeks to buy the wood and ensure that this particular bit of the Slad Valley, immortalised in Lee's writing, was now secure for generations to come to enjoy. Lee's daughter Jessy had led the fight to save the wood, continuing the work that her father had started when he'd bought it.

We finish back at the church opposite Laurie's favourite pub, The Woolpack, at his graveside, but not before Chantelle had taken centre stage and with knitting put away and with a glint in her eye had read a few lines from the climax of *Cider With Rosie,* "The first bite of the apple," Laurie's first tryst with Rosie, who was even prettier than Betty Gleed, "Never to be forgotten, that first, long, secret drink of golden fire, juice of those valleys and of that time... never to be forgotten, or ever tasted again."

Lee had hinted later on in his life that it may not have been himself under that hay wagon and the girl might not have been Rosie, "I was a watcher, observing everything. I sprawled in the long grass and saw what was going on."

Chantelle, for me, has now been rechristened as Rosie and she leads us on to our lunch in the enchanting grounds of the Hawkwood Centre. Our food, like our morning, is organic, biodynamic and utterly delicious. No cider though, just apple sauce on the side.

I linger at the end of the lunch and then go back down to The

Woolpack and look over the valley again to Laurie Lee's Wood. I fell in love with Laurie Lee and his writing many years ago when I was drifting on the cusp of manhood. Recently he had helped me negotiate a crisis in my life. I realise now that on on 26 June 2014, when Lee would have been a hundred years old, the wood will be one year old.

Gloucestershire Wildlife Trust is a county based wildlife conservation charity. The Trust has over 60 nature reserves, including four in the Slad Valley. Laurie Lee Wood opened in 2013.

2014 marks the centenary of the birth of Laurie Lee and Gloucestershire Wildlife Trust will be using this celebration to connect the work of Gloucestershire's most famous twentieth century writer and the landscape that inspired him, by launching a poetry trail. Find out more about the Poetry Trail and The Trusts' work in the Slad Valley by visiting www.gloucestershirewildlifetrust.co.uk. I have chosen to donate 8% of book sales profits to the Trust for the conservation of Laurie Lee Wood.

Bibliography

Works by Laurie Lee

A Moment of War (1992)
A Rose for Winter (1977)
As I Walked Out One Midsummer Morning (1976)
Cider with Rosie (2002)
I Can't Stay Long (1978)
My Many-Coated Man (1955)
Selected Poems (1983)
The Sun My Monument (1961)
The Voyage of Magellan (1948)

Other works

Ackroyd, Peter, *London: The Biography* (2001)
Barclay, Jennifer, *Meeting Mr Kim* (2008)
Baxell, Richard, *Looking Back at the Spanish Civil War* (2010)
Brenan, Gerald, *The Face of Spain* (2010)
Connolly, Cressida, *The Rare and the Beautiful: The Lives of the Garmans* (2005)
De Botton, Alain, *How Proust Can Change Your Life* (1997)
De Waal, Edmund, *The Hare with Amber Eyes* (2011)
Eliot, T.S., *Four Quartets* (2001)
Gallagher, Jock, *Laurie Lee: A Many-coated Man* (1998)
Grove, Valerie, *Laurie Lee – The Well-Loved Stranger* (1999) [Reissued as: Grove, Valerie, *The Life and Loves of Laurie Lee* (2014)]
Haycock, David Boyd, *I Am Spain* (2012)
Hemingway, Ernest, *The Sun Also Rises* (2004)
Hemingway, Ernest, *Men Without Women* (2004)
Hollis, Matthew, *Now All Roads Lead to France: The Last Years of Edward Thomas* (2011)

Holmes, Richard, *Footsteps – Adventures of a Romantic Biographer* (2005)

Howson, Gerald, *The Flamencos of Cadiz Bay* (1994)

Jack, Ian, *Granta 94: On The Road Again – Where Travel Writing Went Next* (2006)

Joyce, Rachel, *The Unlikely Pilgrimage of Harold Fry* (2012)

Kieran, Dan, *The Idle Traveller: The Art of Slow Travel* (2011)

Laing, Olivia, *To the River – A Journey Beneath the Surface* (2011)

Lebrun, Bernard, *Robert Capa: The Paris Years 1933-1954* (2011)

Lorca, Federico García, *In Search of Duende* (1998)

Macfarlane, Robert, *The Old Ways* (2012)

Madeley, Richard, *Fathers and Sons* (2008)

Marsden, Philip, *The Bronski House* (2005)

Matthiesen, Peter, *The Snow Leopard* (2010)

Machado, Antonio, *Selected Poems* (1988)

Milton, *Paradise Lost* (2008)

Morrison, Blake, *And When Did You Last See Your Father?* (1993)

Motion, Andrew, *In the Blood: A Memoir of my Childhood* (2006)

Preston, Paul, *Franco* (1995)

Sheers, Owen, *The Dust Diaries* (2004)

Simmons, John, *The Angel of the Stories* (2011)

Slovo, Gillian, *Every Secret Thing* (2009)

Solnit, Rebecca, *A History of Walking* (2002)

Tóibín, Colm, *The Empty Family* (2011)

Tremlett, Giles, *Ghosts of Spain: Travels Through a Country's Hidden Past* (2006)

Webster, Jason, *¡Guerra!* (2007)

Wilson, Frances, *How to Survive the Titanic* (2011)

Websites

P. D. Murphy's daughter Daniella sings under the name of Ellie Larke. "Stone-Shaped Locket" and other songs can be found at www.soundcloud.com/ellielarke

Useful Resources

Author Details

Blog: www.thelittlesummerofthequince.wordpress.com
Twitter: www.twitter.com/hotspurman
LinkedIn: www.linkedin.com/in/insearchoflaurielee
Website: www.paulmurphyassociates.co.uk
Publisher: www.silverwoodbooks.co.uk

Laurie Lee Centenary Further Details

Official Laurie Lee Centenary website managed by Curtis Brown
   Literary Agency: www.laurielee.org
Laurie Lee Centenary Facebook page: www.facebook.com/pages/
   The-Laurie-Lee-Centenary-Celebrations/603028139790185

Further Book Information

As I Walked Out Through Spain in Search of Laurie Lee Facebook
   page:www.facebook.com/pages/As-I-Walked-Out-through-
   Spain-in-search-of-Laurie-Lee/864036193626037

Acknowledgements

Where do I start to give thanks to the people who have supported the writing of my first book, especially a book that has roots going back to the beginning of my life?

Well, let's be pragmatic and start near the end and work back. *As I Walked Out Through Spain In Search of Laurie Lee* grew out of my time on the MA Professional Writing course at Falmouth University in 2011. My inspirational tutor Susannah Marriott provided advice and encouragement at every stage of the process and has been one of the driving forces behind this book – I cannot praise her enough. Thanks are also due to Helen Shipman, Jane, Kris, Tom, Paul D and the rest of the team. I have to be nice to them as they are currently molding another writer in the family, my daughter Eluned, more of whom later. I am grateful to Philip Marsden, a great writer and my MA supervisor, who gave me advice about how to craft the initial shape of the book, as did Owen Sheers. Kelly Stephens loved my pitch and Emily Barr advised on seeking out snow leopards.

My fellow MA students provided constant help and encouragement. Lucy Cooper has edited the book from the start and given it structure, Fiona Egglestone has provided the final critical edit, a sharp pair of new fresh eyes at the end. Sheryl Farran, a fellow Spanish studies student has polished the Spanish content. Fran Ford provided the beautiful illustration for the front cover, Marty Whistler, the early graphics and setting. Jill and Simon provided me with a home by the sea in Flushing for my studies in Falmouth, once occupied, it is rumoured, by Lord Nelson himself! Cheryl was my kindred spirit in the village. Great support from all at Café Polyglot, thanks to Vic, Katie, Tony and all there. Julie H talked me through my life changes with great skill and sensitivity, building on the excellent foundations laid by Roz R all those years ago.

Helen, Jo and Emma at SilverWood Books have offered much needed support and calmness.

John Simmons of Dark Angels and 26 gave me the initial confidence to write, Sally Baker at Ty Newydd the base, and the Faber Academy a boost at a critical stage, thanks to Gillian Slovo, Andrew Motion and Blake Morrison. Fellow Faber Memoir students continue to share and inspire, particularly Jas, (The Boss), Harriet, Enriqueta, Harvey and Toots and the other stalwarts, Arun, Jo, the two Sams, Hind and Emmett.

Callum and Tracy from Frontier Holidays – sorry about the hens – and Manni and Lindsay from TomaTours in Spain have been generous in their support both, practical and morale boosting.

I could not have written the book without drawing on the rich detail of Valerie Groves' masterful biography of Laurie Lee, just updated and republished as *The Life and Loves of Laurie Lee*. Valerie has been supportive of my book right from the start. Cressida Connelly's *The Rare and the Beautiful*, a wonderful account of the Garman sisters, was my guide to the family that shaped so much of Lee's life.

My Spanish journey started back in the 1970s in Portsmouth at the Poly. Robin, Patrick, Sue, Aurea, Jay and Terry all helped to develop a love of Spain set in train by Laurie Lee. More recently, David Tolley from Cardiff University revived my love for translation and updated my knowledge of the Spanish Civil War.

As for that girl behind the shuttered window on Santa Lucia, a lovely piece of serendipity has recently put me back in touch with her, welcome back Kay, Spain would not have been the same without you.

Eryl and Joe helped me make the transition from one life to another, along with Nikki, Rachael, Marcus, Henry, Archie and Tomas and all at FlintShare. Kieran Duff showed faith in me at a difficult time. On the road in Spain I have to thank Pepe, Dani, Stephen, Alfonso, Marie, Jeannie, Sam, Heather and especially Pilar and Antonio for looking after me so well in Córdoba. Giles Tremlett gave me supper and a great insight into Spanish society and how it is changing.

I would also like to thank Cherry, Group 2012 and Zool from Blackwell's in Oxford for welcoming me into the group, and Fleur for giving me a chance.

Madeleine Bunting and Radio 3 gave me an insight into forgiveness at a critical time.

I am indebted to Anna Davis and Alice Dill at the Curtis Brown Literary Agency who represent the Laurie Lee Estate for generously granting access to Lee's life works for the purpose of quoting and reproduction of extracts. The British Library, keeper of the Lee Estate Papers, authorised access to the papers. Many thanks to Irish cousins for the loan of St Helen's, a great writing base. From Germany I have to thank Rene, Friedericke and family and Alexander, along with Rolf, Petra and Jan.

In the writing of the book I chose not to contact the Lee family but met with Jessy and Kathy Lee at a celebration of Lee's life and writing earlier this year. Jessy made me feel very welcome and for this I am grateful.

The Gloucestershire Wildlife Trust who manage the Laurie Lee Wood have graciously allowed me to work with them in providing a donation to the wood's upkeep from the proceeds of the book.

I have to end by thanking my family who have always supported me but have been particularly generous over the last few difficult years. Thanks must go to my brothers and their families: Stephen, Adrian, Anthony, Michael and Christopher. My clever niece Elisabeth, a talented artist, now becoming a talented photographer, produced a range of illustrations for me. I am also grateful to my godfather Jack for all his support over the years.

My dad is no longer around. I loved him; I wish I could have loved him more.

Thanks to Reg, Marjorie and Jenny for their support once upon a time.

Eluned, my favourite daughter (and yes I know she's my only one) has been brilliant in supporting the book both practically and emotionally. She has provided much needed online marketing skills. She is already a talented singer and on her way to becoming a great writer.

What would a son do without his mum? Mine has been incredible in giving me whatever was needed at the time. In return she gets a book, which doesn't seem quite fair...

Finally I dedicate the book to Nick, Kathryn, Rhiannon and Richard, without whom I doubt it would have happened (and to Sharon and Richard, my Number 1 fans).

The Quince

Everyone deserves an Indian Summer in their lives, a window of opportunity to make a change.

The phrase for an Indian Summer in Andalusia is "*El veranillo del membrillo*", literally "the little summer of the quince", hence the name of my blog.

The quince is an autumn fruit: a bittersweet creation; it hides itself under a downing of pubescent white hair which is burnt off in the autumn; reaches a zenith of ripeness only in the occasional Indian summer; is sour until bathed in salt water which results in an exquisite melt in the mouth sweet sensation. It embodies a mellowing stage of life, it is not perfectly shaped, it reflects a life lived, it has a faded charm, a hint of honey in its perfume. Laurie Lee penned a lovely poem called "April Rise" that captured the annual renewal of life and second chances:

> *If ever I saw blessing in the air*
> *I see it now in this still early day*
> *Where lemon-green the vaporous morning drips*
> *Wet sunlight on the powder of my eye.*
>
> *Blown bubble-film of blue, the sky wraps round*
> *Weeds of warm light whose every root and rod*
> *Splutters with soapy green, and all the world*
> *Sweats with the bead of summer in its bud.*
>
> *If ever I heard blessing it is there*
> *Where birds in trees that shoals and shadows are*
> *Splash with their hidden wings and drops of sound*
> *Break on my ears their crests of throbbing air.*

Pure in the haze the emerald sun dilates,
The lips of sparrows milk the mossy stones,
While white as water by the lake a girl
Swims her green hand among the gathered swans.

Now, as the almond burns its smoking wick
Dropping small flames to light the candled grass;
Now, as my low blood scales its second chance,
If ever world were blessed, now it is.

Illustration: Elisabeth Murphy

www.thelittlesummerofthequince.wordpress.com

Lightning Source UK Ltd.
Milton Keynes UK
UKOW04f1807020714

234446UK00001B/61/P